Christian No More

Praise for Christian No More

"I'm indeed pleased that Jeffrey Mark and I agree so closely on the riveting issues he courageously dissects in this splendid book, because his impeccable logic is, in my view, irrefutable. This book is a delight to read—both in terms of Jeff's obvious talents as a writer, and in his smooth organization of complex material which, in lesser hands, would not have been so systemically argued and easy to understand. This unique and outstanding book is destined to become iconic in the freethought community."

David Mills

Author of *Atheist Universe: The Thinking Person's Answer to Christian Fundamentalism*

"Jeffrey Mark's engaging new book, Christian No More, is sure to make a lasting impact on every believer who reads it. This powerful work is an intellectual broadside to the world's most popular religion. One wonders how any honest and thinking Christian can confront the material contained in this remarkable book and not come away with a very different view of their religion.

Hard hitting but never bitter or mean, this book addresses a broad range of topics. So much ground is covered, in fact, that I recommend it for nonbelievers as well as believers. Every reader, regardless of perspective, is sure to learn and benefit.

Ultimately, the greatest value of Christian No More may be that it can serve as the perfect manual or guidebook for people who sense that they might enjoy vastly improved lives if only they could break free from the dogmatic belief imposed on them by family and society. Christian No More shows them the escape route."

Guy P. Harrison

Author of *50 Reasons People Give for Believing in a God*

Christian No More

a personal journey of
Leaving Christianity

and how you can leave too

Jeffrey Mark

Reasonable Press
Intelligent Books for Intelligent People
www.ReasonablePress.com
COGSPAGE MEDIA, LLC   CINCINNATI   2008

PUBLISHED BY COGSPAGE MEDIA, LLC.
Copyright © 2008 by Jeffrey Mark
All rights reserved. Published in the United States
by COGSPAGE Media, LLC.
Reasonble Press is an imprint of COGSPAGE Media, LLC

For Angie with Love

Thanks

Thanks to all the wonderful people who stayed by my side while I worked through this book, both on paper and in my mind.

Thanks first of all to Angie and Dylan for being here for me.

And thanks to the wonderful people online who offered amazing ideas and insight, including Lacey Lou, Rita Newton, Chris and Dana, Wendy, Tracy Savagescience, Jen B, Barbara "Lady B", Anna, Christopher Gadfly, Richie McCool and his wife Jen, Brandi and her big family, Dr. W. Sumner Davis, Acharya, John Loftus, David Mills, Izzy, Michael Skowronski, Gyreck, Kwisatz Haderach, ...and so many others; I apologize if I left your name out!

And a big thanks to my editor, Leah Myers for her excellent, meticulous work. Thanks to my proofreader, Amy Page, for her incredibly keen eye in catching the last-minute mistakes.

A note about the quoted Bible verses

For much of this book, I have chosen to quote the King James Version (KJV) of the Bible for two reasons: First, the text is in the public domain. Second, many fundamentalist Christians feel the KJV is the only authentic, inspired Word of God. As such, in tackling the arguments of fundamentalists, I felt it made the most sense to use the version that the fundamentalists prefer.

Occasionally, I have quoted the Young's Literal Translation of the Bible. This translation was published back in 1862, and consisted of nearly a word-for-word literal translation of the early Hebrew and Greek texts. It's an interesting translation, because the word ordering often duplicates the original text, without adjusting for more sensible English rendering. As a result, the text is a bit stilted. But it's useful in that it's easy to quickly determine how some people translate particularly unusual words from the early texts. The Young's Literal Translation, like the KJV, is in the public domain.

I also occasionally make use of the New International Version (NIV) text. This is a modern translation that many fundamentalists criticize due to its supposed lax translation and interpretation. But it's an interesting translation in that it allows for an easier, more understandable translation than many of the other translations. However, I typically only use this translation when I'm purposely pointing out comparisons between the translations.

The New International Version is not in the public domain. However, the publishers of the version have given express permission for up to a certain number of verses to be quoted in a book. (The permission is described in detail on their web site, http://www.ibs.org/bibles/termsofuse.php.) Thus, all NIV verses reprinted here are done so by permission.

Another translation that I occasionally mention is the Revised Standard Edition (RSV). In Chapter 5, I give a detailed description of why the RSV is particularly shunned by fundamentalist Christians. (And I do not have any quotes from it; I only describe it. So although the publisher of the RSV grants permission, it's not necessary here.)

A Note about BC/AD vs BCE/CE

In writing this book, I have deliberately broken skeptic and freethinker tradition by choosing BC and AD to refer to years. Many non-religious people prefer BCE ("Before Common Era") and CE ("Common Era") because such designations remove any religious connotation and are more inclusive, while BC and AD are distinctly of Christian origin. BC stands for Before Christ and AD stands for Anno Domini (which translates to The Year of Our Lord); both are clearly focused on the birth of Jesus.

My reason for using BC and AD is simple: I want this book to be accessible to everyone, including Christians who are struggling with their faith. Considering the terms BC and AD are far more common and understood, I have chosen to use these two abbreviations.

Table of Contents

16   *Christian no More*

one

The Collapsing Tower Of Babel

I spent many years of my childhood believing in him. I knew without a single doubt he was real. I would think about him every day as I sensed his presence. I would pray to him. I didn't just *know* he was hearing me; I *felt* him hearing me. The feeling that he was there was unmistakable. I would close my eyes, picturing him, and he was there, talking to me, and, more importantly, listening to me. He was guiding me.

He was real.

There was no doubt whatsoever in my mind, because I could feel him out there somewhere. This wasn't just my imagination. This was real. He was there.

I could feel him with my heart and with my soul. And I knew he heard my prayers. I had a personal relationship with him.

He was real.

That is…until my mother broke the news to me that he wasn't real. She broke the unbelievable news that no, there really was no Santa Claus.

But how could that be? I felt him. He was unmistakably real, absolutely there.

Or was he?

Fear is the main source of superstition, and one of the main sources of cruelty. To conquer fear is the beginning of wisdom.

- Bertrand Russell (1872-1970)

How could I have felt so strongly, so sincerely, so completely and surely that he was there, when he wasn't? This wasn't just a made-up story; this was much deeper. This was a feeling that came from far within me, as if he was a very part of me. He was real.

But he *wasn't*.

Clearly, there was some bizarre psychological thing going on in my brain that made him real.

And what about Jesus?

He was also real to me.

I remember, at the age of around seven or eight, fantasizing about Jesus showing up at the door to our house. There would be a knock at the door. I would be the one to answer it. I would get to the door, open it, and he was standing right there. I would recognize him, of course, because he looked like the thin, bearded man in the pictures in the museums, and was even dressed in the familiar robe. I would say nothing but would step out and we would both smile and hug. You're finally here, I would think to myself. After all this time, you came to me just as you promised you would.

Even though I was excited at the idea of one day seeing Jesus, I, like so many other Christians, was simultaneously terrified. The church taught that if I did the wrong things and forgot to beg for forgiveness, or if, heaven forbid, I committed the "unforgivable sin," that I would not be allowed to go to Heaven. Instead I would spend eternity burning in Hell.

Yet, I had another favorite daydream when I was a child. I would imagine my family standing among the millions of other families, with Jesus up on a big podium, giving instructions. This, of course, was Judgment Day. He would make the announcement that "All good people please move over to this side." My mother would grab my little sister by the hand and say to the family, "Come on, everyone, that's us."

I was the martyr. I would stand back and say, "No, Mom! That's not us!"

My fundamental thinking, of course, was one of manipulation. I felt that the "correct" thing to do was to say that we're sinners, and that Jesus would take note of this and then accept us into Heaven.

But there was something wrong. Even though this was a manipulative little move, deep down inside, I was really starting to believe the idea of sin. I was starting to believe what the Church was teaching me, that I really *was* a bad, evil person.

That is, after all, what the church was teaching me: I am a sinner. I am a bad person. I must beg for forgiveness. Think of it: As a child, the Church convinced me that I was an evil, terrible person.

Today I'm finally free of it all. I am the happiest I've ever been in my life. I don't sit around dreading tomorrow. I don't spend my days believing I'm a bad person and groveling on my knees for forgiveness. I don't just do good deeds in hope of some selfish reward of eternal glory after I die. I've finally learned how to love on my own instead of attributing it to some deity.

Life is good! Indeed, life is good.

And I'm recognizing the hypocrisy of the way life used to be. I'm seeing that when Christians focus every move they make on the reward of eternal life in Heaven, they are being selfish. I'd rather do good deeds because it's right, not because of some post-death reward. I'm not doing the good deeds for my own benefit. I'm doing good deeds because it's important to.

But getting here was not easy.

First I had to break free of the binding shackles of believing that I was naturally a horrible, bad person, because that was incredibly damaging to my psyche, especially when I was a child. What a horrible thing to do to children— teaching them they're bad, and scaring them with Hell and the Devil!

And what a miserable way to live, focusing all your attention on what happens after you die. And what a hypocritical way to live if your goal is just to impress God and to avoid punishment.

But how did I get to where am I now? How did I finally let go? It didn't happen overnight. It was a whole series of events over several years. I started to realize that Christian theology had some serious flaws whereby the theology couldn't possibly be true. And I started to realize the Bible was a re-hash of other very similar myths from earlier times. Little by little, over time, the whole thing fell apart until finally I realized I could not believe what was in the Bible or what the church was teaching me.

Initially I still called myself a Christian, but would qualify it: When asked, I would say, "Yes, I'm a Christian BUT I do not believe what most

Christians believe."

Eventually, even that fell apart. When asked if I'm a Christian, I would say, "Not really."

Now my answer is an unequivocal, "No."

In addition to letting go of believing the ancient myths, I also had to start accepting myself as I am. I had to accept that I really am a good person, and I gradually started to realize it's true. All those things I was beating myself up over for all those years were nothing more than silly things that are perfectly natural and human nature. So I may not have liked certain people. It's normal, it's natural, it's human.

And during that time I started to notice that the things so many Christians (not all, but many) consider "bad" are quite trivial in nature. For example, I'm usually considerate of other drivers on the road, but if I'm not able to let somebody merge into the highway ahead of me, I'm not going to consider myself a bad person for it and beat myself up over it, and I'm certainly not going to pray to some deity and beg for forgiveness over it. Nobody got hurt, and it didn't make the world a bad place. At most, somebody might have been mildly inconvenienced.

But there are evils in the world, and it surprises me that so many Christians (again, not all, but many) are totally blind to them. The United States has waged wars on other countries, causing their civilians to die, and many Christians see nothing wrong with it. Corporations are destroying the planet and letting poor people die, and many Christians don't believe this is true. Instead they're focusing their energy on trivial little issues that have practically no bearing in the greater scheme of things.

Sure, it's important to be polite to other drivers, for example, and to be considerate to people in general. This planet is packed with people and we need to make an effort to get along and not trample each other. In other words, I'm in no way trying to suggest that it's okay for us to all turn into a bunch of rude, misbehaving people. But there are greater problems that we need to think about, like ending war and poverty. Those are the things that matter, and I'm certainly not going to let superstitious beliefs of eternal punishment stand in my way and force me to get all hung up on whether I should or shouldn't have held the door for the person behind me when I was trying to help my little boy get through. They survived. Really, they did.

It's especially surprising to see self-proclaimed Christians ignoring the big problem of war, and acting like it's a good thing. Is killing the people of other countries really a good thing? People like to ask the question, "What would Jesus do?" Would Jesus go to war, pick up a gun, and blow somebody's head off? How many people did Jesus kill in the Bible? That's the great irony of it all: I don't even believe in the ancient stories in the Bible, yet I agree with many of the teachings of Jesus. Many people who claim to worship Jesus, however, have severely *twisted* ideas about what he would do.

Perhaps questions like this will shock people into understanding: Did Jesus kill anyone in the Bible? And if so, what method did he use? They didn't have guns, so did he just pick up a rock and beat his adversary on the head until his skull cracked open and blood gushed out and he died? Was it good when Jesus killed somebody?

Of course, the Jesus portrayed in the Bible never did such a thing. So why do people cling to this false idea of this Jesus character as a defense for their ideas and deeds, when their portrayal of him isn't even true to the stories?

And people have equally twisted ideas about what's "evil" and what isn't. One person I talked to several years ago said the most evil thing she could think of was a plaque with the Lord's Prayer printed backwards and hanging on the wall upside down. That's not even an *act*, but an *inanimate object!* First, it still says the Lord's Prayer, and even if it didn't, it's just an object on the wall. Deeds can be evil, not objects. Deeds that result in people getting hurt and dying are evil; objects hanging on walls are not.

Consider this: I've written this book that you are reading that spells out in no uncertain terms why I am no longer a Christian. There are people who feel that the nature of not being a Christian is evil, with a guaranteed punishment of eternal damnation. But what is the evil act? How did people get hurt? Will people die as a result of me refusing to accept the dogma of Christianity? Compare that to the millions of people who have died at the hands of Christianity during the various Crusades, for example. People can delude themselves and insist that those acts were not Christian in nature, but the truth is, if Christianity didn't exist in its present form, those people would *not* have been murdered. Christianity caused those murders. Atheism and agnosticism did not[*].

And so what if children want to read stories about wizard kids with magical powers? What harm is a little fantasy like that? World leaders are making heartless decisions that are resulting in the death of thousands or

---

[*] Note the comparison also to 9/11, an act performed by religious people, in that case people who were Islamic fundamentalist, but devoutly religious nevertheless.

millions of people. That's evil. Imagining that you can fly on a broomstick isn't. Why would I do something so horrible as teach my little boy that he's evil if he enjoys reading stories about wizard children? He's doing nothing wrong at all, so why should I permanently damage his psyche and self-esteem by convincing him that he's evil for wanting to read such stories?

And realistically, what harm could possibly come from reading such books? The only reason I've heard for not reading such books is people might turn away from Christianity. Well, as you can probably imagine, I have no problem with that whatsoever.

Laugh A Little

Did Adam have reproductive organs?

Yes, we can laugh at that question, but I'm also serious. The Bible says that God made Adam first, and it was only after Adam couldn't pick a partner from the animals that God created Eve. So did God give Adam reproductive organs in the event he might later have a female partner who he could reproduce with? Or did God add that part later after Eve came along?

Although it sounds silly, I am quite serious, because when you consider this kind of thing, it opens your eyes to some of the logical fallacies and downright silliness of the Bible. The Bible says God created Adam before he created Eve. So did Adam have all the parts necessary for reproduction? If so, why? The story doesn't make sense. Did it really happen? That's something to think about.

Perhaps I was fortunate that unlike so many people, as a child I did occasionally question things, things that just didn't make sense to me. I was a voracious reader of science books, and I saw things in the science books that just didn't connect with what I was taught by the Bible.

I was particularly fascinated by Carl Sagan's book *Cosmos*[*]. It wasn't just the amazing scientific material in it, but the wealth of beautiful pictures that made this a wonderful book. And the series that came on PBS was equally fascinating. I watched every episode of it.

But it bothered me. It talked about evolution, while Genesis talked about something entirely different. Clearly, the two couldn't have *both* happened.

* Sagan, Carl. Cosmos (2002 Edition). Random House, New York. ISBN 0375508325.

I didn't just accept evolution, however. The Bible came first. It had to, since it came from God. But what about the fact that we were seeing light from stars millions of light years away, while the Bible made the indirect claim that the Earth was only about 6000 years old? It just didn't make sense to me.

But one thing *was* clear to me: The Bible's truths came first and foremost. I was not to question it. Somehow, science had to fit with the Bible. If I studied science more and more, I would come to the conclusions that were laid out in the Bible. Right? At least that's what I thought at the time.

Consider that point for a moment, as it's of vital importance to understanding the mindset of today's proponents of Creationism and its sister-idea, Intelligent Design: The science must point to the facts laid out in the Bible.

And what if they don't? Well, let's see what today's Creationists themselves have to say about that:

> *No apparent, perceived or claimed evidence in any field, including history and chronology, can be valid if it contradicts the Scriptural record.*[*]

Is that realistic? Of course not. And in Chapter 3, *Of Science and Logic*, and Chapter 4, *Science and Logic versus Religion*, I'll show you exactly why it's absurd.

Another thing I was keenly aware of as a child was that the only reason I was a Christian was because my parents raised me as one. Of course, back then I considered myself *lucky* and *fortunate*.

I do have to wonder, though, how many people really give much thought to the fact that they happened to be born to Christian parents, and if they had been born, for example, to Jewish parents, they would likely follow Judaism, and if they had been born to Muslim parents, they would likely follow Islam, and so on.

Across the planet, there are people who have absolute belief in their religion, and that religion is exactly the religion their parents chose for them. (And, most likely, their parents belong to the particular religion for the same reason.) And these people feel strongly that their religion is correct.

This is even true with different types of Christianity. There are so many variations of Christianity, and people by-and-large believe that the one they happened to be born into is the absolutely correct one.

---

* From http://www.answersingenesis.org/about/faith, under Part D, number 6.

This should say something to people. This should be a clue that maybe something isn't quite right. You don't have millions of people jumping ship and all converging towards one faith in particular. So how can we automatically assume the faith we were born into is absolutely true and correct if our next door neighbor belongs to a different faith and also feels his or her faith is the only true one?

It's easy to feel strongly that your own religion is absolutely true, but when you notice that somebody else with a different religion also feels unequivocally that *their* religion is true, shouldn't that be a pretty good clue that a deep feeling of truthfulness doesn't necessarily imply the feeling is correct?

Certainly, though, people have heard that argument before, but I have to wonder why it hasn't caused them concern. It has for me. I noticed that the Jewish boy in my high school (there was only one as far as I knew) was absolutely sure in his faith; just as sure as I was.

I knew without a doubt that Jesus was real and the Son of God, and my Jewish friend knew without a doubt that Jesus was *not* the Son of God and the messiah was yet to come.

And interestingly, my feeling that Jesus was real was just as strong as when I was younger and felt that Santa was real. But Santa wasn't real.

That gave me something to think about.

I Was a Bad Child

I was a bad child. Even though I got straight A's, and I never did drugs, and I was never sent to the principal's office, and I treated adults with respect and I never got in fights, and I never stole anything, each Sunday at church it was laid out in perfectly plain English: I am a bad person. A *really* bad person.

I was reminded again and again that we're all sinners, and that we have sinned against God in both thought and deed. I was taught that I had not loved God with my whole heart. I was taught that I was, in short, a very bad person and that it was absolutely vital to my salvation that I *beg* God for forgiveness—because if I didn't, I would never enjoy everlasting life, which meant, in short, I would burn in hell after I died.

Although I never got in trouble at school, I knew plenty of kids at school who really did seem like bad people. I knew kids who would get in fights and beat up other kids, and who would come to school showing off the things they stole from the store. These kids were constantly getting taken to the office. They would cheat on their tests, and they would lie.

But the church taught me not to judge. And so I would see them doing these things and I would do all I could in my power to avoid passing judgment on them. I would avoid saying they were bad kids.

So if they weren't bad kids, then, in my mind, the only other possibility was that they were good kids! I would convince myself that: Even though they did things that seemed wrong, I didn't want to judge them, so I convinced myself they were fine and were doing nothing wrong.

I, however, knew that even though on the surface I was a good kid, I did occasionally think bad thoughts. I wanted to see these bullies get what was coming. I imagined that one day I would finally prevail and win against one of them in a fight. It was only in my mind, but that didn't matter. The church made it clear to me that I was a *sinner*, a bad person, and even thinking about such things was wrong.

And I knew the occasional bad thoughts were there, and it was clear to me that goodness wasn't in my heart. The church told me so.

And every once in awhile if I did actually say something nasty to one of these bullies or say something nasty about them, I would immediately have friends and family coming down *hard* on me, pointing out that that was *wrong*.

Yet, my friends would do the very same thing that they were criticizing me for. And worse, it seemed like they were also doing something else wrong: They were judging.

But: Judge not, lest you shall be judged. That's what the Bible said. So I would look the other way and not criticize people for doing bad things, while enduring their criticism, which I also avoided judging them by. They were good people. I wasn't.

This, of course, was totally warped, and if I presented these ideas to most adult ministers or pastors, they'd probably explain that I had the wrong ideas, and that today I'm presenting a rather unfair depiction of the whole theology. After all, the idea is forgiveness, that Jesus died for my sins, and so even though I'm a bad person, as long as I pray and confess that I'm a bad person, all will be fine and I can look forward to an eternity in Heaven.

But regardless of whether I'm being fair now or not, the fact is, what I'm describing here is exactly what went through my mind over and over as a child, right into adulthood. Even on those occasions where I felt confident that Jesus still loved me, it ate at me: I was convinced I am a bad person, a *sinner*.

It was taught to me by the church, and indeed ask any Christian today: Am I a sinner? Yes, so the religion says. We all are. And as a child, the point was more than driven home for me. And at that time, in my own warped little world, the bullies and mean kids at school were the good people. All the people around me who would so quickly point out the bad things I did were the good people. It doesn't matter if a trained theologian would tell me today that my thinking as a child was wrong. The fact is, that's the way I viewed the world, thanks to the church.

I was the bad kid. I was the one who was destined for Hell.

Now really: Is that a healthy attitude? Is it really good to teach this kind of *nonsense* to a mere *child* who has not yet developed the life skills necessary for coping with such horrible criticism? Should we really be teaching children that they're *bad?*

But I grew up believing it. Throughout childhood, and even as a young adult, I was filled with guilt for silly little things, things that I knew without a doubt made me a bad person. I liked women and found them physically attractive. (That was called *lust*. I was a sinner, a bad person.) I wanted to get a good job and make good money so that maybe—just maybe—I could live a decent lifestyle and pay off my debts and maybe buy a couple nice things. (That was called *greed*. I was a sinner, a bad person.)

And I did other things, too, like occasionally seeing somebody with a broken-down car and not stopping to help. (Although out of guilt I would offer a quick prayer to God to bring the police to help them, convincing myself that praying *was* helping. Today I take the easier route and just call for help on my cell phone. Still, I was filled with guilt.)

All these things ate at me. I would pray for forgiveness constantly, every day, many times a day. And when I would see other people misbehaving, I would accept it, because it wasn't my place to judge. And in my mind, it was clear that I was destined for Hell, while all the people around me were forgiven.

Face it: I was seriously messed up, all thanks to what the church was telling me. This was affecting my everyday life. Although I hid it from others, I privately spent most of my 20's in a severe depression. I hated myself, and my self-esteem was only getting lower by the day. All because of what I was told in church over and over since I was a child. Every Sunday we said:

Most merciful God, we confess that we are in bondage to sin and cannot free ourselves. We have sinned against You in thought, word and deed, by what we have done and by what we have left undone. We have not loved You with our whole heart; we have not loved our neighbors as ourselves. For the sake of Your Son, Jesus Christ, have mercy on us. Forgive us, renew us, and lead us, so that we may delight in Your will and walk in Your ways to the glory of Your holy name. Amen.

And I believed every word of it.

And today, frankly, I have an enormous amount of anger for what they did to me. They taught me to hate myself. That was the Christian way. Do we really want to continue teaching children to hate themselves? Is that really acceptable? Do we want children growing up with psyches and self-esteems that have been crushed and destroyed? Is that a *good* thing?

I say no. Absolutely not. It is *not* acceptable, and no self-respecting adult should think it's a good thing. It is an abomination to teach children such an obscene, disgusting theology. But it continues as it has for a couple thousand years.

And growing up I believed it all. I was a bad person filled with evil.

I hated myself for simply being human. And today I can only wonder how many hundreds of millions of people have gone through the same thing. That is nothing short of a global tragedy.

Of course, there's a bit of a problem here. Just because we might not like something doesn't make it untrue. In my 20s, I was starting to hate the religion and theology that I so much believed in. But I still believed it to be true. How could I possibly let go of something that was real, even if I didn't like it?

It wasn't easy.

Long ago I had decided to write this book, but at the time I was only upset with Christianity, and wasn't ready. So I began researching and reading and talking to people and studying everything I could, both for and against Christianity. And then it all started to make sense to me, how it came about and why it just isn't real. I had no idea that I would learn so much about mythology and Christianity's history, and that I would end up with a 300 page book—not just about why I didn't like Christianity, but why, in fact, Christianity isn't even real.

This book is about a journey, about my own journey of coming to realize that the faith I so long embraced isn't real, and hopefully this book will help others work through similar struggles.

But You Are Going to Hell (Not Really)

If you're a Christian reading this, I truly hate to be the one to tell you this, but I must. You are going to Hell. That's all there is to it.

Okay, I don't really think so. But if you're a Protestant, then there are at least some Catholics who believe you're going to Hell. And if you're a Catholic, there are some Protestants who believe you are going to Hell. I have met some Baptists who believe anyone who isn't Baptist is going to Hell. And there's a fringe group of extremist Christians in Topeka, Kansas who feel everybody who doesn't believe the way they believe is going to Hell.

You don't have to search very far, and you will find *somebody* out there—a self-professed Christian, no less—who believes that you are going to Hell.

And typically it's more than one person gathered together making the claim that you are destined for Hell. Often it's a group of people meeting together. And indeed Jesus said:

> *For where two or three are gathered together in my name, there am I in the midst of them. (Matthew 18:20)*

So we must presume that Jesus was there, egging them on. And they say you're going to Hell, and if one person says it's true, it must be true, right, especially since the Bible says Jesus was there with them?

That's just something to think about, some food for thought. No, I no longer believe that this imaginary character named Jesus was there. But if you're a Christian reading this, do you believe he's with the people saying YOU are going to Hell?

Now let's get started, shall we? Let's start by exploring a bit of the theology of why you and I are worthless pieces of crap destined for Hell.

two

I am Worthless (and So Are You)

erhaps the biggest aspect of Christianity that is singled out for attack from non-Christians is the self depravation which, to many of us, is not only dangerous, but horrible and out-right abusive. When I see Christians tormenting their children with threats of eternal punishment and damnation through hellfire, I become completely disgusted. And I get even more disgusted, to the point of anger, when I see people teaching their kids that they are fundamentally bad; that they are sinners and must bow to a deity and beg for forgiveness.

I'll get right to it: It is absolutely rotten the way the Christian church destroys the self esteem and psyche of children by teaching them that we are all sinners, and by terrifying them with threats of Hell, and by referring to Bible verses that imply that the vast majority of humans will end up in Hell.

How's that for an introduction to this chapter? But it is the heart of why I find Christianity appalling. I must raise this question, however: Just because I don't like Christianity, does that make it untrue? Indeed, it is untrue, as you'll see particularly in Chapter 6. For now, I want to address the dangerous theology of Christianity.

Indeed, the Dalai Lama has criticized the self-deprecating aspect of Christianity as well. In the pages that follow, I give you a summary of what exactly this theology of self-worthlessness is, why it's dangerous, and why I simply cannot accept it as truly coming from a supposedly loving God. Then I'll show you exactly why other aspects of Christian theology simply can't be true, neither logically nor morally.

The Promise and the Threat

One of the rather enticing features of Christianity is the promise of eternal life in an amazing, beautiful, loving place called Heaven.

But you won't automatically go to Heaven. In fact, there's a good possibility you'll end up in the other place, a place called Hell—according to the theology.

Hell is a place run by Satan, the antithesis of God, the evil one, the so-called Prince of Darkness. When you are sent to Hell, you are doomed to spend all eternity in misery.

One particularly odd thing about Christianity is that many of the fundamentalist Christians tend to spend more time talking about Hell than Heaven. The sermons are more about threats of what will happen to you if you don't get accepted into Heaven.

So while the promise of Heaven is certainly enticing, the threat of Hell may be more motivating: If you don't do what the Bible says, you will be sent to Hell forever, where you will be tortured and punished for all of eternity. And your chances of going to Hell are extremely high, considering only a tiny percentage of people have been chosen by God to go to Heaven*.

But how do you get into Heaven? The Bible offers many different answers to this, and they don't all totally fit together.

On one hand, the Bible teaches that all it takes is a belief in Jesus, the Son of God, to get into Heaven. Indeed, the single most famous verse in the Bible is probably John 3:16, which goes like this:

"For God so loved the world, that he gave his only begotten Son, that whosoever believeth in him should not perish, but have everlasting life." (John 3:16)

But it's clear that what's preached by the majority of Christian churches goes beyond this; to get into Heaven, you must confess your sins to God. That is, you must *repent*. Indeed, by and large, the main theology that runs throughout Christianity is "Repent or go to Hell."

For fundamentalists, the threat is usually expressed even more severely:

Repent or Burn.

* The book of Revelation in Chapter 7 states that 144,000 people are going to Heaven. That's a tiny percentage of all the Christians who have lived.

In other words, the entire Christian faith is built on a single threat: Do as God says, or you will burn in Hell for all eternity.

Here's the problem I have with this theology. If there is a God, he is certainly much wiser and more powerful than any of us. So why, then, would he do something so trivial and superficial as to use threats to get us to do good?

There is no sane way to approach this flawed theology with respect. After all, if God uses a severe threat like this to coerce people to do good, then the people who do good simply because of this threat are behaving as hypocrites. They don't actually *want* to do good; they're doing good for no other reason than to impress God. The good is not in their hearts. It is nothing more than superficial and hypocritical. And if God is all-powerful and all-knowing, then is this really going to fool God? Yet God was the one who supposedly made the rule! That makes no sense at all.

To me, the reason for this not making sense is clear: It's wrong, not true, and created by superstitious human leaders of ancient times who had agendas, not the least of which was to control the masses of people.

Sin and Self-worth(less)

Fundamental to the entire Christian theology is the notion of forgiveness. On the surface, this sounds like a really nice idea: You screw up; you pray to God and confess that you did something wrong; God forgives you; all is good. Sounds great, doesn't it?

But that's only on the surface. Beneath this sugar-coated layer is a much darker layer that has resulted in severe psychological trauma for millions of people—including children. And it's the trauma on that latter group, children, that angers me the most.

Allow me to explain. In Bible-talk, the word "sin" refers to wrongdoings. Unfortunately, the concept of sin is actually terribly vague. Ask a hundred Christians what the word "sin" means and you'll get 100 different answers. Ask them to provide some examples of sins, and you'll again get 100 different lists.

Nevertheless, I've taken the time to ask many Christians to provide examples of sins, and almost every time they mention things that I consider rather trivial. For example, one answer I heard was that it's a sin if you're driving on the expressway and you don't let somebody merge in in front of you. Other people I asked talked about "being nice" as the opposite of sin, and how it's important to be nice to people that you encounter in your daily life, such as in the grocery store.

Of course, I have also heard of some rather strange ones. One person I spoke with many years ago even said that she felt it was important to stop and pick up every single hitchhiker on the road, for to drive past would be a sin. (That's pushing the realm of *danger* in my book.)

But interestingly, these "sins" that people refer to almost never cause actual harm to anybody beyond a simple annoyance. Sure, it's nice to let somebody merge in front of you onto the highway, but if they have to tap their brake and drop in behind you, it's not the end of the world. Nobody got hurt, and life goes on. (Assuming, of course, you don't run them off the road and hurt them.) And if you're at the grocery store, it's nice to let the person with one item in the checkout lane go ahead of you and your $300 worth of groceries. But if you don't, they'll survive. They might be annoyed, but they'll survive.

Now I'm not saying you should be rude like that. As I said before, I think it's important for us to try to get along. But I'm asking in all honesty: In the greater scheme of things, does it really make a difference if on occasion little things happen like this where nobody gets hurt? Certainly they're annoyances, but it's not something we should be beating ourselves up over, running to church and confessing our sins over, considering ourselves evil people, while ignoring the *real* evils of the world where people really *are* getting hurt and really *are* unable to find food and shelter and really *are* dying.

Now compare these ideas to a few things I really *do* consider evil. For one, suppose you're a politician and you push some laws through Congress that limit help to poor people, and as a result, thousands of poor people—including children—die because they can't afford food. That's evil, because people get hurt.

Or, how about this: You're the President of the United States, and to avenge something that happened to your father, who was a former President, you invade a foreign country, topple the leader, have him killed, and in turn cause over four thousand US soldiers to die, along with hundreds of thousands of citizens of that country[*]. Yes, hundreds of thousands of people died—possibly

---

[*] Estimates of how many people have died as a result of the Iraq War vary greatly (spanning from a hundred thousand up to over a million), and the estimates aren't immune to political agenda. Many organizations who support the war are inclined to reproduce statistics that show lower counts, while anti-war groups tend to reproduce statistics showing higher counts.

even a million or more—because of your decisions.

Compared to that, is it really going to change much if you don't let that car merge in? Now I'm not saying we should all become a bunch of self-absorbed people who refuse to look out for each other. I do let people merge in, and I have let people go ahead of me in the checkout lane. But if for some reason I don't do it, I don't lose any sleep over it, and I certainly don't pray for forgiveness. And more importantly, if somebody doesn't let me merge in, I don't expect them to pray for forgiveness, and I certainly don't think they'll be condemned for all eternity to Hell for it!

And this brings me to my point: We are humans with natural, built-in human qualities, and we live in a crowded world. There are things we do that are normal and perfectly human, and the churches teach people that these things are wrong and sinful. People then beat themselves up and mentally torture themselves when they don't behave as a Perfect Human, and they convince themselves that they are not very good people, and they come to church and beg God for forgiveness—for being human.

Unfortunately, this type of mental attack takes place often among those who are least equipped to mentally defend themselves: children.

I already mentioned in Chapter 1 how I would imagine overtaking the bullies, but then feel guilty. Now we certainly don't want to teach children that fighting is good, because it isn't. But the problem is, from week after week of sermons at church, I started feeling incredibly guilty about these thoughts I had towards the bullies; so guilty, I was developing self-hatred.

But the sermons also taught that God knows what's in our hearts, and that we had to truly have goodness in our hearts, and that we had to love our enemies. And that's where I fell apart mentally and psychologically.

Think of it! I was just a child, and it was perfectly normal for me to imagine overpowering the bullies and to finally be treated with respect. And it's certainly human to not like certain people. As I said, I had no fantasies of killing them or gunning them down; I simply imagined winning a few battles and being treated as an equal, and throughout it I obviously didn't find myself exactly *liking* those other kids, much less, *loving* them.

But the church taught me not only that this was wrong, but made it pretty clear to me that God can see through me and know that deep inside I wasn't being compassionate and *certainly* I wasn't loving my enemy as Jesus instructed:

But I say unto you, Love your enemies, bless them that curse you, do good to them that hate you, and pray for them which despitefully use you, and persecute you. (Matthew 5:44.)

...nor was I turning the other cheek, as Jesus also instructed:

If someone strikes you on the right cheek, turn to him the other also. (Matthew 5:39, second half)

This all added up to one thing: *I was obviously a bad person inside.*

And these thoughts were running through my head before I was even 11 or 12 years old! What on Earth did these Christians think they were trying to accomplish, teaching a child that in his heart he was a fundamentally bad person? That is a horrible, terrible thing to do to a child. And that is exactly what many churches continue to do to people of all ages. They convince people that they are bad.

Then the theology of forgiveness comes in. The people are then taught that the only thing that they can do is to pray—no, *beg*—for forgiveness. In the Lutheran church that I attended, we would actually get onto our knees in a groveling position, and beg for forgiveness. It was pretty easy to beg at that point, because the notion that we were bad people was pretty well ingrained into our heads by then.

And so we would beg, week after week.

But that's where things got interesting. Different churches have different ideas on what happens next. In our Lutheran church, the preacher would then declare our sins completely forgiven. And so suddenly, after all the horrid feelings of being a bad person, we would feel happier, like we were transformed. And it was a good feeling! But then the cycle would continue, week after week after week. I remember showing up and reaching rock-bottom, believing I was total scum. Then suddenly I would get this uplifting feeling as I was forgiven. Up and down; up and down; up and down. Unfortunately, the up part only lasted a few hours, because by Sunday evening, I would start to see myself being "bad" again, and that's how I would feel the rest of the week. So most of the week was spent knowing I was a bad person.

The end result was years upon years of major damage to my psyche and my self-esteem. By the time I reached my 20's, I was pretty convinced I was a lousy excuse for a human and that I was fundamentally bad and evil. And I was constantly asking God for forgiveness. In fact, looking back, it was pretty pathetic.

I can't speak for other people, but I can say that most Christians I have met, if asked, "Are you a good person," would hesitate to answer yes. They would have loads of self-doubt. They would question whether they're a good person. They would be leery of answering in the affirmative. Many would even say, "No. I'm a sinner."

Now is that really healthy? Is it really good for an entire population of people to be filled with such self-hatred? Well, actually, it is a good thing, if you're an evil politician trying to control the masses of people. Let's consider that next.

Built-in Control Mechanisms

Although I'm not much for the idea of socialism, I do have to say that Marx was onto something when he wrote that religion is like an opium for the people*. I can attest that there was this amazing feeling inside me during that moment when I believed I was suddenly forgiven for doing all those things that are perfectly normal.

Forgiveness was like a drug to me. And I'm sure it is to other people. How often do they return to the church again and again to get their drug? Many return every week, some even more often.

And they need it, because they truly believe that they will not be granted everlasting life without it! Indeed, the church teaches them that they must repent and be forgiven or they will burn in Hell for all eternity. What a serious, terrifying threat!

But that "repent" idea presents a problem in itself, because the church teaches that you must truly feel sorry for what you did. You're not just begging for forgiveness; true repentance comes from deep within the heart.

But that's a problem, because, as I said, many of these supposed "sins" are perfectly normal human characteristics. One has to wonder how many people sit there in total fear and dread, knowing that deep inside they *like* doing these things. (Sex in all its different forms certainly comes to mind here.)

---

* This phrase appeared in Marx's *A Contribution to the Critique of Hegel's Philosophy of Right*. You can find an English translation at http://www.marxists.org/archive/marx/works/1843/ critique-hpr/intro.htm.

When I was a child, I *liked* the idea of overpowering the bullies. It felt good to imagine that for once in my life I would be regarded as an equal among my peers. Why wouldn't that feel good? Yet, I was supposed to feel sorry in my heart in addition to verbally asking for forgiveness. How could I truly be forgiven, then, if I wasn't truly feeling sorry in my heart?

The solution, of course, was to keep going to church, and keep "working on it." This started in my childhood, and moved forward right into my adulthood. As an adult, it wasn't about overpowering bullies. Instead, it was other "sins," such as disliking my coworker who treated everybody like crap, and really hoping he would get fired. Other people commit other sins, of course; other people feel guilty when they eat junk food. How can they truly repent if they love junk food? What a position to be in! And I already mentioned sex, which alone has certainly provided tons of guilt for millions of people.

And let's not forget that all these are normal human characteristics. Even more so, they are important survival mechanisms in our society! We need to move up in our positions at work if we want to maintain a decent lifestyle. Yet that in itself could be construed as greed, which is, again, a sin.

And that's why this is such a trap and a control mechanism in our society, whether it's a conscious decision on behalf of the leaders or not. (I tend to think not, as I'm not much of a conspiracy theorist.)

As a result of such mechanisms, people ultimately become serious prisoners to the church, and, ultimately, to society. People who subscribe to a Marxist belief could even, with good cause, take it a step further, and note that by forcing people to believe they are evil and greedy, they will not attempt to move up the ladder at work. And by teaching them to repress their jealousy (and beg for forgiveness when they don't repress it), workers will simply step aside and not try harder when their coworker does get the promotion they were hoping for, or, even more likely, not go and start their own company and compete with their former boss.

In short, through all these control mechanisms, it would be very easy for a country's leaders to keep the people right where they want them to be, as hard-working laborers who have no aspirations other than to work hard and make the boss rich.

Such control mechanisms pretty much encompass the entire Bible. The Old Testament provides a perfect example—a testament, if you will—of how easy it is for a government to control people by adding a little religion. Consider this: suppose you're the governor of a primitive tribe, and there's a certain plant that tastes really good but makes people sick when they eat it, and can even kill them. You can't get the people to stop eating it. What do you do? You try telling them it's wrong, but all they do is keep eating it anyway. (Look how many of us love junk foods that aren't healthy; it's *normal* and part of our biological survival mechanism to crave high-calorie foods.) As the ruler of the tribe, you want your tribe to grow and become strong with lots of healthy people. What do you do to get them to stop eating these plants that are making them sick?

Easy: You tell them God doesn't want them to eat it. Bring religion into the picture and it's a done deal. If the people believe that you speak for God, then they will easily do what you say. This has been done since the beginning of human history and continues to happen to this day.

Indeed, the Old Testament is filled with such warnings. The Old Testament tells us not to eat shellfish. Today, most of the more modern governments, such as that of the United States, have rigid laws in place for safe food handling. We know that shrimp, when not properly handled, can make us *very* sick. But back in ancient times, they didn't have safe handling methods. So the only real option was to not eat such foods at all. Shrimp, therefore, was outlawed in the Old Testament, and is still outlawed in most Jewish traditions, which continue to use the Old Testament's rules.

Religion has proven over and over that it's a powerful tool for controlling people. And the Bible has many additional control mechanisms built into it, mechanisms that ensure that after the people are under control, they won't stray.

The Bible is filled with verses that tell us not to question God. That, of course, is easily interpreted to mean we shouldn't question the leaders of the church. Indeed, many Christians I've spoken to have an almost unhealthy respect for the pastor or minister of their church, to the point that borders on absurdity. But the verses are clearly there. Here's one I refer to a couple times in this book:

It is better to trust in the LORD than to put confidence in man. (Psalms 118:8)

Many Christians take this as a warning against people who might question Christianity. But certainly the single, ultimate built-in control is this famous gem:

*Verily I say unto you, All sins shall be forgiven unto the sons of men,
and blasphemies wherewith soever they shall blaspheme:
But he that shall blaspheme against the Holy Ghost hath never
forgiveness, but is in danger of eternal damnation. (Mark 3:28-
29)*

Or in the New International Version:

*"I tell you the truth, all the sins and blasphemies of men will be
forgiven them. But whoever blasphemes against the Holy Spirit
will never be forgiven; he is guilty of an eternal sin." (Mark 3:28-
29, NIV)*

This is known as the unforgivable sin, and it is used as a grave warning to
Christians: Don't sin against the Holy Spirit, or you will burn in Hell forever,
and there is *no chance* for forgiveness. None. You can repent all you want;
you can feel bad about it; you can beg God to forgive you, but he won't listen.
You will burn forever.

This single verse has probably caused more terror in Christians than
all the other verses combined. This is the single most severe warning in the
entire Bible, and people do *not* take it lightly. I've personally known people
who have been *terrified* into submission, and they don't dare question Christianity in the least, for fear of committing the unforgivable sin and burning
in Hell for all eternity.

Not only is this the ultimate threat in the entire Bible, it's the ultimate
control mechanism. Think about it: Once you start believing the Bible and
you start believing the theology of the unforgivable sin, *you are effectively
trapped from ever leaving.* It is nearly impossible to let go.

And most people I've talked to who have managed to let go agree that
this one threat was the biggest stumbling block. Because even though they
might have decided they don't believe in God and the Bible, there's still the
"what-if" factor: What if it's true? What if I'm wrong? And if I am wrong, then
my leaving the church is pretty much a guaranteed ticket to Hell.

In fact, I'm sure that there are many people who figure that I, by writing
this book, have basically purchased my own one-way, non-refundable, per-
manent ticket to Hell. (I've talked to many fundamentalist Christians who

have made it clear that they believe I have.)

> **If you're in the same boat, questioning your beliefs, and not sure you dare walk away due to these threats, then I can offer hope. Please read this whole book. You will see that what's taught in the Bible simply cannot be true. Not "probably isn't" true. But *can't* be true. It isn't true.**

(If you're in a hurry and want to see why the theology of the Bible can't be true, read the short section, "Who is Working with Whom" in Chapter 5. Then read as much of the rest of Chapter 5 as you care to.)

Man is Evil?

When you start looking at the history of the Christian Church, this whole concept of us being evil and needing to beg for forgiveness has a long, miserable history. But it wasn't always that way.

Where did this idea come from? It goes back to early disagreements on the fundamental nature of humans. St. Augustine, an early theologian who was born in 354 AD, taught that sin began with the first man, Adam, and continues through each and every one of us. This idea has spawned the theology of *total depravity*, which means that humans are, by nature, evil.

Think about that for a moment: The church is saying that you and I and all our friends are fundamentally evil to our core; that we were all born that way. And there are plenty of Bible verses to back it up.

To be fair, this theology isn't universally accepted among the Christian churches. But those that differ only differ on one part of it, and that's how people can overcome this fundamental nature of evil, whether it can be done through free will or whether it can only be done with God's help. Regardless of this little difference, the common theme is still present throughout, that you and I are fundamentally evil.*

As I've already mentioned, telling people—especially children—that

---

* This theology wasn't always in place. During Augustine's times, others presented opposing ideas, such as the thought that people are fundamentally neutral. But they were quickly quieted and called heretics.

they're evil is a horrible thing to do and damaging to children. Besides, if there is a God, why would God create something that is fundamentally evil? Why not fundamentally good? Or why not fundamentally neutral, that people have both good and bad?

Sure, we all make mistakes. Nobody is perfect. But that's a far cry from suggesting that we're each filled with evil.

But that's what churches teach. And that's where the theology of *divine grace* enters. (A lot of churches don't use this particular term, but they do teach the basic idea.) This is the forgiveness part. One common definition taught in the Lutheran church where I grew up is that "divine grace" is "undeserved forgiveness."

To me, that just reiterates the basic idea that we're just a bunch of evil scumbags. But it piles more on the heap by saying that even though we're evil scumbags, God will still somehow manage to forgive us. But the kicker is the "undeserved" part. Even though God will forgive us, we must not forget, so the teaching goes, that *we don't deserve it.*

Again, that's yet more assault on the psyches of the people, including the children. I can't stress enough just how disgusting I find this belief: teaching children that they are incredibly bad people by nature, and that only through God's grace will they receive forgiveness, because without it, they are such bad, horrible people that they certainly don't *deserve* the forgiveness.

But why do the churches do this to people?

Easy: They have to. Because if they don't, people might actually start to think they're decent people. And if they think they're decent people, they might stop coming to church because they won't feel they need to beg for forgiveness. And then people might stop buying into the religion and will stop putting money into the collection plates.

And when the people stop believing, the churches will lose their power, their hold, and their control over the people.

Therefore, the early leaders of the church clearly recognized that they had to keep the people in check by reminding them that they are, at heart, fundamentally bad, corrupted, evil, dirty, morally bankrupt, downright disgusting people. And that's why people who opposed Augustine's ideas of us being fundamentally evil were quickly quieted. It all fits together like a puzzle.

And you know what? I categorically reject this. As you'll continue to see throughout this book, I refuse to accept the idea that you and I are fundamentally bad people. Anyone who has spent time around children has seen that most children have a lot of good points, a natural caring and compassion. Of course, many also have a natural selfishness, but that's simply human and by no means evil. Looks at animals: They fight over who gets the food. It's normal, and the result of a survival instinct, and certainly not evil. And when children fight over who gets to play with the toys, they're just being human. Not evil—just human. And we, as parents, teach them to be less selfish. And they quickly and easily learn right from wrong on their own, which again, is natural and human.

Sorry, I don't buy that people are fundamentally evil. It just isn't true.

But, as I said in Chapter 1, just because I don't like the theology, does that really mean it's not true? Not necessarily. But there are many reasons why Christianity cannot possibly be true. Let's talk about the starving people in Africa.

The Starving People: God's Blessing in Disguise?

Not only has the church convinced people they're evil, it has spawned some truly warped and demented ideas.

I have yet to see a reasonable response from a Christian to the question of why there are so many starving people in Africa. Probably the most absurd, selfish, obscene response centers around the notion that God has chosen us Americans to help them. While I think it's important that we do our best to help the people in Africa, I think it's ridiculous to believe that a deity intentionally set it up that way. And here are many reasons why.

First, if this supposed God is able to feed the people of Africa, why doesn't he? Is he unable to? Or is he just ignoring them?

Too often the response I get is that this is a perfect opportunity for us to be good Christians and help feed the people. Sorry, I cannot in good conscience accept that as an answer. While I applaud each and every one of us who is making an effort to feed the people in Africa, I think that this answer about God's plan is a total cop-out simply because it shows the arrogant, self-centered nature of the Christian who is providing the answer.

Put yourself in the shoes (or bare feet, more likely) of the starving child in Africa, and look at the Christian response from her perspective. The supposed Christian God has intentionally set up a situation where you, the African child, are going through the pain of losing family members to starvation, unable to find food yourself, so that some arrogant white Christian in the United States who has plenty of food can demonstrate to God that he or she is a good Christian by helping you.

Imagine the thoughts of the poor woman as she holds the body of her baby who died of hunger when told, "It's okay. God did this to provide a good lesson to the Christians in America."

To the Christian I say: You *can't* be serious. That is a morally reprehensible way to look at the problem. Is this all about *you?* Did your supposed God set up this whole situation so that *you* can look good and impress God and get accepted into Heaven after *you* die, so *you* can go from one plush life to an even plusher life, while simply using the starving Africans as nothing more than human tools to help *you* get into Heaven?

Unfortunately, after much dialogue (typically online) with Christians, I have seen many responses to this statement I just made, and they only get more disgusting. For starters, typically the Christians I've spoken to totally miss the point. They think that I'm somehow blaming God for the starving people in Africa. But that is *not* the point.

I am not blaming God for the starvation in Africa. How can I when I do not even believe in the Christian God?

Instead, I am recognizing that there is a very real problem that our entire global society has created, and I'm using that as an example to show that this God character that our ancestors created and Christians believe in simply cannot be real, because if he were, he wouldn't allow it to happen. And further, I'm pointing out that all your explanations are nothing more than silly rationalizations that put the focus on *you* and your own salvation and present the starving children as nothing more than collateral damage in God's plan for *your* salvation.

I have yet to see a good explanation for this one. All the explanations focus on either me blaming God (which misses the point) or on why it is up to us as Christians to help those people starving in Africa, which is at best an agnostic viewpoint in that it implies God is not helping and instead expects his people to clean up the mess (that he apparently created, or, at the least, allowed to happen). After all, in common usage, "agnostic" refers to people who think there might be a God but that he doesn't interact directly with people. And isn't that what Christians are saying when they say it's up to them to do God's work and take care of the people in Africa?

I want to be clear, however: I *agree* we need to help the starving people of this world. But let's drop the Christian part, because frankly, I don't care to listen to Christians expressing how this little act of kindness of feeding the kids is actually more about you and your eternal salvation than actually giving a damn about the starving children.

The situation of the starving people in Africa is definitely a bad one. But let's look at another bad situation: The tsunami of 2004. This tsunami caused 225,000 people to die.

For a Christian, there are many ways this incident could be interpreted. Some Christians might look at it simply as an unfortunate natural disaster, and not factor God into the equation at all. But how can they do that when they believe God is absolutely there? Surely if God exists, either he was involved in it or he wasn't. If God wasn't involved in it, then he was ignoring the needs of the world, and such a view is, again, very agnostic in nature, and if somebody claiming to be a Christian feels this a way, they should seriously consider whether they truly believe in such a God.

The other alternative is that God was involved in one way or another. The "nice" version is that God was not responsible for the tsunami but was involved in the goodwill that people from all over the planet extended in helping the victims. But this view is hardly different from the agnostic view, because one must ask: Where was God? Why did God sit back and watch the tsunami but do nothing? A very common answer here is to brush it off and say that God works in mysterious ways. But is that realistic? That God somehow had a "plan" to kill all those people in one giant swoop so that the Christians would have a chance to demonstrate to God they're good people? That's pretty disgusting if you ask me. What a horrible thing to do. But if it was God's plan, then why did he want all those people to die together in the first place?

That brings me to what's probably the most obscene response of all, which came from the fundamentalist preachers, particularly the famous ones that make their vile presence a regular occurrence on cable TV. Many such preachers actually said that the tsunami was some kind of warning or punishment to the world for allowing "evils" to occur such as homosexuality. (Apparently to these people, two men enjoying some physical time together in the privacy of their own home without anyone else knowing is the worst evil of all, far more, than say, the CEO of an oil corporation destroying the lands of native people in Africa so that people die simply so the corporation can profit.)

On one hand I would like to just brush this off with a pleasant "fuck you" response to these televangelists. But I do feel compelled to go beyond just telling them off and actually tackling the response head-on. So here goes.

The problem I have with this is once again the standard selfishness that I laid out regarding the starving people in Africa, because once again, the focus is on the *us* and the *me*—the Christians of the world, primarily America. It is what I would call a Christocentric theology that is morally repugnant in its self-centeredness.

Think about it: Suppose the tsunami was a "warning" from God. But who is this warning supposed to be for? The people who died? Hardly; they're gone and can't heed a warning. If there was a warning, then it was for the people who survived, and, I would venture to guess that the televangelists feel the warning was primarily for Americans. So if this were truly a warning from God, then God's focus (and "love" I suppose?) is, once again, on the Westerners who sat back and watched it on TV. And this, like the problem of the starving people in Africa, is again at the expense of innocent people, in this case the quarter million people who died. Wouldn't you love to be one of those random people God picked to stomp on like ants just so he can make a point to his chosen people, the Christians of America, warning them not to allow homosexuality?

Once again, that is disgusting, and the people who suggested such a thing should be utterly ashamed of themselves.

Now again, I commend the people who actually worked to help those that were displaced and hurt by the tsunami. I'm in no way belittling their efforts. But once again, can we please leave religion out of it so we can focus on what really matters? Let's not take this huge disaster and place the focus on the salvation of somebody who wasn't hurt by it. I hardly think that the focus of this tragedy in the South Pacific should be on the eternal salvation of some John Doe sitting on a couch in the middle of America. To suggest it is would be nothing short of selfishness.

Invariably, though, there are people who looked at those who managed to survive and made this statement I've heard all too often after other disasters:

"It was a blessing nobody else died."

It was? It was a *blessing*? Recently I saw on the news a story about a maniac who opened fire in a shopping mall, killing several innocent people. What a horrible thing to do. The guy ended up killing himself, so he couldn't stand trial for his heinous crimes.

The evening news, of course, interviewed people afterwards. Several people who were at the mall made statements along the lines of, "It was a blessing from God that we were spared." I'll get right to the point on that one: So if God blessed these people who survived, what does that say for the people who didn't make it? That God ignored them? Or that God purposely wanted them to die and that the gunman was simply fulfilling God's will and working as an agent for God? Once again, that's a pretty selfish thing to say.

I've thought about this a great deal, and I've come up with what I think is the best story to make the point. Suppose there are two families, each having a very sick child staying a children's hospital. Both children have the same ailment. Both families pray desperately to God to save their child. One child suddenly starts to recover and ultimately gets better and survives. The other child, unfortunately, dies.

While the family of the child who dies all sit in the lobby of the hospital crying and consoling each other, the other family happily passes by on their way out, loudly proclaiming that their faith in God healed their child, and what a miracle it is and how much God loves them.

Now think how the other family will feel when they hear this. Not only are they having to deal with a horrible event—losing their child—but they must also listen to this other family say that God saved their child. And imagine what might go through their minds. Did God ignore their pleas but not the pleas of the other family? Did God somehow "like" the other child better? Many Christians would try to comfort themselves (or others) by suggesting, once again, that God somehow has a greater plan. (I would hope they wouldn't be so vile as to suggest that God was punishing the family whose child died. However, I would dare say that if the child was a teenager and homosexual and the disease was AIDS, there are a good share of people who *would* suggest such a thing.) So is that really God's plan? To take down an innocent child and somehow teach people something? That's pretty sad if that's what they believe, and I can hardly accept such a thing.

But once again, I want to be absolutely clear here about this: I am not saying I'm mad at God or blaming God. Rather, I'm saying that people get sick, and people die, and it's disgusting when those that survive try to imply that God somehow favors them, or, worse, is trying to issue a warning to *them* at the expense of another human being.

Internal Terror

Although what I just said was quite harsh, there is a huge group of Christians that I have a huge amount of sympathy for, and that's the group that is experiencing the same enormous internal torment that I experienced.

Recently I read a news story where a man in his 50's was violently murdered. The murderer was caught; he stood trial and went to prison for a life sentence. The victim's wife, a woman also in her 50's, said, "I know that I have to forgive him for killing my husband or I won't be able to go to Heaven."

That is a tragedy and the church is to blame. This woman has been through enough. Her husband was murdered and she has to live the rest of her life without him while knowing that the last minutes of his life were total terror. And now the Church has taught her that *she* could be the one to receive the ultimate punishment as the final result of this horrible act!

Think about it: It would be very easy for the murderer to sit in prison and start to feel guilty about what he did, and finally confess his sins and accept Jesus. Christianity teaches us that if he does that, he'll probably go to Heaven.

It is far more difficult, however, for this woman to forgive the murderer. How can she? Some say it can be done, but it's far from easy. And now she's scared that she could be the next victim—not the murderer's victim, but God's victim when he sends her to Hell! She's worried she's the one who will ultimately be punished and sent to Hell for all of this! And it wasn't even her fault!

I know that people will feel that what I'm about to say goes totally against what we're taught, and some will even say it will earn me a shortcut trip to Hell. But I'll say it anyway: This murderer killed a man and destroyed a woman's life. And people honestly think this woman is required to forgive the murderer? I disagree. While it would be to her benefit to somehow try to move on with her life and try to find some happiness and not destroy herself with anger, she is under no obligation to do something good for this man. It is certainly noble and admirable if she *wants* to, but that is strictly her decision, and she should not be punished if she chooses to not forgive him. And I cannot believe that a reasonable God would disagree with me on this, and that's just one of the many reasons I cannot accept the Christian idea of a God.

However, I should probably clarify something. Some people consider the act of putting the anger behind them forgiveness. Some people say that forgiveness means not living with anger and simply forgetting the person who did it. That's fine, and an extremely healthy thing to do. But regardless, to force people into thinking that they will go to Hell and receive eternal, severe punishment if they *don't* make this step of moving on acts as a form of punishment itself and is wrong. Would a truly good, loving creator really do such a thing? (But remember: At this point people could easily say that just because I don't like it doesn't mean it isn't real. But as I've said before, throughout this book you'll see why the Christian idea of God isn't real.)

No Moral Compass

Non-believers get abused again and again by Christians for supposedly lacking morals. I've heard all the arguments over and over. At least twice I've been told via private email by fundamentalist Christians that non-believers live horrible lives filled with sex and drugs. (Yet at the same time, many of these fundamentalists think that Christians make up a tiny percentage of the population, and so you have to wonder why they don't see drug-laden, sex-filled behavior by the rest of the population in places like the grocery stores.)

And other claims come from more mainstream Christians, claims such as the need for God to give us a moral compass so we know what is right and what isn't. I'm not kidding, I've met people who say they need the preacher at the pulpit to tell them what's right and what's wrong. Is it okay to play cards?

To respond to this, let's return to the starving children in Africa. Why are the Christians feeding them? In all fairness, I know many Christians who are sending money to charities to feed the starving children simply because they care. That's good, and I commend them for that. But I also know that many Christians I've talked to are doing it because God wants them to do it. And why do what God tells you to do? Why, eternal salvation, of course! Who wants to piss off their maker and end up in Hell forever?

Doing good just because God wants you to, to me, seems like a case

Laugh A Little

I swear this is true: Growing up, I had a Baptist friend tell me that although Christians aren't allowed to play cards, his pastor had deemed it acceptable to play the card game Uno (from Mattel), because that one didn't suffer from the same moral problems that other card games did. And so my friend and his family partook in regular Uno matches with their fellow parishioners. I'm not making this up.

Although, oddly, this guy's parents didn't go to church anymore. "They were saved years ago," was his explanation. Again, true story.

study in Hypocrisy 101. Do people only do good acts because they want to impress God? And are they incapable of determining what is good and evil until God tells them so?

Consider the case, for example, of robbing an elderly lady leaving a grocery store. Who would want to do that? Nobody, I hope. I don't want to. Why? Because I think it would be a horrible thing to do to somebody. If I see an elderly lady walking to her car causing no trouble at all, the last thing I would do is wish something horrible on her like getting robbed or killed. And I'm sure most people would agree, regardless of religious background.

But why do I feel that way? I'm not looking to a god for an answer on whether that's wrong. I just know it's wrong.

And why do Christians feel it's wrong? Hopefully a good share would agree that it's just wrong. But there are plenty who say that the moral compass comes from God and that us non-believers have no moral compass. Translation: They feel it's wrong because God said it's wrong.

Really? Because if the only reason they say it's wrong is because God says it's wrong, then that is no different from saying that without God telling them it's wrong, they would just as soon do the deed. Secretly, in their hearts, they would have no problem beating up and robbing that poor old lady walking to her car, and the only thing that stops them is that God doesn't want them to do it.

That might seem like an unfair assessment, but it's not. They are, after all, saying the *only* reason it's wrong is because God says it's wrong, and that without that little warning from the old man in the sky, they would see nothing wrong with it.

Either that or they *must agree* that they see that it's wrong on many different levels. They could say God says it's wrong, but they might also agree that regardless of religion, it's still just plain wrong and even if God didn't warn against it they still wouldn't do it. And if they reach that point, then they are admitting that things can be wrong *without* God saying they're wrong, and then they're admitting that it is perfectly reasonable and possible for a non-believer to feel that certain things are wrong. And that means they agree that it is possible to have morals without religion.

I'll sum it up like this in a rather shocking, pointed, possibly unfair manner: "Unlike you Christians who would prefer to rob and kill harmless old ladies buying groceries where the only thing stopping you is God, I personally care about that old lady and really don't want to hurt her."

Feel free to quote me on that. And do you find it unfair? Then you might want to re-evaluate the logic in saying that your moral compass comes from God, because that is ultimately what you are saying.

Consider the following choices:

1. You do good because it is right.
2. You do good because it makes you feel good.
3. You do good because you want to impress God.
4. You do good because you are afraid of burning in Hell for all eternity.
5. You do the Church's official definition of good (even if it's not) because you are afraid of burning in Hell for all eternity.

It might be hard for some people to imagine this, but I put myself and other non-believers squarely in the first two slots. And I perceive Fundamentalist Christians as being squarely in slot number 5. And I perceive mainstream Christians (for the most part) as living in slots #3 and #4.

I'm not saying it's correct; I'm saying it's how I perceive most Christians. To me, it is so painfully obvious that a great majority of Christians perform their acts of good based first on what the Church defines as "good" and second, because they're afraid of burning in Hell and, possibly, because they want to impress God.

They can say I'm wrong until they're blue in the face, but they'll have an extremely difficult time convincing me I'm wrong. Actions speak louder than words, but when combined with words, the true intentions are clear.

And at some point they must ask themselves: Is it wrong to rob somebody at the grocery store, and if so why?

The Ten Commandments

Is it just me, or is everybody sick of hearing about how the United States Government is based on the Ten Commandments? I've even heard some atheists concede that even though they don't believe in the Bible, they do at least agree that the Ten Commandments are a pretty good starter for a moral code.

I disagree. As Sam Harris points out in his controversial (but excellent) book *Letter to a Christian Nation*, the first four commandments have nothing whatsoever to do with morality. Take a look at them and you'll see what he means. They're all about making sure you don't stray from worshipping the God who supposedly wrote them.

And that is anything BUT American. In the US, we have freedom of religion, and our laws do not require us to worship any god in particular. So US law is definitely *not* based on the first four commandments.

But what about the rest of the commandments? Surely, people ask, you must agree that *Thou shalt not steal* is a pretty good rule. Sure it is. But come on; we all know that stealing has been wrong for ages, and that we don't need the Ten Commandments to tell us it is wrong. Other cultures that have spawned separately from the ancient Judaic culture of the Ten Commandments have also decided that stealing is wrong, without the Ten Commandments to tell them such.

And besides, as written, the rule against stealing isn't particularly useful. Many state and local laws in the US exist that allow stealing under certain situations. For example, if my next door neighbor plants a tomato garden, and one of the plants grows through the fence in my yard, many cities and towns make it legal for you to pick the tomatoes on that part of the plant. The law states that it becomes yours.

I presented that argument to a Christian and he said to me that even though it may be legal, it's still wrong and still stealing. But apparently he forgot to read the New Testament where it clearly states that we must follow the earthly human laws. Here's the quote, from Paul's writings:

Let every soul be subject unto the higher powers. For there is

* Harris, Sam. Letter to a Christian Nation. Vintage; Reprint edition (January 8, 2008)

no power but of God: the powers that be are ordained of God.
(Romans 13:1)

This is from the King James Version; modern translations typically make reference to governing authorities or rulers for "powers that be," as in the New International Version:

Everyone must submit himself to the governing authorities, for there is no authority except that which God has established. The authorities that exist have been established by God. (Romans 13:1, NIV)

In other words, this verse clearly says to obey your government.

And what about the IRS? Many people consider the government to be stealing from us. But, Jesus also told us to go ahead and pay our taxes:

"Tell us then, what is your opinion? Is it right to pay taxes to Caesar or not?" But Jesus, knowing their evil intent, said, "You hypocrites, why are you trying to trap me? Show me the coin used for paying the tax." They brought him a denarius, and he asked them, "Whose portrait is this? And whose inscription?" "Caesar's," they replied. Then he said to them, "Give to Caesar what is Caesar's, and to God what is God's." (Matthew 22:17-21)

So that's a situation where stealing is allowed. So the phrase "Thou shalt not steal" isn't particularly useful, in fact, because modern laws are much more complex than just that.

And what about the commandment about coveting your neighbor's property? Who hasn't driven around and admired somebody else's house and wished they had a nicer house? Is that illegal in the United States? No! Not at all. Remember, to "covet" simply means to want something. There's nothing illegal about wanting things. So clearly the rules about coveting are not a basis for US law.

Indeed, the laws that we have today are not at all based on the Ten Commandments. There might be some similarity in some cases, such as making it illegal to kill somebody, but just because there are some similarities does not mean the founders of our country based their ideas on the Ten Commandments.

In fact, they *didn't*. They based their laws on many earlier laws, including English law, as well as ideas from ancient Greece and Rome. But definitely *not* the Ten Commandments.

Need further proof? Look at what the Bible says is the punishment to people who violate the Ten Commandments.

Deuteronomy 17 states that if somebody violates the first commandment by worshipping other gods, he shall be put to death by stoning. In the United States, we have freedom of religion. Are people who claim our law is based on the Ten Commandments really saying that we shouldn't have freedom of religion, and that those who break any of the Ten Commandments should be put to death?

And if somebody works on the Sabbath, thereby breaking the third (or fourth depending on your ordering) commandment, again, you must be put to death. In fact, the Bible has a rather graphic (and disgusting, I might add) story about a man who was indeed put to death for simply gathering up some sticks to use in a fire. The book of Numbers, Chapter 15:32-36 tells the story of how the man was taken before Moses, who asked God for help, and God said he must be stoned to death. (Somehow Moses apparently had a face-to-face conversation with God.) And that's what they did: They violently and brutally killed the man. For gathering wood for a fire?

Do people who insist our country is built on the Ten Commandments also hope that we start enacting the punishments?

Richard Dawkins, in his book *The God Delusion*, makes what I consider an excellent argument about basing our laws (and morality) on the Bible. Unfortunately, the argument won't hold up in the senseless, mindless eyes of so many Christians. His argument is that if people decide that they'll accept certain aspects of the Bible as basis for our laws and morality (such as the Ten Commandments) but reject the more outdated ones (such as death by stoning for people who work on the Sabbath), then they are using some other basis to decide what parts of the Bible should serve as moral guidelines and which should be rejected—a basis that is outside of and separate from the Bible. And thus, they are using some internal, non-Bible basis.

Unfortunately, that's too logical for a lot of Christians to understand. When posed with exactly that argument, one woman I encountered online made the argument that when God commanded the people to kill the man who worked on the Sabbath, we should not question it, for God works in strange and mysterious ways and is far superior to us, and was perfectly allowed to occasionally break the laws.

My personal feeling, which I base in logic and reason, is to reject the Bible outright. I've explained why the Ten Commandments are trivial at best and certainly not a basis for the US laws and government. There are better laws today than these archaic, barbaric laws created by an ancient, superstitious people.

Before closing this section, however, I want to address a comment I've heard made more than once, and that's that the Ten Commandments are the oldest known laws. They're *not*. The Sumerian literature far predates the Ten Commandments, and contains many similar laws, including the famous "Do not steal" law, as well as a law forbidding a man from having an affair with a married woman. (They even have a rule forbidding cursing strongly.) And another set of laws was created in Babylon, again, well before the Ten Commandments (possibly a thousand years earlier).* Sorry to be the one to break the news, but the Ten Commandments were *not* the first such laws.

And while we're on the topic of the Ten Commandments, the list people usually refer to isn't even called The Ten Commandments in the Bible. Don't believe me? Read Exodus 34 to see what the Ten Commandments really are. (One of them is a warning not to cook a goat in its mother's milk. I'm not making this up. Go read Exodus 34. If you're a Christian, you might be surprised.)†

Moral Absolutes and Moral Compasses

The concept of "moral absolutes" is a bit of an oddity in that different people have different ideas about it. Typically, from what I've observed, the most fundamental Christians are usually the ones who most believe in moral absolutes. By *moral absolutes*, I'm referring to things that people consider wrong—a sin, if you will—regardless of time period, setting, culture, and situation.

---

* You can read about the Babylonians' Code of Hammurabi here: http://www.wsu.edu/~dee/ MESO/CODE.HTM What's interesting is that these laws may well have provided a basis for much of the laws in the Old Testament book of Leviticus. That would imply, of course, that the laws that Moses received were not written by God but instead inspired by earlier laws.

† To be fair, many Christian scholars are well aware of the two sets of "Ten Commandments" in the Bible and distinguish between them as the "ethical" and "ritual" commandments. But how many regular Christians are aware of the difference and realize they only follow one set and ignore the other, which are just as clearly spelled out and required by God's people as the first?

Here's a timely example: Some people consider abortion wrong, period, under all circumstances, even in the case of rape or if the pregnancy is jeopardizing the woman's life. That's a moral absolute. Other people, however, disagree. Some people feel that abortion is usually wrong, except should be allowed in extreme situations such as those mentioned. That's *not* a moral absolute. And, of course, other people feel abortion should always be allowed. Although that could also be considered a moral absolute, in the current discussion, I'll use it primarily to refer to situations when people consider something always wrong or always sinful (as opposed to always good or always allowed).

And now I'll explain why the concept of moral absolutes is senseless and sketchy at best. The Bible makes many laws, mostly in the Old Testament, including the Ten Commandments I was just talking about, which includes the commandment outlawing stealing.

Earlier I talked about how certain municipal laws allow stealing in the situation of, for example, a vegetable plant growing into a neighbor's yard, and the neighbor legally being allowed to take that which grew into his or her yard.

When talking to people about that one, however, I found that most people take a definite opinion on that; many Christians I spoke to still felt it was wrong for the neighbor to take the vegetables. Fine. But what about something on a bigger, grander scale?

Consider this scenario: Suppose I own a large company that sells fine china dishware. In the operation of the business, I need to decide what price to charge for the dishes. I need to factor in the costs to run the company and to pay the employees, and also how much I want to profit.

I don't want to price the dishes too low, or I'll make very little profit or even lose money. But I don't want to price them too high, or people won't buy them. I have to find the highest price people are willing to pay that will maximize my profits. That's the goal, anyway: To maximize the profits.

Let's get right to it then: How many Christians believe their God would send me to Hell for that? Should I pray for forgiveness? And is it even obvious why I'm asking that question?

I'm asking because I have a range of prices I can charge for the dishes while still making a profit. I can charge at the lower end and make minimal profit, or I can charge at the high end and maximize my profit. The goal for most business owners is to maximize the profit.

Now suppose that range is $20 for a plate at a minimum to $30 for a maximum. If I choose to charge $30 for something that could just as well be sold for $20, then I'm taking $10 more from the consumer for the same product. (And I'm assuming that the competitors are charging the same as well.)

In other words, I'm taking an extra $10 from the customer than what I could have. The customer is getting, conceivably, a $20 product, but giving me more money than it's worth.

Is that stealing? Most people would agree there's nothing wrong with that for many reasons, including the fact that the customer has a choice and doesn't have to buy it. But the biggest reason is cultural: It's simply business, and it's the way things are done. It wouldn't even occur to most people that there might be something *sinful* about it.

But the fact remains, I would be getting $10 extra of the consumer's money, and if we try hard enough, we could make it seem like it's stealing—even though it's not to most people. So is it stealing or not?

And what exactly *is* stealing? It's not always clear. Earlier I also mentioned the case of taxes. How many Christians feel the IRS employees must go home and pray for forgiveness just for doing their job? While I imagine there are a good number of people who do feel the IRS employees are evil, the fact is, it's the law in our country, and indeed the Jesus character even said that it's okay for the government to tax people.

But what if I, as a business owner, intentionally did something that was well within the letter of the law, such as cut back the payment of my employees just before Christmas so that I could give myself a handsome bonus? That may be legal. Would it be stealing and sinful? The way I just presented it makes it sound wrong. But "cutbacks" are often viewed as sound business sense and not considered *sinful* by most people, and certainly not something that people feel requires confession before God.

Is stealing right or wrong, then? It depends on the particular situation as well as the definition of stealing. In other words, it's not always clear or *absolute*.

Let's look at this a bit further. What of killing? The Bible says *Thou shalt not kill*. It's easy to say killing is wrong. Most of us agree: If a guy takes a gun and goes out and kills somebody, he has done something wrong. That's pretty clear.[*]

But what about this: President George W. Bush, launched a war on Iraq, which in turn resulted in the deaths of US soldiers, Iraqi soldiers, US civilian

---

[*] But what about issues of self-defense? Is it always clear?

contractors, and Iraqi civilians, as well as soldiers from other countries help-ing in the cause. Did George W. Bush personally kill those people? George W. Bush made a decision that resulted in the deaths of people, because certainly had he not decided to invade Iraq, those people would not have died. Did he kill them? Well, he made a decision that resulted in their deaths. But should he confess his sins? I have met *many* Christians who feel what he did was right and just. Yet those same Christians typically also preach the theology of moral absolutes!

But what about me: I'm paying taxes, and, presumably, if you're an American, you are too. My taxes are going to fund the war effort, where people have died. Does that put blood on my hands? Does that make me a murderer? While I did not vote for George W. Bush, I did vote for his pre-decessor, Bill Clinton, who also ordered invasions where people died. Does that make me equally guilty?

Consider this: There are large corporations that have polices that hurt people. Corporations have policies that have resulted in people getting sick, hurt, or killed. Sometimes it's cheaper to pay the fine and pay off the family than to fix a product that may one time out of a million cause a death. Some corporations have policies that lead to pollution of the air and drinking water in inner cities, causing people to get sick. Personally, I feel that's wrong. But how many Christians are preaching against this and saying that the busi-ness owners must confess their sins? To be realistic, there are plenty of more liberally-minded Christians preaching against this, but they seem to be the minority these days. The majority of Christians, especially the fundamen-talists, see nothing wrong with this and do not criticize the corporations and certainly don't write the CEOs letters telling them they'll burn in Hell if they don't repent.

Moral absolutes simply don't make sense and invariable result in a con-tradiction. To believe in moral absolutes is narrow-minded and absurd.

Finally, consider my lack of belief in the Christian religion. People feel that will guarantee me a quick trip to Hell. I have been informed quite eloquently more than once that I must get on my knees and pray for forgiveness if it isn't already too late to try to prevent my eternal damnation. Now compare my mindset, which is not hurting anyone (except me, perhaps, in the eyes of the Christians who feel I'll fry in Hell) to the CEO who creates the policies that really do hurt people. Where are those Christians who confronted me calling evil? Who are they saying will go to Hell? Certainly not the God-fearing CEO who goes to church every week and donates his time and money to the local chapter of the Grand Old Republican Party. No, it is not the CEO who must suffer through persistent threats of eternal damnation and hellfire. I am the one, for simply not believing as the fundamentalist Christians do.

Sensible? Logical? Try none of the above. Moral absolutes don't make sense.

Indeed, who is hurting whom: Christians claim to be repressed, even though they make up some 90% of Americans, while many atheist writers and organizers feel compelled to use pseudonyms to protect their identity and location due to real, live threats from Christians who are making their lives miserable—not just through threats of eternal damnation, but real, *physical* threats of violence.

One person I know quite well online who speaks out quite loudly against Christianity has received actual death threats from people. And the famous atheist Madalyn Murray O'Hair, whose activism led to the removal of organized prayer in school, received thousands of death threats from Christians. (She was ultimately murdered, although the man convicted of her murder was angry at her for other reasons*. Nevertheless, many Christians celebrated her murder.) The fear is real. If these people think that God is going to send us to Hell for eternal punishment, then why would they have any scruples against inflicting their own pre-Hell suffering on us? They do, after all, think that we worship Satan.

Is that a surprise? I'll take that up next.

Kill the Satan-Worshipping Non-Believers

This is a concept that a lot of shallow-brained fundamentalist Christians just can't seem to wrap their minds around: People who don't believe in God and Jesus do *not* worship Satan.

How could they? Satan is the invention of Christians. People who don't believe in God and Jesus also don't believe in Satan.

Yet, for some reason, people seem to think that it's one or the other: If you don't worship God and Jesus, then certainly you must do the other thing, and that's worship Satan. People seem to think that we non-Believers

---

* Wikipedia has a pretty good description of the motives in her murder, as well as alleged apathy from the police towards investigating the case. See http://en.wikipedia.org/wiki/Madalyn_Murray_O'Hair.

go home and light a few candles surrounding some satanic symbol while we kill a few goats and sacrifice a few virgins all in a good fun-filled evening with the family at home.

A friend of mine who is a rather radical atheist had this experience. He was at home and the doorbell rang. He answered it to find two women at the door holding Bibles. He was polite and spoke with them briefly. They wanted him to read some of their literature (which, I should add, was not the Bible; rather, they were religious brochures and what-not). He identified himself as an atheist and said that he would like to make a deal with them: He would read their books if they would read a book that he gave to them.

He said the look of horror on their faces was almost comical. These women honestly thought that the word "atheist" and "Satan worshipper" were the same thing! And as such, believed that this book that my friend was going to have them read must be some horribly frightening book detailing the evil goat-sacrificing rituals my friend almost certainly partakes in quite regularly.

In fact, the book my friend was hoping to present to them as a gift was his own copy of *Cosmos* by Carl Sagan! When he told me this story (which was some ten years ago), I was skeptical that the book would really change their minds. However, on hindsight, I think his idea was sound, because no book would change their minds. Rather, perhaps a book like Cosmos would at least open their minds to the vastness of the universe and how the world could not possibly be only 6000 years old.

Although some Christians seem to think that non-Christians are secret, closeted Devil Worshippers, it's fair to say that many don't think that. However, a good number of Christians do believe that any non-Christian beliefs (in which they lump atheism) are the result of a scheming and conniving devil name Satan.

They believe that although non-believers may not be consciously aware of it, their beliefs are the result of Satan, who is trying to corrupt the minds of the people and lead them astray from the Truth of Jesus Christ. (And again, in fairness, there are a good number of Christians who do not believe that, but it does present a problem for them, because they aren't sure if non-Believers *can* go to Heaven since they have rejected Jesus Christ. When I was a practicing Christian, that's the position I was in as I considered non-believers.)

And so one of the reason for the vicious attacks and very real threats of physical violence is that many of these fundamentalist Christians truly believe that non-believers are children of Satan, whether the non-believers realize it or not, and as such deserve no compassion or sympathy whatsoever. To such fundamentalist Christians, we non-believers are fair game and deserve threats at the very least, and even sometimes more than threats.

Frankly, it is disgusting that people who claim to be all high and mighty and moralistic would behave that way towards other people. But it's no surprise. This is certainly going to anger some people, but it's a fact: The people who bombed New York City on 9/11 were religious fanatics, and so it should be no surprise to see fanatics of other religions behaving similarly. Look at the people who bomb abortion clinics. They believe *sometimes* killing is necessary in the name of God. (Yet many believe in moral absolutes. Figure that one out.) How is that any different from the Muslim extremists who also kill in the name of their God?

To people with ideas like mine, there is no difference. Killing people for not believing in their religion is wrong any way you cut it. And so we have to ask: Who has a seriously warped moral compass?

Before I end this section, I should point out yet again that not all Christians agree with the acts of those who bomb abortion clinics. Indeed when I was a practicing Christian, I was appalled the day I drove past a Planned Parenthood in college on my way to class, only to see that the building was destroyed, having obviously burned to the ground. Today I have many Christian friends who agree that such behavior is appalling.

But like it or not, it is the same religion and the same Bible—just different interpretations of this same ancient text that has been the excuse and justification for so many murders and killings in centuries past. How can we truly use this book as a guide when its words can so easily be used for hatred and killing?

Jesus or a Life of Sin

The audacity of some Christians amazes me. I've been informed that I'm living a life of sin because I no longer accept Jesus Christ as my personal savior.

Let's see. I work a day job; I have a wife and a little boy, both of whom I love dearly with all my heart. We all have fun together and I try to make sure my little boy has the best life possible, one filled with happiness and compassion. And I make sure he has plenty of clothing and food and a good home.

I pay all my bills. I don't steal. I treat other people with respect, doing unto others as I would have them do unto me. I'm honest, almost to a fault. (This book alone should be a testament of the fact that I'm honest, as it certainly takes a great deal of honesty to admit that you've ditched your religion!)

I live a good life, and I'm good to those around me.

I don't do drugs; I'm not even much of a drinker, and I have never smoked a cigarette in my life.*

And, most importantly, I, and my family, are *happy*.

Is that a sinful life?

If a Christian believes I'm a child of Satan, is this the honest life that Satan wants me to live? Does Satan want me to take care of my family and pay my bills and treat people with respect? Is that what Christians think? I find it hard to believe that a Christian would object to these aspects of my life I've described. So what exactly do they mean by a "life of sin"?

To the best of my knowledge, this "life of sin" phrase refers to something not real. It's just an abstract, meaningless phrase that refers to somebody who has not embraced their religion. That's all. Of course, the word "sin" refers to an act of evil, so perhaps what they're really saying is they consider anybody who doesn't subscribe to their particular dogma as evil.

But now compare the lifestyle I just described to the somebody who scares the living daylights out of children by threatening them with eternal damnation after they die. Personally, I think *that's* a pretty sinful life.

And now consider the Dalai Lama. This is a man who grew up in Tibet under the Buddhist religion. When he was a young man, he and the other Tibetan monks were displaced from their homes when Communist China invaded Tibet and claimed it as their own. The monks then moved to the mountains of India where they live to this day.

The Dalai Lama—whose real name is Tenzin Gyatso; the Dalai Lama is a title—is a wonderful human being. He has traveled the world over teaching about peace and love. He has done wonderful things, and I have nothing but pure respect for the man. He's a good man. *But:* He has not accepted Jesus into his heart. Does that mean that he is living a life filled with sin and evil? Does that mean his acts of good came from the Devil? Does the Devil occasionally dabble in goodness just for fun? That, of course, is pretty absurd, but it shows the flaw in logic when saying that a non-believer, by default,

---

* I should probably add a caveat here: Even if I did smoke, I think that's a personal issue that people need to deal with and by no means makes somebody a bad person. And if somebody does illegal drugs, they need help for their addiction, rather than being told they'll go to Hell.

lives a life of sin.

Next consider Mahatma Gandhi, the man who helped bring independence to India from the hands of Great Britain. He taught peace and nonviolence and, like the Dalai Lama, was a wonderful person.

Gandhi died in 1948. The Dalai Lama was born in 1935, and as of this writing, is still with us. Gandhi did not accept Jesus as his personal Lord and Savior, nor has the Dalai Lama.

I can't speak for all Christians, but many Christians I've asked have made it absolutely clear that Gandhi is in Hell today, and that the Dalai Lama, unless he accepts Jesus into his heart, will end up there after he's gone.

Compare that to a criminal who has raped and killed 50 people, and on his death bed repents and asks for God's forgiveness and accepts Jesus. According to most Christians, the criminal, who left a legacy of evil, will go to Heaven, while Gandhi and the Dalai Lama are condemned to Hell for all eternity. Why? Not because of their "bad deeds," which are few and far between (if any at all!), but rather, because they haven't accepted Jesus.

So clearly, there's no way around it. To people who make such claims, it's not about being good at all. It's about accepting Jesus, and clearly, being good and accepting Jesus are two separate acts, and it's the second of those two—not the first—that gets you into Heaven.

But remember: The standard Christian theology is that you *must* accept Jesus as your personal savior, or you *will* go to Hell. So, by that rule, there's no way around it: A perfectly good person could be punished for all eternity for *doing nothing*. And sorry, but that simply isn't sensible. Why would a perfect deity who supposedly created us and is supposedly far superior to us in love and knowledge send his own people that he created to Hell simply for not believing he exists? It makes no sense. In fact, it's attributing a very backwards, very *human* (and flawed) behavior—an egotistical, narcissistic behavior—to a deity. It's absurd, irrational, senseless, and obviously a man-made construct, and just one more reason I can no longer believe in the Christian theology. It's not real.

The Dawkins Cause: Defense of Children

I mentioned this briefly in the previous chapter, but I want to re-iterate it.

Richard Dawkins, author of *The God Delusion*, devotes an entire chapter to the mental abuse carried out by the Church. I agree: I think it's an abomination to terrify a child with threats of eternal punishment. Dawkins provides many examples of the kind of mental abuse that has gone on in the church.

But he also makes an excellent point and encourages people to bring this up over and over, which I'll do. He says that there's no such thing as a "Christian child" or a "Muslim child." Children can not possibly have matured enough to make up their own minds about what they believe and don't believe regarding religion. Rather, they are simply "children of Christian parents" or "children of Muslim parents."

Indeed, most people would be a bit alarmed if somebody introduced a four-year-old child as, for example, a Socialist. "My four-year-old child is a Socialist." Imagine that. Has the four-year-old studied Marx and decided to embrace Socialism? Just the same, what if a parent claimed their three-year-old is a "Devout Republican." Did the three-year-old study the Reagan presidency and make a conscious decision to agree with the policies put out by Ronald Reagan?

You never hear a Christian parent saying, "We're Christians, but my three-year-old has instead decided to embrace Taoism." Or, "We're Christians but my four-year-old disagrees with us when we claim Jesus was the Son of God and instead agrees with the Muslims that he was a Prophet; therefore, our child, unlike us, is a Muslim."

There's a video that has made its way around the Internet and YouTube featuring an interview with various Muslims about their attitudes towards Jewish people. In the video, a child is interviewed who says some rather disturbing remarks towards Jews, remarks that are racist and hateful, encouraging the killing of Jews. And this little girl is maybe four or five years old! And what's also disturbing is the adults in the video then say what a wonderful little girl she is for being so devout to Muslim beliefs!

One could argue that this child is certainly a devout, fundamentalist Muslim. But I disagree, as I'm sure Dawkins would. Rather, this child has been brainwashed by her parents and is simply restating what her parents have told her to say. She has not on her own made any conscious, informed, educated, rational decisions about what she believes or doesn't believe.

Children can't be of a particular religion. They are the children of parents of a particular religion. There aren't "Christian Children" or "Jewish Children" or "Muslim Children" or "Hindu Children". They are children whose parents belong to a particular religion.

I'd Like the Gift of Eternal Salvation

I've been asked more than once why I would reject a gift of eternal salvation. And I've seen a question posed along the lines of, "Christianity has lots to offer. What do atheism and agnosticism have to offer?"

The problem is that's an illogical question that makes no sense. As a non-believer, I'm not "offering" you anything. I'm simply stating the facts: The god described in the Bible isn't real. But one does have to wonder: If a Christian wants to get somebody to join up and become a believer, is enticing them with eternal salvation really going to bring in a new recruit? Most sane, reasonable people would first want some kind of evidence or proof that the offer is even real. It's as if somebody shows up at your front door and offers you some beautiful land in Florida for dirt cheap. Would you really just abandon logic and reason and instantly believe it? I would hope not. And just because somebody shows up offering you eternal salvation, does that enticement alone cause you to believe it's real? Seriously: if somebody wants to offer you something, before you can accept the offer, you would have to *first* know if what is being offered even exists.

I'm not a psychologist, so I can't say what exactly would cause a person to suddenly start believing in what Christianity teaches. In my own case, it was simply a matter of being taught since I was a child that it was true and only later starting to question it. I can't know what goes on in the mind of somebody brand new to the faith and how they would suddenly start accepting it as real. (I have heard that the missionaries to primitive countries are faced with exactly this. Although I haven't seen it firsthand, I've heard anecdotal stories where the primitive people are actually led to believe "God" is an actual person in the United States who sits on a big throne and people worship him.)

The nonbelievers aren't offering something that first requires a leap of faith to accept something that seems unbelievable and will result in some kind of eternal reward. And yet, when I heard the question posed online, and nonbelievers expressed what I'm expressing, some Christians laughed and said they didn't think we'd be able to come up with a good answer. But the problem is the question isn't even a legitimate question. Nonbelievers aren't offering something. Rather, they're asking for proof of this outrageous offer of eternal salvation that the Christians are making. It's like somebody accepting the offer for cheap beachfront land in Florida simply because the person doubting the offer has nothing better to offer. Does that make sense? "Since you're doubting the validity of this offer for cheap land and have no better offer, clearly the offer must be real." That's some seriously flawed logic.

I already spoke of how the majority of Christians base their faith on various teachings in the New Testament that insist the *only* way you can get to Heaven is by believing in Jesus. So it doesn't matter how good of a person you are, if you don't believe in Jesus, you won't go to Heaven.

Seriously. Is that what an all-powerful deity who created the universe would want? I talk about this in more detail in Chapter 5. But for now I must ask: Is that realistic? If there's a deity who could create the whole universe from which all love supposedly comes, would that deity be so arrogant and narcissistic that he would demand that we believe in him, and that such belief would trump the moral value of all our deeds?

I am "only" human and I can tell you that I could come up with a better system of justice than that. Now imagine what a perfect, amazing system a deity would come up with. Certainly not the one I just described. And so I must ask you: Is it realistic? Is the justice system of Christianity really one created by a deity or, rather, by ancient, superstitious humans?

People in ancient times had not yet developed a reasonable justice system, although some philosophers had toyed with some ideas. The people back then lacked much of what we know today in terms of political systems and technology and science. Today we know so much that we didn't know back then. Yet, the "God" described in the Bible seems to prefer the barbaric, selfish justice systems of ancient times.

A lot has changed since then. Human culture has progressed far beyond, and our movement forward is partly due to an understanding of science and logic in ways ancient people could not possibly have imagined, and in ways, therefore, that the ancient writers of the Bible similarly couldn't have included. Let's look at some of the modern facts of science and logic next, followed by a discussion of why even many people today still can't accept them.

And in the process, you'll see why I personally have had no choice but to move beyond the ancient, superstitious beliefs of Christianity and ultimately walk away. I had no choice, when I realized it isn't real.

three

Of Science and Logic

hen I was a child, I read every science book I could get my hands on. I loved the book *Cosmos* by Carl Sagan, and the TV version on PBS.

But there were things that I found troubling. In Sunday School, the teachers were saying that humans were created in the first week of the Earth's existence.

But the science books were saying something very different. It didn't fit together. Something was wrong. Initially I just ignored the differences, thinking they really didn't matter. But over time, the differences *did* start to matter.

To help understand why these things matter, it's important to take a journey through science and see why science and religion simply *can't* get along, even though some people insist they can.

Facts do not cease to exist because they are ignored.

-Aldous Huxley (1894 - 1963)

Misconceptions about Science

A common misconception is that scientists think they have all the answers. Another common misconception is that scientists are convinced their ideas are perfect and written in stone. And yet another common misconception is that the way scientific ideas spread is that some guy comes up with some crazy idea and starts pushing the idea on other scientists who blindly believe it.

None of the above beliefs are true. Granted, there are some scientists who are incredibly arrogant and feel very strongly about their ideas, but science as a whole is about recognizing what it doesn't know and learning new information.

The beauty of science is that it continues to grow and change as scientists learn more about the universe. As new data comes in, old ideas get refined and replaced by newer ideas.

This is contrary to the Bible, which does not change. You don't hear churches announcing, *"In light of new scientific advances, we've decided the Book of Genesis is completely wrong and we will therefore be removing it from the Bible."*

Science, however, *does* make such changes. Early on, scientists observed the Sun moving across the sky as if it went around the Earth. That was all the data they had, so that's what they went with: The Earth is fixed and the sun revolves around the Earth. But eventually, through observation and data analysis, they realized the situation was more sophisticated and, in fact, the Earth and all the planets revolve around the Sun, which in turn revolves within the rotating Milky Way, and so on. As such, they threw away the old model, admitting it was wrong, and replaced it with a newer model. Would a church do that to parts of the Bible? Of course not.

Science has also freely modified and fixed other models that weren't quite right. Einstein's Theory of Relativity caused scientists to rethink the way objects move through space. The older ideas, developed by scientists such as Isaac Newton, still hold true, but have been modified to allow for extremely fast speeds. The theories of motion were adjusted and modified as new observation and discoveries were made. Does Christianity modify its ideas when people find parts of the Bible to be wrong? Absolutely not.

One argument I've heard many times against science is that scientists think they have the whole world figured out and that it takes faith to believe the ideas put out by scientists. I have much more to say later in this book about "faith" and what it is, but for now, let's just squelch that argument once and for all: Scientists do not claim to have all the answers yet. Scientists freely admit that we're still learning how the universe works. But what science doesn't do is blindly fill in the unknown with "God did it." That's called the "God of the gaps" argument, something I cover in detail in the next chapter. And further, scientists only accept ideas that can be *demonstrated and tested*. It's not about faith. In fact, it's quite the opposite. Let's take that up now.

Scientists Blindly Following Others?

The National Science Teachers Association has released a statement *endorsing evolution*. The statement is from the organization, not the individual members. However, the individual members have not started leaving the association in response to the statement, and so one can surmise that the members agree with the statement. How many members are there? The National Science Teachers Association currently has more than 55,000 members.

Of course, this organization is made up of science teachers. Typically science teachers are teaching science, but not necessarily doing original research in science. This gets to the heart of an argument I've been making for some time: I myself have taught and tutored in the sciences, but I have not done original research in science. Therefore, I have to choose who I am going to trust: The scientists doing original research in evolution, or the Christian creationists who are disputing the findings of these researchers of evolution?

But how many scientists are there? A few? A dozen? A few hundred? A thousand? A few dozen thousand?

The American Academy for the Advancement of Science (AAAS) consists of about 120,000 members, and it has also released statements supporting evolution.

Compare the size of the AAAS to the so-called "Scientific Dissent from Darwinism"*, a statement put out by The Discovery Institute, a group that pushes Intelligent Design (another name for Creationism). This list includes signatures of scientists who say they do *not* accept evolution. It would be easy for the general public to look at this list and be impressed to see such a large number of scientists who oppose evolution. This in turn could easily give people the impression that a large percentage of scientists don't accept evolution and that there is continued "debate" within the scientific community and by no means a consensus between scientists.

But in my opinion, the list of dissenters is nothing but deception. At the time of this writing, the list consists of about 700 signatures of scientists who do not accept evolution. To somebody just stumbling upon the list, they could

* The statement is available online at www.dissentfromdarwin.org.

easily be swayed, thinking the list is huge. But it isn't. It's tiny. The AAAS consists of 120,000 scientists, and the best The Discovery Institute could do was find 700 scientists to sign their list? That is about a half of a percent of all scientists, if you only factor in American scientists.

In fact, it's an even smaller percentage. The AAAS consists of primarily American scientists, and not all scientists are members. Is this the best The Discovery Institute can do? If there was truly a huge disagreement among scientists, and there are hundreds of thousands of scientists on the planet, shouldn't they easily be able to find 50,000 or even 100,000 scientists who disagree with evolution? Over the past several years, the best they've been able to muster up is 700, a fraction of a percent of the scientists of the world.

The other side, then, contains a *huge* number of scientists who accept the reality, the *fact* of evolution. We can't know the exact ratio, but if the 700 out of 120,000 is any indication, then that means *at least* 99% of scientists agree on the reality of evolution.

Clearly, there is not a debate and disagreement among scientists; there is an *agreement*, a *consensus* among scientists that evolution is real, that evolution has happened, and that evolution is happening.

Evolution is a fact.

But aren't these scientists just riding the bandwagon and blindly following Darwin? This is another misconception that I alluded to earlier, one that gets to the idea of faith.

One of the tenets of science is that scientists do *not* blindly accept each other's ideas. They do not sit and worship the words of one scientist. Quite the contrary, in fact. Consider Einstein. Today we know that Einstein's Relativity is absolutely correct. It has been demonstrated and proven. Want simple proof? The television is proof—not the newer LCD and plasma TVs, but the older ones that contain a picture tube. When engineers originally developed televisions, they hit a snag. The pictures were ending up severely distorted. The reason, it turned out, was the electrons in the picture tube were moving through the tube at close to the speed of light, resulting in something called *time dilation* for the electrons, something predicted by Relativity. This dilation was causing the pictures to be skewed and distorted. And so the engineers had to make an adjustment to the device, one that factored in the math formulas of Relativity. Then the picture was not distorted.

But scientists have also done actual experiments with Relativity involving rocket ships. They have used carefully synchronized, highly accurate clocks, leaving one clock on Earth while an astronaut goes into space with another clock. Upon return, the clocks were no longer synchronized. That was the result of Relativity. The amount of time that passed for the astronaut was not exactly the amount of time that passed for the people on Earth. The difference was so tiny that it took a computer to see the difference. But it was there.

Relativity is real.*

Relativity has shown up in many other places as well. Many people now have GPS systems in their cars and wireless phones, and Relativity has caused minor issues as the GPS information travels near the speed of light from satellites down to the GPS receivers in your car.

Relativity has been *demonstrated.* Therefore, relativity is real.

But when Einstein published his original paper on Relativity, it was by no means widely accepted by scientists, not by a long shot. Scientists are skeptical by nature and do no blindly believe every new idea. It took many years before scientists as a whole accepted it, and it was not the result of Einstein trying to convince people it was real. Einstein didn't hire a bunch of lawyers and fight to force scientists to believe it and teach it in schools. Rather, it was only after additional research and experiments were conducted, thus *demonstrating* Relativity was real, before scientists accepted it.

As I said, scientists are, by nature, skeptics. They have to be, because otherwise any crackpot could come up with some speculative idea and preach it from a pulpit, and then thousands of other scientists sitting in the pews could easily embrace the nonsense. Rather, when a scientist comes up with an idea, the idea must go through rigorous testing, often over years or decades, before scientists as a whole accept the idea. Scientists didn't simply embrace Relativity "just because Einstein said it was so." (In fact, when Einstein first developed Relativity, he was a nobody. He didn't have his PhD yet and he worked in a patent office in Germany.) Instead the scientists exhibited healthy

---

* For the more scientifically minded readers, a fascinating demonstration of Relativity is in the actions of muons. Muons are elementary particles created in the upper atmosphere when cosmic rays headed towards the Earth react with atoms. First pions are created, which almost immediately decay into muons and neutrinos. The muons continue traveling towards the Earth, and they should decay well before reaching the surface of the Earth. But they don't. Time dilation takes place, and the time that passes from the muon's frame of reference is much shorter than that of the observers on Earth. As a result, the moun doesn't appear to decay as quickly, and makes it to the Earth's surface. If you're interested in studying this, simply Google muon relativity.

skepticism towards Relativity, and at first outright refused it, just as they do towards all research, including evolution. Only after experiments proved Relativity is real did they accept it.

Before ideas can move forward and be accepted by scientists, they must go through many steps, including the use of the scientific method to physically test and verify the idea. Further, the new research must go through a huge beating in the form of peer review where other scientists look at the research, and put it through the wringer, looking for flaws and problems.

The scientific method is the standard method used for testing ideas, and it uses anything but blind acceptance. It uses solid methods of testing an idea (an idea is called a *hypothesis*), and one of the most important rules is that it must be possible to show that the hypothesis is *wrong*.

That's correct. Before you can apply the scientific method, it must be possible to show that your hypothesis is *wrong*. That seems backwards to a lot of people, because it would seem the goal is to show that the hypothesis is right, not wrong. But that's the beauty of the method, because it gets to the very reason science does not blindly accept an idea. Science is built on growing new ideas by proving that bad ideas are wrong, by "falsifying" ideas, to use the scientific term. Only if an idea survives the attempts to prove it wrong does it move forward. And of course, in the process of testing, the hypothesis is slowly verified and demonstrated to be correct as well. That, in turn, makes for a very strong proof: A scientist has an idea and numerous, repeated tests have shown it's true, and no testing has been able to demonstrate it's false. (If it is found to be false, the scientist is forced to reject the idea and go back to the drawing board. From there the scientist can throw it out completely, or modify the idea, or try a new idea.)

All scientific research goes through this. Relativity went through it. One of the aspects of Relativity is that light travels at a fixed speed, no matter how fast you are going when you measure the speed of a beam of light. How can that be proven wrong? Easy. Measure the speed of light. If it's not going precisely the known speed of light, then you've proven it wrong. But after years upon years of experiments, scientists have not shown the contrary. Light always goes the same speed. (That is, light that's traveling through a vacuum. Light does slow down when traveling through other things like glass or water.) Relativity has stood the test of time. And remember, it is easy to test if the idea is wrong: Measure the light speed. Is the idea wrong? A scientist can easily find out.

But it gets better: Because of the importance of being able to prove an idea wrong, the scientific method continues to operate. Suppose 100 years from now scientists find an instance where light in a vacuum traveled at some speed other than the known speed of light. Then there would be a problem. Scientists wouldn't just abandon Relativity altogether; instead, they'd likely need to verify many times over that the particular test was valid and that nobody screwed something up. And if they see that the test repeatedly holds and that under the particular situation light travels at some other speed, then Relativity would have to be adjusted for the situation. Relativity wouldn't be thrown out altogether; it would be modified. It would evolve; it would grow into a bigger, more complete explanation of the universe.

In fact, that's exactly what Relativity did to previous theories. In the late 1600s, Isaac Newton developed what are now known as Newton's Laws of Motion. These are a set of mathematical formulas that precisely predict the motion of moving objects. Although most people think of the three laws of motion, the most famous being, "For every action there is an equal and opposite reaction," the laws actually include precise mathematical formulas that have been shown to accurately predict how things will travel when pushed. (And also, it's important to note that the action and reaction statement applies to movement of objects, not to psychological events, even though some people seem to think they do.)

Prior to around 1900, Newton's laws were all scientists had to describe motion. But then Einstein developed and demonstrated Relativity, and showed that at extremely high speeds, the laws change, and don't apply exactly as-is.

And so what did scientists do? Did they throw away Newton's laws? Absolutely not. They revised them to take into account Relativity. They knew Newton's laws still held. The difference is they found that Newton's laws only held under typical conditions such as the speeds and sizes we encounter in everyday life. When car accident investigators need to do their calculations, they use formulas built on Newton's laws, because Relativity has virtually no part in it since the speeds of the cars don't come anywhere close to the speed of light. Only when speeds get extremely high (such as the electrons in a TV picture tube) does Relativity become a factor. And so Newton's Laws still hold; scientists just have to factor in Relativity in the cases of extremely high speeds.*

In summary, then, Newton's Laws weren't thrown out; they were modi-

* Technically, Relativity does exist at slower speeds, but its effects are so tiny, it's virtually impossible to detect them.

fied to accommodate the newer understanding of science.

This also gets to a misconception people have about evolution (and science in general). People seem to think that if one little tiny aspect of evolution is shown to be wrong, the whole thing will come crashing down. But it just isn't true. Relativity didn't cause Newton's Laws to come crashing down, and neither will changes to evolution as new data comes in and scientists continue to learn even more about it. Rather, the theory gets modified to account for the new data. The theory grows and itself evolves.

And it has happened many times. Researchers are constantly finding new data as they learn more about evolution. Occasionally they find something they previously thought was true wasn't exactly correct, and the idea is replaced with the results of the new data.

I couldn't possibly fit all the examples in this book of where the science of evolution has itself evolved and grown and changed in the past two centuries. But I can say that as science has moved forward, so has the science of evolution, and today we have mountains of research: not just Darwin's original book, but volumes of research in the 200 years since Darwin. One extremely important area of research is that of DNA studies. As researchers have learned an enormous amount of information about DNA, the result has only reinforced and confirmed the science of evolution, even though evolution was discovered before DNA. There have certainly been modifications to the overall ideas as DNA studies have brought in new data pertaining to evolution. But these are changes and have by no means displaced the theory. Rather, the theory continues to grow (much to the chagrin of the Creationists) and become even stronger and more solid.

In fact, I can't help but wonder if Creationists constantly monitor the activities of scientists, ready to try to debunk the massive amount of new research that comes in every week!

Science Isn't Determined by Debate and Government

The whole Creationism and Intelligent Design movement has created another misconception of science, that acceptance of scientific ideas is determined by debate and by government and courtroom decisions.

For example, if two people are debating an issue (such as Evolution vs.

Intelligent Design), whoever shines in the debate does not "win" in the scientific world. Just because somebody happens to be a better talker doesn't mean the scientific community will embrace his or her ideas. Rather, winning over the scientific community requires facts and data and tests that can be reproduced.

And further, scientific consensus certainly isn't determined by government regulations and courtroom decisions. We're fortunate that when the school board went to court in Dover, Pennsylvania to battle over whether Intelligent Design should be taught in the classroom, the court ruled in favor of science. But even if the court had not, and instead forced Intelligent Design into the classroom, that would *not* mean scientists would embrace it. Not by any means.

Earlier I mentioned peer review. This is an example of where scientists use healthy skepticism, and is another area where laypeople are typically misinformed.

When a scientist comes up with a new idea, the scientist must do several tests and experiments to make sure the idea is correct. After careful testing, and careful determination that the idea is correct, the scientist then details all the findings in a written article. The scientist carefully describes the ideas, the data, the experiments performed, any related mathematical formulas and diagrams, and the conclusions. Then the scary part begins.

The scientist submits the article to any one of a number of reputable scientific journals (such as a journal called Nature, for example). These are not popular magazines like you would find at a nearby bookstore. These are journals that cost a few hundred dollars a year to subscribe to, and are usually associated with an organization that scientists pay money to belong to.

Before the journal publishes the paper, however, the journal selects several scientists to carefully go through the article and find anything and everything wrong with it. This is called peer review. The article is reviewed by the scientist's peers. The scientists reviewing the research are highly trained people with PhDs, and they go into the review *expecting* the research to be *wrong*. The article must be so good and so convincing that these scientists change their minds and decide it must be correct. Think about that: They are the first ones to doubt the idea. The article must change their minds! The scientist reviewers may even perform further experiments to test out the assertions made in the article.

Basically, the scientists give the article a beating. And if they find anything wrong, any mistakes, any errors in calculations—whatever—the article will be rejected. Only after the article survives the peer review will it even be considered for publication in the journal.

But it doesn't end there. When the article is published, it will be read by thousands of other scientists, many of whom are experts in the field of the article. And these scientists won't just blindly accept the article either. They will also look for problems in it. Like the peer review, they will put the article through the wringer, and look for any problems they can find, usually in the form of their own tests which may go well beyond the original experiments.

Clearly, then, science is not decided by debates and courtroom rulings, nor is it decided by popular opinion. It is decided by facts and data and proofs.

It's Just a Theory?

When dealing with the issue of evolution, people who buy into the Genesis account of creation like to say something like, "Evolution is just a theory."

A statement like this shows a total ignorance of science. In science, the word "theory" has a profoundly different meaning than it does in everyday language. In everyday language, a theory is just an untested idea somebody is tossing around, a *conjecture*.

In science, however, a theory is not just a conjecture. One science professor I know put it something like this: On a scale of 1 to 10, how would you rate a "theory" with 1 being "it's just an idea and could be thrown out," to 10 being "it's a definite fact"? He had the class vote and most students felt a "theory" belonged somewhere in the middle.

The teacher then pointed out that the students were wrong. A scientific theory is at 10, and no less. In order for something in science to be officially deemed a "theory", it must have been demonstrated over and over and it must be accepted by the scientific community as being true in the manner I described already. That is, if an idea is a theory in the scientific world, then it is fact.

No, a theory is not just an idea a bunch of scientists sitting around smoking pot come up with. A theory is tested and verified, and can accurately make predictions about future tests.

Evolution is a scientific theory. It has been tested, and has survived thousands upon thousands of tests over two centuries. It is verified, and it can and has been used to make scientific predictions of the outcome of future tests. Evolution is a fact and scientists have shown it to be. To say it's "just a theory" demonstrates ignorance towards the meaning of the word *theory*.

But how exactly is evolution tested? Many ways. Evolution, remember, is not something that can be fully described and detailed on a single sheet of paper. Massive books have been written about it. It's an enormous idea covering multiple disciplines. One way (out of thousands) that it's been tested is through archeology. Evolution makes predictions about the way bones and dead organisms should be arranged throughout the crust of the planet. When archeologists arrive at a new site that's never been explored and dig extremely deep into the Earth's crust, they see exactly what evolution predicted they would see. That is how evolution makes predictions that can be tested.

In my own journey, recognizing how evolution is more than just some silly idea was an important step for me. I used to not "believe in evolution." I remember in high school kids mumbling in shock and disgust that our biology teacher "believes in evolution."

Today I don't just believe in evolution. I accept evolution as fact. Further, I don't even like to use the word "believe" because it's not accurate. Scientists don't "believe" in evolution in the same way that Christians believe in God and Jesus. Scientists have proven to each other that evolution is true. To say they "believe" in evolution implies that it hasn't been proven and that they blindly buy into it. But that's not the case at all.

I don't believe in evolution. Instead, I accept that it is a scientific fact.

The Logical Method of Science

A couple years ago I heard a friend make this statement:

"A friend of mine and her husband wanted to have a baby. They wanted to make sure their baby would be a girl, so they did the exercises and positions to ensure a girl… And it worked!"

Now wait a minute here. How does she know it worked? "How do you know it worked?" I asked.

"Because they had a girl."

"Well how do you know they wouldn't have had a girl regardless of the exercises?"

She got silent and changed the subject.

Is the logical flaw here obvious? There's more-or-less a 50/50 chance of having a boy or girl. They would have had one or the other, and just because they had a girl does not in any way mean their method *worked*. All it means is they did the exercises *and* they had a girl. It was a coincidence.

A proper test would have involved hundreds of volunteers doing the exercises prior to conception and then watching how many of them gave birth to girls. Then the study would likely be repeated many times over before it was found to be correct. But until then, we have no reason whatsoever to believe it's correct. And so until then, I refuse to say it's a fact or a scientific theory. Rather, it's a coincidence, and some people believe it for no reason other than they witnessed the coincidence.

I'll say that again, because it's a vitally important concept:

Until the test is proven to be true, we have no reason to believe it's true.

That's the way science works. Scientists do not blindly believe things just because somebody (such as Darwin) said it's true. Scientists need to see observations and data and tests and analyses and logical conclusions before they'll accept something. And they certainly can't be looked down upon for doing so. Why should people be criticized for wanting proof before blindly believing something exists? Yet so many religious people think scientists have blind faith in science.

What's sad here, though, is that so many people would have made similar observations like the woman made about choosing the sex of a baby. Many people would have thought that the couple's supposed exercise "worked." By and large, people don't understand science and logic, and they base their understanding of the world on superstitions instead of rational thought.

Imagine if the drug industry behaved that way. Imagine if somebody heard of some bizarre tropical plant that someone else claimed cured cancer, and the drug industry did no testing at all and started marketing a pill containing ground powder from that plant as a cure for cancer.

Think of the actual drugs we have right now. Consider the acid blockers, for example, which help people who suffer from acid reflux. These drugs are highly-tested and carefully formulated chemicals that do their job. The scientists who created them have a deep understanding of the chemistry of the human body, and they know what chemicals will react with the chemicals in our bodies to stop the flow of acid in the stomach. The scientists carefully determined the chemicals and the amounts and then had to do a long series of tests to make sure they really worked. Then the drug company needed to send the results to the Food and Drug Administration which used its own complex procedures to verify the findings before the drugs were finally allowed to be sold to patients.

Compare that now to the idea of "I know somebody who said this worked." Which is more rational? Which is more logical? Which is more *realistic* and *sensible*? I think the answer should be obvious.

What does this all come down to? If two different people present me with ideas, one based on faith or anecdotal hearsay and one based on science, I am going to trust the one based on science.

Most of us are in this same position: We are not scientists, and we must filter through the information thrown at us. Am I going to listen to a preacher tell me why evolution is wrong, or am I going to listen to a scientist tell me why evolution is right? We owe it to ourselves to determine who we can trust and to use logic and reason in making our assessment.

Although I've been focusing on the data-collection aspect of science, there is another aspect that many people do seem to be vaguely aware of, the creative process in science. But many people also don't understand how this process fits in.

I mentioned how scientific theories aren't just the result of a bunch of people sitting around waxing philosophical and coming up with outrageous ideas. However, there is a shred of truth to it, and that's in the creative process. Scientific theorists do often come up with new ideas before data is analyzed. Many of the most brilliant scientists are said to have had *aha!* experiences.

However, that's not the whole story. In fact, their ideas came about only after making real, live observations. But it's true the idea might have come before extensive data. But after the *aha!* experience, experiments and testing begin; then from the experiments, data is gathered. And if the data shows that the idea is wrong, then the idea is discarded as I've described already, otherwise peer review follows, and publication and further review.

Intelligent Design, on the other hand, has *not* gone through this process. It has not passed rigorous testing. Rather, its advocates are trying to force it into the world through court battles.

The ideas behind Intelligent Design have not been tested by scientists and have not gone through peer review, and have not been published in reputable journals, simply because the ideas don't hold up. And the courts are recognizing that as well, fortunately.

And even if the courts did side with Intelligent Design, it still would not be used by scientists, because it's *not* science. Even if they force schools to teach it, scientists will not use it or accept it.

Burden of Proof

As I see people argue online in the various blogs and forums about religion, a common theme is *burden of proof*. What it comes down to is this: Religious people claim there's a god. The atheists respond that it's up to the religious people to prove there's a God. In other words, the burden of proof lies on the people who claim God exists.

Unfortunately, the religious people quickly turn it around by saying, "No. You say there's no God, so prove there's no God. The burden of proof is yours."

From a purely logical standpoint, this is incredibly flawed. I could make the outrageous claim that the universe is controlled by a guy named Jim who lives at the center of Jupiter, and it's up to everybody to prove me wrong, and until they can, it's a fact.

Of course, that's absurd; if I make such a claim, other people are under no obligation to believe it until I prove this guy named Jim really exists.

Facts are facts and will not disappear on account of your likes.

-Jawaharlal Nehru
(1889 - 1964)

Unfortunately, however, this purely logical approach doesn't exactly fit the situation for two reasons. First, to the religious person, it doesn't matter if other people don't believe in God. *Dis*belief in God doesn't mean God doesn't exist. Just because you don't believe in my God doesn't mean my God doesn't exist. Or, to put it into perspective: Just because you might not believe in Antarctica (have you ever seen Antarctic?) doesn't mean Antarctica doesn't exist. So by same token, just because somebody doesn't believe in God doesn't mean God doesn't exist.

In the mind of the religious person, that makes perfect sense. They will say: *Until you can prove me wrong, I will keep believing in God, because deep inside I know God exists. And the fact that you can't prove he doesn't exist just reinforces my belief, because he is real.*

So really, not disproving God's existence just adds to their own personal conviction. *See,* they could say, *the reason you can't prove he doesn't exist is because he does exist.* And further, in their mind: *I may not be able to prove he exists, but it doesn't matter if you believe in him or not. Your lack of belief doesn't change anything.*

That's the first reason pure logic doesn't fit the argument. The other is the approach that a lot of atheists take. For the burden of proof idea to fit, a person is not obligated to accept a claim until it's been proven. This is the case in science. When one scientist makes a claim, other scientists aren't obligated to accept it until it's been proven. But that doesn't automatically mean the claim is false. A scientist may make a claim, for example, that some energy can escape from a black hole. The scientist might not have yet proved it. That means other scientist aren't obligated to accept it yet. But that also doesn't mean it's false and that there is no energy escaping from black holes. It just means *we don't yet know if it's true.*

When applied to the existence of God, the burden of proof argument becomes: You are claiming there's a God, but because I haven't seen any proof, *I don't know if your claim is correct or not and I'm under no obligation to believe it.*

To the strict atheist, this doesn't work. And that's what the religious person will latch onto, because to many atheists, God absolutely doesn't exist. Many atheists say, "God absolutely does not exist." And to the religious person, the atheist is now making a claim of his or her own, one that the religious person is under no obligation to accept until the atheist can prove that claim. The claim is: God absolutely does not exist. And that's something the religious person could respond to with, "I'm under no obligation to believe your claim."

But see what happened? The religious person ultimately twisted it around and placed the burden of proof on the atheist, even though doing so essentially violates the rules of logic. But does it?

Really, the atheist is making a rather strong claim: There is no God. Or, equally, *The hypothesis that there is a God is false.* And that's what the religious person will latch on to and reply with: "Prove it."

The conversation typically goes like this. I'll use R for religious person, and A for atheist:

> **R: There's a God.**
>
> **A: Prove it.**
>
> **R: I can't.**
>
> **A: Then there's no God.**
>
> **R: Prove there's no God.**
>
> **A: No. The burden of proof is on you.**
>
> **R: But you said there's no God. So the burden of proof is on you, and I ask you to prove it.**

And the argument will go on, *ad nauseum*.

I pointed this out on my myspace blog, and I then mentioned Richard Dawkins' approach to the argument. Dawkins is well aware of the logical issues here. And as such, Dawkins, who calls himself an atheist, doesn't say, "There is no God." Instead, he says, "There almost is certainly no God." (That's actually the name of Chapter 4 of his book *The God Delusion*.) Dawkins does not accept the existence of God and will not unless there is proof. There's a subtle but highly important difference here. He's not making the reverse claim that there is no God, and as such, isn't opening himself up to abuse from religious people. Rather, he's making it very clear the he does not believe in God, and will not unless solid scientific proof is presented.

For the burden of proof argument to work, then, the atheist would do best to follow Dawkins' example and respond to the claim of God's existence with something along the lines of: I am under no obligation to believe in your God until you prove he's real.

Unfortunately, this whole argument I'm making is not well-received by either side. Some atheists were quite angry when I said this, and said I'm just twisting words. And some religious people were oddly thrilled by it; at least one person said he was glad that Richard Dawkins is leaving open the possibility of God's existence.

But that's not an accurate portrayal of Dawkins. I can't speak for him, but it's pretty clear Dawkins is 100% atheist and doesn't believe in God. But the scientist in him knows better than to state the logical argument, "God definitely does not exist." The atheist in him, however, is convinced God doesn't exist, and he makes some pretty solid claims to that effect in his book, *The God Delusion*.

But of course, this book I'm writing here is about my own personal journey of leaving Christianity. Where do I stand on all this? And what does this all mean for my journey?

In the final chapter of this book, *Letting Go and Walking Away*, I talk about whether God exists or not. After reading my thoughts, many people would probably label me an agnostic, although I don't particularly like labels, especially that one. But I can say this: After reading the remainder of this book, if you're a Christian who is struggling, I think you'll have some pretty strong ideas yourself that are similar to my ideas.

Let's continue with the discussion of science. The Creationist and Intelligent Design community has essentially launched an assault on the science classrooms of America. I will address that in the next chapter.

four

Knowledge, Religion, and Society

ewis Carroll, the man who wrote such famous stories as *Alice's Adventures in Wonderland* and *Through the Looking-Glass*, wrote a wonderful short story that pretty much demonstrates what people who are well-versed in logic are up against when arguing with somebody who lacks a sense of logic. The story is called *What the Tortoise Said to Achilles*. (Google it for the full text in several places online. I highly recommend reading it.)

I've shared the story with people, but if these people aren't skilled in logic, they unfortunately often miss the point. Completely. So I've had to simplify the story to convey the same meaning. Here's my version of it. (In this version, I'll play the one who isn't very bright.)

Supporters of Intelligent Design seem to believe that the science classrooms should be a free-for-all where any idea, no matter how outrageous or absurd, should be allowed in.

- me

Fred says to me, "A polygon that has exactly three straight sides is a triangle"*

I then say, "Yes, I will agree to that."

Fred then shows me a picture of a triangle and says, "See, here is an object with three sides."

---

* Really, to be more accurate, I should have Fred say, "A polygon with three sides…" but remember, I'm trying to dumb it down a bit.

I say, "Yes, I agree it has three sides."

Fred says, "So you agree it's a triangle."

I say, "No, that's not a triangle."

Fred says, "But it has all the properties of a triangle. Don't you agree that a polygon that has exactly three straight sides is a triangle?"

I say, "Why yes, I do agree."

Fred says, "Well you can see this is a drawing that has three sides."

I say, "Yes! I agree it has three sides."

Fred says, "So you MUST agree that this is a triangle!"

To Fred's dismay, I say, "No. I don't believe it's a triangle."

See the trouble I'm causing in this discussion? I'm being totally bullheaded. The story could also be constructed where Fred gets me to agree, for example, that when you have twelve things it's called a "dozen." He then presents me with twelve apples and gets me to agree that there are twelve apples, but I refuse to agree that the twelve apples are a dozen.

The original version of the story, however, didn't just revolve around word definitions. In the original story, two characters, The Tortoise and Achilles, argue over logic. The Tortoise plays devil's advocate and refuses to accept a rather obvious logical argument and wants Achilles to force him to accept it. Achilles nearly goes out of his mind trying to force The Tortoise to accept it.

Some people claim that Lewis Carroll has created a logical paradox. I disagree; I don't see it that way at all. I think he is making a social commentary on human nature, human knowledge, and even education, by suggesting that given all the facts laid out in front of them, some people still don't accept what logically must be true.

And that is a huge problem with society today, and I feel religion is directly responsible. Religion has taught people to be skeptical of science, to doubt science.

Why? That's easy. The Bible is filled with stories that could not possibly be true, as I discuss in Chapter 5, *Bible Facts and Myths*. If people accept science at face value, they will start to question religion. And that can be very dangerous for religion, especially if you look at early Christianity when, for example, Rome was a powerful political center, and the church essentially had total control over all of Europe. If millions of people start to acquire knowledge of science and logic, and then begin to question the religious beliefs (and doubt the threats of Hell), they could easily band together and take down Rome, causing the Pope to lose his power.

This, of course, was in times past, when it was very easy to keep people superstitious, because by and large, education was severely lacking throughout Europe. People were grossly uneducated; most people couldn't even read. When people got sick, it was easy for them to believe it was God's plan, rather than, say, the result of people drinking water containing contaminants that can't be seen by the naked eye.

But this started changing about 400 years ago. Most people know of the story of Galileo and how he was sent—by the church!—to prison for his scientific advancements that showed the Earth was *not* the center of the universe. (He was later moved to "house arrest" but remained under such arrest for the rest of his life—again, by the church.)

Why did this particular idea of Galileo's bother the church so much? By itself, it probably didn't. What did they care if the Earth moved through space? Rather, it was the bigger threat that science was starting to prove the church and its Bible wrong. And if they're wrong, there goes their stronghold. And being a political center (with prisons and courts!), they were, naturally, opposed to anything that might weaken them.

Even today people are taught to distrust science, and to be leery of obtaining too much knowledge. Although they might be aware of it, people are still learning to distrust knowledge thanks to their Bible studies, going right back to the beginning of the Bible. What was the name of the tree that had the forbidden fruit? The Tree of Knowledge of Good and Evil.

Of course, the name of the tree isn't just "Tree of Knowledge" yet it would seem people fear knowledge. And indeed the Bible *does* warn people against knowledge:

It is better to trust in the LORD than to put confidence in man. (Psalms 118:8)

Trust in the LORD with all thine heart; and lean not unto thine own understanding. (Proverbs 3:5)

For it is written, I will destroy the wisdom of the wise, and will bring to nothing the understanding of the prudent. (I Corinthians

1:19)
Let no man deceive himself. If any man among you seemeth to be wise in this world, let him become a fool, that he may be wise. For the wisdom of this world is foolishness with God. For it is written, He taketh the wise in their own craftiness. (I Corinthians 3:18-19)

Even the story of the Tower of Babel includes a warning against human ingenuity and creativity. God says the following (apparently to other gods, as it's not quite clear who he's talking to, a particularly odd point people seem to overlook):

And the LORD said, Behold, the people is one, and they have all one language; and this they begin to do: and now nothing will be restrained from them, which they have imagined to do. (Genesis 11:6)

Clearly, in this story, God was afraid of human imagination and ingenuity. Does that sound like a real god, or does that sound like a jealous, frightened, mythical god created by ancient, superstitious tribal people?

During discussions and debates, many people who study reason and rational thought find themselves unable to proceed when the people they're debating finally resort to these Bible verses. The fundamentalist Christians are ultimately saying that they don't care *how* correct science and logic are, that ultimately the ideas go against God, and are, therefore, wrong.

The assault against reason and thought here, then, is two-fold: The Bible explicitly warns against such knowledge, and further, science clearly contradicts many things in the Bible, proving such stories wrong. Science and truth, therefore, has to be terribly frightening for a fundamentalist Christian! They see the truth, they hear it, they know it's true, they know it challenges their basic faith, and they know they've been warned against it. The immediate defensive response, then? Call it "Satan" and turn your back on it.

I've heard these arguments from fundamentalists myself during discussions, and I've been told that because I "worship" science that I'm turning my back on the "ultimate truth" of God, and therefore giving my heart to Satan. Yes, I've actually been told that. And the implication, therefore, is that science comes from Satan.

Now, to be fair, not all Christians believe that. In fact, from my own experience it's only a tiny percentage that takes it to that extreme.

However, when push comes to shove, the majority of Christians (at least in America), do reject science when it counters the teachings of the Bible—science such as evolution.

As such, science continues to be the enemy of many, many Christians, even when logical, reasonable arguments are put right in front of their face. And it's only getting worse, as science advances and explains more and more phenomena that were once covered by religion. These areas of knowledge are what many freethinkers call the "gaps". We'll take that up next.

God of the Gaps

When scientists are trying to find how something works, they perform many experiments, and gather large amounts of data. The data they gather must point to only one conclusion. If it doesn't, scientists don't just randomly pick one of the different conclusions and go with it.

Consider this: I might park my car outside and in the morning find a large crack in the windshield. That's an observation, a piece of data. I might then take the data and come up with one possible conclusion that explains what happened:

A rock was kicked up by a passing truck, and the rock broke the windshield.

The more I study religions the more I am convinced that man never worshipped anything but himself.

- Sir Richard Francis Burton (1821 - 1890)

Is that the only possible conclusion? Is that the only conclusion the data points to? No. Here are two more possibilities:

Somebody walked by and hit the window with something and broke it.
Somebody was playing baseball and the ball hit the window.

Clearly there are many choices. I could just pick one and go with it and blindly refuse to budge and to not allow for any other possibilities. But that's not what science is about. Science doesn't just randomly pick one and accept it. Now consider this possible conclusion:

God broke the window.

In the same way, I could just randomly pick this one and hold onto it, completely refusing to let go of it. But the truth is, until I have more data, I don't know how the window broke. Unfortunately, too many people operate by filling in the unknowns with "God did it."

This failure of sound reason is what many people call the "God of the gaps" problem. If there's something people don't understand, it's common to just attribute it to God. But that is fundamentally flawed, because at its heart, it is nothing but circular reasoning, mixed with sheer randomness (and perhaps hope).

Here's one place where it breaks down other than the obvious random nature: Why does it have to be specifically the God described in the Christian Bible? Why not Zeus? Why not Isis? This flaw is demonstrated perfectly in the "watchmaker" argument used by Creationists.

The "watchmaker" argument was originally described like this, by William Paley, in a book he wrote in 1802:

> *There cannot be design without a designer. … Design must have a designer. That designer must have been a person. That person is GOD.*[*]

Here's the problem: If you have something that appears to be designed, such as the Earth itself, and you insist there must be a designer, does the data absolutely undeniably point to one designer in particular, the Christian deity named God? No. Remember, to be scientific about this, the data must point to only one conclusion. If it doesn't, an intelligent, reasonable person doesn't just randomly pick one.

So if the Earth were designed by some intelligent designer, who would that designer be? Here are a few of the infinite possibilities:

- Zeus
- Satan
- Aliens living on Mars
- Aliens from another galaxy
- Aliens from another universe
- Humans who went back in time
- Some unknown deity that I'll randomly create
- My friend Fred who lives at the center of Jupiter

---

* William Paley, *Natural Theology: or, Evidences of the Existence and Attribute of the Deity, Collected from the Appearances of Nature.* (1802)

...and so on. The people who buy into Creationism, unfortunately, have randomly picked a designer: The God of the Christian Bible. But why that one? *Because that's the one they already believe in.* And here's where the circular reasoning comes in: They already believe in the Bible. And they look for proof that God exists. They look to the amazing things they see in the world around them and feel that these things are clearly created by God. Therefore God exists and therefore they believe in the Bible. It's totally circular, and it is *not* scientific, nor is it logical, reasonable, or intelligent.

But let's return to the broken car window for a moment. What if we literally found a trail of data: The damage happened when there was snow on the ground, and we saw footprints leading out of a neighbor's house, up to our car, and then back to his house. And sitting next to the car was a rock. We now have a trail of information that suggests our neighbor did it: Footprints from his house to our car, a broken window, a rock lying beside the car, and footprints leading back to his house. Does that prove our neighbor did it? Not necessarily yet, although it offers some evidence pointing in that direction.

But what if we found another trail of information? Suppose the police interviewed various people, and it turns out somebody across the street saw our neighbor going out and doing it. That's another piece of important evidence. By itself, it might not be reliable, because the guy interviewed might not be telling the truth; he might simply dislike the neighbor and want to get him in trouble. But we have two pieces of evidence that together strongly support the conclusion that our neighbor is the one who did it.

But now what if we found even one more piece of evidence: We have a video camera on the front of our house recording everything going on. And right there on the video is a recording of our neighbor leaving his house, going out to the car, smashing the window, dropping the rock next to the car, and going back in.

Now we have three separate trails of evidence that converge to form only one conclusion: Our neighbor is guilty.

And so now, what if I *still* insisted, against all the evidence, that God did it? Wouldn't people find me rather stubborn, or even a bit crazy? Wouldn't it frustrate people in the same way that Achilles frustrated the Tortoise in Lewis Carrol's story? Imagine if I told the police that I refused to press charges because even though all the evidence suggests this particular neighbor did it, I don't really believe it and instead I think God did it.

But that's exactly what Creationists do with evolution and other scientific theories. What Creationists don't want to admit is that there aren't just a few pieces of evidence possibly suggesting evolution might have happened. Further, there's not just a single trail of evidence that points to evolution. Rather, there are many, *many* trails all leading to evolution. And the trails exist in several different fields of science, not just one. The evidence spans many diverse fields of study, such as biology, genetics, microbiology, archeology, paleontology, chemistry, and even physics and other fields built on these fields, such as medicine and dentistry. And within all these fields are thousands upon thousands of peer-reviewed articles covering experiments that either deal directly or indirectly with evolution. Not just one article written by Darwin, but thousands upon thousands: Mountains of data and evidence.

Creationists don't seem to realize the mountain of scientific data and articles they would have to climb over to truly debunk evolution. But they try anyway. That's something I'll cover in the next section.

Instead, the Creationists just resort to saying God created us as outlined in the book of Genesis. In fact, people have used "gaps" arguments for ages. In ancient times, anything people didn't understand was attributed to God (or God's enemy, Satan). If somebody was mentally ill with a condition such as schizophrenia, they were said to be possessed by Satan or one of Satan's demons. And if people found amazing things, such as the highest mountain ever seen, they attributed it to God: God put it there, apparently forming it literally with his own hands. This "God did it" approach to explaining how mountains form is in contrast to what we know today: that huge continent-sized blocks of land bump into each other, causing gigantic waves and earthquakes, as well as land to lift, forming mountains).

The data does not even point to God. That is an assumption. And further, as science becomes more advanced, we understand much more of how the universe works. We have scientific explanations for things we never had explanations for in the past. Previously scientific phenomena was attributed to God and brushed off. Today scientists understand how so many things work and don't just blindly attribute it to God.

In other words, the gaps are getting smaller. Science is learning more and more. Unfortunately, people still use the Gaps argument. There are, of course, things scientists still haven't figured out. And people (Creationists in particular) use those in their minds as clear indications that not only did God do it, but that God must, therefore, exist, and, even further, scientists must be completely wrong.

Again I appeal to the sound logic: Just because scientists don't yet understand something, does that *imply* that the *only possible explanation* is that it *must* have been done by God?

No. That is not an absolute, automatic conclusion. For example, if scientists don't know where the planet Neptune came from, does that mean the *only possible answer* is that God put it there? Of course not. There are many possibilities, and scientists won't automatically accept any single conclusion until they have enough evidence and data to support a particular conclusion. And so if scientists don't know where Pluto came from, they'll leave it as an open question until they get more data and really figure out the origin of Pluto .

One argument I've heard too many times goes like this: But people during Biblical times didn't yet know about modern chemistry and physics, so how could they have included it in the Bible?

Indeed, how could they, as that is exactly the point we non-believers make. But when Christians say this, they seem to fail to recognize the inherent contradiction: On one hand, they're claiming that an all-knowing, all-powerful God wrote the Bible, but at the same time they are saying the writers of the Bible could not have written in terms of modern chemistry and physics, and so that's why the topics are absent from the Bible.

Now pause for a moment: As I write this chapter, I have to consider who I am writing to. Are the fundamentalist Christians who are strong in their faith going to read this? Doubtful. So clearly you, dear reader, likely understand the contradiction I am presenting. But in the unlikely event a fundamentalist Christian wishing to expand his or her narrow worldview is reading this, I'll try to explain the contradiction again, albeit in slightly simpler terms.

If you say God wrote the Bible, why didn't God include modern physics and chemistry in the Bible? You say people didn't know about it back then, and in doing so, you are admitting that the writing in the Bible was created by men. By saying the writing *couldn't* contain modern physics and chemistry, you're admitting the Bible was authored by mere humans. If you're insisting God wrote the Bible, then certainly God could have written it in terms of modern chemistry and physics and put that information into the minds of the people holding the pens in their hands. Yet, oddly, all mentions of modern physics and chemistry and any understanding of it whatsoever is suspiciously *absent* from the Bible.

Am I, as a non-believer, supposed to take a leap of faith and blindly accept that God purposely chose to leave out his knowledge of chemistry and physics? Certainly, the more logical and natural step is to simply recognize that the notions of modern chemistry and physics are absent from the Bible because the authors knew nothing of it. Who were those authors? Men. Not God, but just ancient, superstitious men.

Incorrectly Debunking Science

A quick Google search shows a huge number of sites that supposedly debunk various aspects of science, most typically science that deals with either evolution or the Big Bang. With almost no exception, these sites are run by Christians or, on occasion, Jews or Muslims. First, should it be any surprise that the only science these people purport to debunk is that which stands in direct conflict with the teachings of the Book of Genesis? These people don't single out other science to attempt to debunk, such as the fact that atoms contain a nucleus that includes neutrons and protons. They only attempt to debunk those ideas that *don't work with their religion*. And they go through long, complex discussions that claim to show why evolution or the Big Bang could not possibly have happened.

To the untrained reader, it would be very easy to look at these articles and feel respect for the person who wrote them and to blindly accept them as fact. And the more intelligent readers might even be able to read the articles and understand them.

But there's a problem. Typically the people who write these articles are not trained in science and have studied only a little on their own. And a trained scientist with a PhD in the field in question could easily look at it and find all kinds of holes in it. Remember what I said about peer review; these layman's articles do not go through peer review. Instead they are dumped out onto the internet (and not published in any journals) for people to eat up without question. These articles are not published in reputable science journals and are not accepted by the scientific community.

And if the readers without advanced training can understand these articles, they will often be presented with something that makes good sense, something that really does seem to debunk evolution or the Big Bang. But the problem is the methods used in these articles are not sound, even though to somebody untrained in the field they seem to be.

Let's show how this works. Here's a demonstration that I came up with recently. I'm going to do what these people do in their articles. I'm going to disprove an important theory in science—at least it will seem that way to people who aren't trained in this particular area of science.

The theory I'm alleging to debunk is Einstein's Relativity.

Earlier I talked about Relativity. One of the main tenets of Relativity is that nothing can move faster than the speed of light. Imagine you're in a rocket ship going extremely fast and another rocket ship passes you going even faster. You will never be able to measure that rocket ship as going faster than the speed of light—no matter what.

So let's debunk that and see how it goes.

"Scientists say nothing can go faster than the speed of light. No matter how fast you measure something, it won't go faster than the speed of light, even if you're moving as well.

Now imagine two ships taking off from Earth. You're in one of them and it shoots off at three quarters the speed of light in one direction. Just as you take off, another ship takes off in the opposite direction. It's also going three quarters the speed of light.

To somebody standing on Earth with some kind of high-tech speed measuring device, they would see both ships going three quarters the speed of light, but in opposite directions, and away from Earth.

To you riding on the first space ship, the Earth will look like it's shooting away from you at three quarters the speed of light. That's how fast you would measure the Earth to be traveling away from you, even though you're the one doing the moving, Just as if you're on a boat leaving the dock and it looks like the dock is moving away—actually it's the boat moving. And then what happens if you measure the speed of the other space ship? How fast does it appear to be traveling away from you?

That's easy. If you're driving down the interstate at 70 mph, and you pass a car going in the opposite direction also going 70 mph, and you aimed a radar gun at that car, you'd show it going 140 mph away from you. Your two speeds would add.

So you would see the ship going away from you at your speed (three quarters the speed of light relative to Earth) plus its speed (also three quarters the speed of light relative to Earth). Add those up and you get one and a half times the speed of light. To you, as the rider on one ship, the other ship will appear to be going faster than the speed of light, nor can anything appear to be going faster than light. Obviously, Einstein didn't think of this when he came up with his Relativity, and scientists all across the planet just blindly accept Einstein and accept it without question, while totally missing such an obvious point. Einstein was wrong."

To somebody not trained in physics, this makes perfect sense and seems logical. You can just add speeds, and if you add two ships going in opposite directions, their speeds relative to each other would be faster than light, something in opposition to Relativity. It would be so easy to simply accept this argument and believe it, and to doubt the quality of all the scientists that have lived in the past century, and to create web sites proclaiming how stupid scientists are for blindly "believing" in Relativity, and, therefore, why religion is right. (Of course, even if science is wrong about something, that doesn't automatically mean religion is, by default right.)

However, the "proof" I just gave is absolutely, completely wrong. I used logic and simple math to debunk Relativity. However, the math I used is, in fact, incorrect. In Relativity, you don't just add speeds like that. Scientists have found it doesn't work; adding speeds like that doesn't apply to objects moving extremely fast. The calculated numbers end up wrong compared to actual measurements. And scientists know that and have proven that. Rather, you have to apply a special formula that Einstein used that was based on some earlier work done by a scientist named Lorentz. The equations are called the Lorentz Equations, and they are very carefully formulated, and they *do* take into consideration the scenario I presented of two ships traveling in opposite directions.[*]

But do you see what happened? I played the role of somebody with very little training in science and purported to debunk the science. And to somebody with little scientific training, it sounds believable and sensible. But it's not. It's *wrong*.

That's what these Creationists who post these "anti-Evolution" articles on the web do. These are *not* scientists and they do *not* fully understand the science they are attacking. But they think they understand it and will argue they do, and, unfortunately, convince other people that they know their stuff. But they don't.

But it gets even worse, unfortunately. In addition to claiming to debunk

---

[*] For the mathematically-inclined reader, the way to add velocities using relativity is $(u + v) / (1 + uv/c^2)$ where u and v are the two speeds and c is the speed of light. Try it out and you'll see that two numbers less than the speed of light never add up to more than the speed of light using this formula.

science, they convince other people that scientists are wrong, and they convince these people to distrust science.

But in the eyes of so many Christians, it has to be that way; they must claim science is wrong. Science has, after all, proven beyond any doubt at all that the Creation story in the book of Genesis is nothing but a total fabrication. It is not a literal story, and it did not happen. For the Bible-thumping literalists, this is a problem indeed! And that is exactly why they spend so much time and energy trying to debunk it.

What I'm about to say is going to sound incredibly arrogant, but there's not a very gentle way to say it: I'm surprised how many times I've tried to gently explain to Christians lacking scientific degrees that they do not understand evolution, and that they do not understand advanced scientific concepts, and until they further their education at a reputable university and obtain at least a bachelor's degree in a scientific topic, they probably never will understand it, much less *debunk* it.

People get very angry when they hear that. But why? Imagine you have a problem with the plumbing in your house. You try to fix it yourself, but after awhile it gets too complex and you realize you don't have the plumbing training necessary to complete the job. So what do you do? You admit you're not an expert, and you call an actual expert, a plumber. Now imagine the plumber is working away on your pipes and the whole time you're looking over his shoulder, telling him what to do next. Will he appreciate that? Hardly. Do you know as much as he does about plumbing? No, because otherwise you wouldn't have called him; you would have done the work yourself. At some point you need to concede that the plumber knows more than you do about plumbing.

The same is true with scientists. Unless you've done graduate work in biology, then you do *not* know as much as a scientist with a PhD in biology. There's a point where you have no choice but to accept that the people with PhDs in various scientific fields know more than you do about the particular field, unless you *also* have a PhD in that field.

Recently in a discussion online, somebody tried to call me out on that, saying, "So you're trying to say that I don't understand the the science." My response: "That is exactly what I'm saying."

Take physics, for example, which is where my training is, along with mathematics. I just talked about how one can incorrectly debunk Relativity. And I suggested that there is more advanced mathematics involved. But how advanced is the mathematics? Consider this: In elementary school, kids learn arithmetic—adding, subtracting, multiplying, dividing, fractions, decimals, etc. In high school, students are expected to have mastered arithmetic as they learn Algebra. In college, engineering and science students take Calculus, where they use Algebra as a tool that they have mastered. To study physics, you start your college studies with four semesters of Calculus. That's just the start. By the end, you're expected to have mastered all four semesters to the point that you can easily use Calculus as a simple tool. And *then* the advanced math classes begin.

That's right—Calculus, which is more advanced than arithmetic and algebra (and geometry and trigonometry, for that matter) is not advanced to a Physics student. Physics students then continue their math studies in both the Mathematics and Physics departments at school. They will take courses that require a complete mastery of Calculus, to the point that Calculus is *easy* and *just a tool*. They will continue their studies in math fields with names like Real Analysis, Partial Differential Equations, Complex Analysis, and other cryptic-sounding names. (You've seen pictures of physicists standing in front of a chalkboard filled with strange symbols and equations. Do you understand what the symbols mean?)

In order for Einstein to have fully formulated Relativity, he had to go well beyond what mathematics at the time offered. He had to take Calculus and build on it and develop a new, more advanced form of mathematics based on earlier work called Tensor Calculus. That's right: As a side project, Einstein had to develop an entire field of Mathematics just so he could get his work done.* How many of these people spouting Creationist ideas have a background in such advanced mathematics? They don't.

Of course, physics isn't totally a prerequisite to do research in genetics and other fields that pertain to evolution. However, other equally complex studies are required. For example, Organic Chemistry is as important to biology and chemistry as Calculus is to physicists. Organic Chemistry is extremely advanced to non-scientists, but important to biologists and chem-

---

* And don't believe for a moment the legend that Einstein was no good at math. He was a genius in math. That's just a legend people have invented to make kids feel better when they're struggling with math.

ists whose work has gone well beyond Organic Chemistry to the point that it's a simple tool for them.

And ask anyone who has suffered through a college course in Organic Chemistry: Is it easy? They'll tell you unequivocally, no.*

One man in particular who has made a life's work of trying to debunk evolution and other theories about the beginnings of the universe is a man named Ken Ham, who lives in Kentucky. Let's consider him next.

The Creationists' Small Universe and Backwards Science

Not far from Cincinnati, Ohio, in the northern edge of Kentucky near the Cincinnati International Airport is a place called The Creation Museum. This world-famous museum is the creation of a man named Ken Ham and his organization called Answers in Genesis.

To be clear, the ideas put forth by the Creation Museum do not represent all of Christianity. However, many, *many* Christians, especially those in the US, do believe what is being taught there.

What is being taught? That the book of Genesis is a literal, historical account of the beginning of the universe. People who subscribe to such beliefs are called Young-Earth Creationists. These people believe the world is no more than about 6000 years old, and that the story of Genesis, including the first book, detail exactly and *literally* how the world began. "Young Earthers" (as some of us call them) believe that the world was created in exactly seven literal days.

Many Young Earthers are people with science degrees who are trying to debunk evolution and the Big Bang theory. But the problem is that the approach they are taking is anything but scientific.

Look at it this way: Suppose you're not feeling right, and you go to the doctor. The doctor goes through all your symptoms, and puts them together

---

* If you encounter a Creationist who thinks he or she is an expert but find they haven't studied Organic Chemistry, have them go to **http://en.wikipedia.org/wiki/Electrophilic_aromatic_substitution** and tell them to explain it to you. That will put them in their place (maybe, assuming they aren't too stubborn).

and discovers they point to a particular, single problem. The doctor prescribes medicine to fix that one problem. You take the medicine, and sure enough, all your other symptoms go away.

But what if all the symptoms together point to several possible problems? One problem might be with your kidneys. Another problem might be with your liver. Still another problem might point to a viral infection somewhere in your body. The symptoms don't clearly point to a single problem. What is the doctor to do?

The doctor could just pick one problem and go with it. But that's not a good idea, because what if that diagnosis is wrong, and you end up taking medicine for the wrong problem? Instead, if the symptoms point to multiple problems, the doctor will probably order more tests, such as blood tests. Then the doctor will factor in the data acquired from those tests until a diagnosis is clear.

Medicine is, in fact, a science, and that's how science works: As I said in the previous chapter, the data points to a conclusion. In the case of medicine, the data is the set of symptoms, as well as the results of any tests the doctors perform, such as blood workups. From the given data, the doctors can usually come to a conclusion about what is wrong.

And if the conclusion isn't clear, then more data is acquired. In general, only after the data clearly points to a conclusion do the scientists agree on the conclusion. All science works this way, even areas of study we don't immediately think of, such as history, archeology, sociology, and psychology.

But now consider this: Suppose the doctor comes into the office one morning and says, "Today I'd like to treat a case of kidney disease."

You then come in because you're having some aches in your abdomen. The doctor checks you out, and clearly your aches are inconclusive. More tests are necessary to determine what's wrong. Certainly kidney disease is one possibility, but there are many possibilities. But without ordering further tests, the doctor makes the abrupt conclusion that you have kidney disease and he wants to start you on a treatment plan to heal your kidneys.

Any doctor who works that way deserves to have his or her license revoked. Doctors can't start the day expecting a conclusion. Rather, the doctors must go in with an open mind, check out the data, and determine the conclusion.

Unfortunately, people who study what they call "Creation Science" are doing exactly what this quack doctor is doing. They are going into their studies expecting to find answers that perfectly coincide with what's in the

Bible. (Of course, they would likely deny that, but to many of us, it's clear that's what's likely happening.)

People have been guilty of this for centuries. Prior to the last few decades, when archeologists would explore the Middle East, they were performing what they called Biblical Archeology. They were going into their digs looking for evidence to support the conclusions they already had in their minds, that the Bible was literally true.

People contributing articles to the Answers in Genesis web sites often use the word *presuppositions*. They claim that in analyzing data, scientists use their preconceived ideas; what Ken Ham and others call presuppositions.[*] They claim that scientists supporting evolution have presuppositions based in what they call "naturalism," which they define as a belief that denies any supernatural significance. They then admit that they have their own presuppositions, but theirs are based in the absolute truth of the Bible.

In other words, they are going into their studies with the advanced expectation that the studies will match with the Bible. But they even take it a step further: If the data doesn't match what's in the Bible, then they feel the data must be discarded. In their eyes, apparently, if scientific data, no matter how carefully and accurately obtained, contradicts the Bible, then the data is necessarily *wrong*.

Many creationists write about presuppositions on their web sites. It appears to me, however, that they are simply trying to appeal to the Bible-believing folks who have not yet learned what science is really about. But I also see that as a fundamental flaw in their arguments. It appears they're trying to defend against scientists the fact that they're starting with the Bible as a basis for all facts and knowledge, for no reason other than that they believe the Bible to be true.

But isn't that simply admitting that they're going against science? Probably not in their eyes, but to me it seems like they are.

In one article on the Answers in Genesis site[†], a writer tries to further defend this notion of presuppositions, by arguing that scientists have presuppositions that we take for granted, such as moral laws and our own existence. But he doesn't stop there. He then adds to these presuppositions the *laws of logic and induction.*

[*] Chapter 1 of *Evolution Exposed by Roger Patterson.* http://www.answersingenesis.org/articles/ee/what-is-science.

[†] *Feedback: Are scientists really biased by their presuppositions?* By Dr. Jason Lisle. http://www.answersingenesis.org/articles/2007/07/13/feedback-interpreting-facts.

This is a sure sign of major trouble. *Of course* scientists rely on the accuracy of the laws of logic and induction. The article also makes the claim that science expects our senses to be reliable. Of course it does. Is that a problem?

Oddly, however, the article is vague because on one hand, the author makes it sound like he agrees in the importance of the painfully obvious "presuppositions" such as sound logic and reason. But later in the article, he says that scientists and creationists (which he considers a form of scientist) have *different* presuppositions.

And this is where the article becomes rather disturbing. The author describes induction and how if you create an experiment that results in a particular outcome, you can expect an identical experiment to produce an identical outcome. That is true. But the author gives the credit to God, saying that God will uphold the future universe. During this discussion, the author then refers the reader to a particular verse in Genesis (Genesis 8:22). And he claims that scientists, without bringing God into the equation, have no good reason to assume the experiment will be repeated in the same way!

That's where this diverges from science altogether. Science stands on its own without the need for an external deity to factor into the equation. The scientists don't rely on the Bible to make sure the experiment will work again. Rather, they rely on *experience* that tells them the universe behaves in a particular way and that the laws that we know to be correct will *continue to be correct.*

Let's put this in perspective: Cars and computers work by the laws of physics. Will they continue to work tomorrow? We have no reason to worry that tomorrow we might wake up and find that all the laws of the universe have changed and cars and computers no longer function. (Besides, it's the laws of the universe that hold our molecules and atoms together in our bodies. If the laws all fell apart, we wouldn't survive to worry about the broken computers and cars.)

And further, science isn't built on presuppositions. Any facts that scientists have that provide a presupposed basis are so trivial and simple that they're barely cause for any consideration, or else they are factored in logically and intelligently. For example, the author of the article mentions a presupposition that your senses are accurate. Yes, I'm going to trust that when I see the number "20" on the screen of the computer that measured the weight of something, that the screen isn't secretly showing a different number and I'm only dreaming the 20. And I'm also going to trust the equipment works: If the scale measured 20 grams, the material really is 20 grams.

But you know what? Scientists are well aware that their equipment isn't perfect. And they factor that into their experiments. They carefully calibrate their equipment, and they make sure that their formulas take into account how accurate and precise the scale is. For instance, they know the range of precision the scale can handle, and recognize that if the scale says 20.00 grams, that could mean anywhere, for example, from 19.995 grams to 20.005 grams. And they repeat the experiments many times over to be sure. There's no guesswork here, and there are certainly no *assumptions*, which is probably a better word to use than *presuppositions*.

Pulling the Bible in, then, as a factor, is more of a random assumption than a presupposition. There's no reason to factor it in, other than personal taste, and that has no place in science. Otherwise, a scientist could just as easily declare that some primitive medicine man's writings were inspired by God and are holy, and that any claims made by the medicine man must, therefore, be factored into a modern pharmacology experiment as a "presupposition". In the realm of science, such an absurdity is no different from trying to force something as random as the Bible in by claiming it as a presupposition. One scientist could add the Bible into an experiment as a presupposition; another could add ancient Vedic scriptures of India; and another could add some ancient Mayan writings. Should we really trust any of these three scientists' results? Of course not. They are all equally random, and none of them belong there.

Besides, assuming the Bible is accurate and that, for example, the world was created about 6000 years ago and that dinosaurs existed at the same time early humans did is a *huge* assumption that would need some serious evidence before being used in scientific experiments, much more so than a silly little assumption such as the physical laws of today will work the same as tomorrow; or that when the scale says 20, it's not lying to me and really measured 40. (And the latter can be tested: Use a second scale and compare the results. But let's be realistic and not make more silly presuppositions, such as that the two scales are going to become conscious and conspire together to lie to us.)

So after covering this, I must ask: Is it *really* objective and reasonable to factor the Bible into science and assume that it's more accurate than anything scientists can do, or is it simply wishful thinking and forcing one's religion into science for no reason other than it happens to be the researcher's own personal religion? (And one must also ask: What if two scientists working together have very different religions? Which presuppositions do they fall back on?)

Back to the article I was describing, unfortunately, the article is a response to a letter. The people who wrote the letter were challenging the Creationist view, and end it with the rather nasty, "Choke and die on your bibles already." That's unnecessary and unfortunate, as it does nothing to further the cause of debunking Creationism, and greatly undermines the true intentions. I sincerely hope that people who are trying to further real science will abstain from such senseless attacks.

After reading some of these articles, I was curious about this odd term *presupposition*. It's obviously a real word and not made up by these guys; you can see the word is simply a combination of "pre" and "suppose". But it's not a commonly used word.

In fact, the word does have a use in logical arguments, often from a linguistic approach. But I decided to Google it to see how common it is on the Web, and how it's most often used.

I first Googled the plural, *presuppositions*. And my own presupposition was that the results would be primarily pages dealing with logic. In general, I was right. But guess what: On the first page of results, the *third* result linked to a page that's an excerpt from a book about Christianity. And the seventh result links to a page about whether Jesus was an actual historical figure. The second page of results, showing numbers 11-20, starts off with number 11 being a link to a page about...Creationism. Number 14 is a link to a page about faith. Number 17 is again about Creationism.

So why would this word be so commonly used among Creationists to the point that a seemingly simple word that appears on nearly 700,000 pages would have top hits mostly related to religion, and particularly Creationism? It turns out this word *does* have a history in Christian theology.

In the early 20th century, a Dutch theologian named Cornelius Van Til came up with ideas that rely on presuppositions that the Bible is always true: that is, when in doubt, the Bible is ultimately true. Van Til didn't use that term himself, but others used the term in reference to his ideas, which they called *presuppositional apologetics*. The idea is that if you're arguing with somebody who accepts something that contradicts the Bible, then your opponent must be wrong, because the Bible is true *by default*.

This is obviously in line with ideas about Intelligent Design: If there's any discrepancy between science and the Bible, IDers (as people call them) automatically goes with the Bible. That's exactly what Van Til's presuppositional apologetics is all about.

But this kind of theology clearly doesn't work. In order to use the Bible as a basis in an argument, both parties to the argument would have to believe the Bible is the infallible truth. Otherwise the argument will convince nobody. I don't believe in the Bible anymore, so why would I believe an argument that relies on a verse from Genesis?

Going the Wrong Way

As I mentioned earlier, Science is about analyzing data and *then* drawing conclusions, regardless of preconceived notions and biases. Creationists and IDers are going about it backwards. They already know what they want to prove: The Bible. They already have their conclusions. All that's missing is the data to back it up. Science does not work that way, and suggesting it does is an abomination *and* an insult to science. And it's deceptive. It deceives people into thinking science is something *other than* what it is.

> *Truth is what stands the test of experience.*
>
> *-Albert Einstein*

Science is about finding the answers, and accepting them whether you like them or not. Creationists don't do that. They start with the answer that they refuse to budge on and then plow forward and try to prove it, meanwhile totally undermining science. Unfortunately, they can't prove things like Intelligent Design, so they gather together bits and pieces of data into something that looks like a proof, and present it as-is, even though there's not even a single line of evidence, only a sprinkling of weak ideas. Do they submit it to other scientists for peer review and get it published in a reputable, widely-accepted journal? No. They never have, because they know it won't survive the peer review. Other scientists would find numerous flaws. But they know that the mass of people out there with no training in science, on the other hand, won't know the difference, and so they put these papers on the Internet for people to come across and point to when trying to prove Intelligent Design.

Of course, people with training in science see right through it and refuse to blindly accept this false science. But then the Creationists just get mad and call us arrogant and closed-minded, and then accuse us of being the ones who hold onto a theory without any rational reason for doing so. Yet they're the ones who hold onto ancient, nonsensical stories about talking snakes that have no basis in rational thought, and they refuse to let go of such ideas even when the evidence against such stories is overwhelming.

But the fact that people so blindly accept the nonsense spewing out of the Creationists and IDers is no surprise given that people in the US aren't being allowed to get a real science education.

Using the Wrong Formulas

Earlier, I showed how, with only a partial understanding of a subject, one can incorrectly debunk a scientific topic. But when somebody has even more understanding of a subject, that person can do even more damage to it.

There's a small group of people who maintain primarily an online presence who are convinced the world is not spinning and that the world is stationary, and that the rest of the universe rotates about the Earth—just as people believed prior to Galileo and other great scientists proving the notion wrong.

Some of the people who are perpetuating the myth that the Earth is stationary actually have scientific degrees, even PhDs, in fields such as physics. In other words, these are people who should know better. There are various web sites run by these people that include supposed research articles that claim to back up the incorrect ideas with scientific formulas.

But again, they get it wrong (and they should know better, too). In addition to going the wrong way by starting with the presupposition that the Bible is correct, they also use math incorrectly.

Here's how: Physics makes heavy use of mathematical formulas. Physics is very much about finding a math formula that accurately describes how the world works. Consider human inventions that fly, such as planes, missiles, and rockets. Scientists use math formulas to figure out exactly how much push these objects need and for how long and in what directions to know exactly how to control the objects. To make these calculations, scientists and engineers make use of many different formulas, including those developed by Newton as I explained earlier—Newton's Laws of Motion. These are highly accurate, detailed formulas where you plug in a set of numbers (such as the path you want the missile to fly in) and you get back another set of numbers (such as the direction to point the missile, how much fuel to put in, and so on).

Now the thing about these formulas is that they fit with reality: When you plug in where you want the missile to go, you get back another set of numbers, and all the numbers fit with the missile's initial conditions (such as the amount of fuel it needs) and the path the missile flies in. The numbers all work and are correct, and as such, the formulas used to calculate the numbers are right.

But are these the *only* formulas that can be used? This is where things get tricky and confusing, and it's where people can start to deceive other people, either intentionally or unintentionally. In fact, often you can find other formulas that more-or-less work. But there are two problems: First, the formulas might only work under certain conditions, and second—and this is where the real trouble comes—often in order to force the formulas to work, the scientists must add other factors into the situation, such as particles and forces and physical entities that don't even exist.

And that's where the geocentrists go wrong. I carefully read through several of these supposed research articles online (which, I might add, were very beautifully done to look like actual, formal journal articles). Because I have a degree in mathematics and have done graduate work in physics, I was able to understand all the formulas put forth. And the formulas were, for the most part, sound. They worked. They correctly predicted the motion of the planets and stars "around" the Earth.

Except there was one huge problem: In order for the formulas to work, there had to be an additional "undiscovered" force pushing down on the Earth, some strange thing emanating from above, something that scientists haven't yet discovered or detected.

See the problem there? In order for the ideas to work, the guy developing the formulas had to introduce additional physical items that don't actually exist.

Compare that to the actual formulas that the engineers at NASA use to launch their spacecrafts. Their formulas don't rely on any additional physical entities that haven't yet been found.

Logically, then, which is correct? While it could be possible that there's a force out there that scientists haven't yet discovered, the fact that there are formulas that *work*, that don't rely on such a force, leaves scientists little choice but to accept these latter formulas as being the correct ones.

Here's a case in point: Prior to Einstein discovering Relativity, scientists accepted that there was some unseen *thing* that permeated all of space, something that provided a means for light waves to travel "through" in the same way water is what ocean waves travel through and air is what sound waves travel through, and that this thing—which scientists named the aether—was stationary and all moving objects had a fundamental speed relative to the aether, and, with careful calculations, scientists could figure out the speed of any object through space.

Turns out that's not at all the case. Einstein's formulas work without the need for an aether. The only speeds you can calculate on objects are their speeds relative to something else. We usually calculate speeds relative to the Earth, which, in turn, is also moving.

We know Einstein's formulas are correct, and his formulas remove the *need* for an aether. Prior to Einstein, advanced formulas relied on the presence of an aether, but nobody had ever been able to detect the aether. By all accounts, it didn't exist. Yet, the formulas required it. But Einstein's formulas worked without the need for this physical thing that nobody had ever detected. That simplified things greatly for scientists, as it removed the need for this hypothetical aether, and, for all intents and purposes, removed the notion of aether from science altogether. The aether doesn't exist, and the formulas don't need it.

So when the geocentric people model the universe, they have no choice but to add in invisible, undiscovered, hypothetical entities like the aether. But we already have formulas that don't need these hypothetical entities, formulas that work. Which, then, is correct? The answer should be obvious, especially when you factor in why exactly the people are trying to develop a set of formulas that allow for a stationary Earth: The Bible seems to claim that the Earth is stationary, and since they believe the Bible must be right, then they'll develop their formulas accordingly. Unfortunately for them, to make the formulas work, they need to introduce hypothetical things that don't really exist. Seems to me that pretty much invalidates their ideas, now doesn't it?

Limited Science Education

The sad part is, the majority of Americans have no clue that the ideas being perpetuated by the Creationists are flawed and non-scientific. Creationism and so-called Intelligent Design are *not* science and *not* theories and *not* alternatives to evolution.

But people don't know or understand that. In a sense, we've hardly advanced from the time of Galileo when the church had a stronghold on Europe and didn't want people learning real science, lest they question what's in the Bible.

But what's especially sad is that people are given the incorrect impression that even scientists are debating and take a "pick and chose" approach to science. So many people seem to think that some scientists *like* Intelligent Design better and prefer it, while other scientists *like* Evolution better and prefer it. That is not true at all, and is not what science is about. As I've said before, science is about accepting the facts that have been repeatedly observed and tested and verified, and not simply picking one idea over another because it *feels* better.

Even some people who should know better don't. A couple of years ago, a school here in America made national news because two science teachers (who were reborn Christians) decided it was important to teach Intelligent Design alongside evolution. And they said that they felt it was important to teach "critical thinking" and let the students compare both and decide for themselves which they "supported" and then to write papers about it.

Those who seek consolation in existing churches often pay for their peace of mind with a tacit agreement to ignore a great deal of what is known about the way the world works.

-Mihaly Csikszentmihalyi, Flow: The Psychology of Optimal Experience, 1990

That is not science! Scientists do not pick and choose which theories they like better and therefore "support." Science is not about choosing opposing ideas. Yet, people don't seem to understand that. Recently online I saw a Creationist argue that science is about presenting non-scientists with different "viewpoints" and that it's very non-scientific to not allow Creationism in the classroom as an alternative viewpoint.

Wrong.

The fact that this gentleman used the word "viewpoint" shows just how wrong he is. Science isn't about different people taking different "viewpoints." It's about facts and data and only accepting the conclusions that result from the facts and data. Look at it this way: I could present an opposing viewpoint to the hard research being done in the pharmaceutical companies. Here's an opposing "viewpoint" some crackpot might propose: *Cyanide, which is commonly believed by scientists to be deadly, can, in large quantities, cure any and all disease.*

That's an opposing "viewpoint." Of course, cyanide would kill any patient being treated for a disease, and there is absolutely no data to back such an outrageous, absurd claim. Would it be scientific for science teachers to present this opposing "viewpoint" to students in a classroom? Of course not. Yet, that's exactly what these people are trying to say, that the science classrooms should be a free-for-all where any idea, no matter how outrageous or absurd, should be allowed in.

Scientists do extensive studies and tests to determine which ideas are correct. I already talked about the process of peer review, and that's the first step to scientists accepting another scientist's work. They don't pick and choose based on what feels right. They accept theories and ideas based on data that can be tested and verified, and then used to make predictions.

Simply choosing between two ideas, therefore, is not "critical thinking" by any means, and suggesting it is is nothing short of ignorance. And *teaching* it as such has no place in the science classroom. But apparently the science teachers who were teaching Creationism believe it is critical thinking, which demonstrates their *own* misunderstanding of science.

But how many people in America even realize that? How many people in this country truly have an understanding of the scientific method and the process by which new ideas are formulated and tested? And worse, how many parents don't understand it, and don't like the teachers at the schools teaching scientific facts and prefer they teach false science that proclaims Intelligent Design is a legitimate scientific theory that is embraced by half the scientists, and that scientists pick and choose their theories?

It's hard to say, but I would venture to guess that the majority of Americans do not understand what science is really about. Even a large number of college graduates don't understand it, because many majors don't require any courses that teach the scientific method. (I myself have gotten into arguments over the scientific process with people with college degrees in areas such as math or computer science.)

Knowing how people lack understanding here shows just how easy it is for Americans by and large to see things like "Intelligent Design" as a viable "alternative" to evolution, when it *isn't*. And it's easy to see why they'll say that science classes should teach "both theories," when Intelligent Design is *not* a scientific theory. (Besides, if they're going to teach both ideas, why not a gazillion other "competing" ideas, such as the idea that Zeus created the world last year and filled our brains with false memories? Again, it sounds like Creationists are looking for a free-for-all here.)

But how can we teach people what science is and is not, when they're trying to control what we teach? See the problem? They won't let us teach the children what real science is all about, and that way if the science classes are forced to teach non-science like Creationism, the students won't be prepared to look at it critically and see that it is *not* science and will just eat it up. Talk about frustrating!

And sadly, it's more than just frustrating. It is holding our country back by limiting the science education of our children, and keeping them from becoming scientists and researchers. Sure, the court in Dover might have forced ID out of the classroom for now, but there are still people trying to teach Creationism and Intelligent Design in the science classrooms.

Interestingly, today the Catholic Church claims to admit that Galileo was right. But is the Church as a society, as a huge collective of people across the planet (especially the United States, anyway) willing to say as much? Hardly.

What can we do then? This is where politics comes into play. Even though science is not decided in the courts, the educational system is. Therefore, we must keep writing letters to the editors of the newspapers, and we must keep writing to our politicians, and we must support groups such as the Freedom From Religion Foundation (FRFF) that wage battles in the courtrooms to keep non-science like "Intelligent Design" out of the science classrooms.

But Isn't it Okay for a Scientist to be Religious?

If a scientist wants to "believe" in Creationism, then that means he's not subscribing to the scientific method. But what about engineers and other people building things that make our lives easier? Shouldn't they be free to be believe how they want?

Well, in our country, the correct and appropriate answer is Yes. We have freedom of religion. But their religion can only get them so far. Here's why.

Suppose a team of engineers is designing the circuitry that runs dialysis machines. They have the designs 50% finished, but they're having some problems with that last half. What should they do?

I've worked in some engineering fields, and I've known a few engineers who go home and pray about their problems. They may or may not come up with a solution, but if they do, it's easy to attribute the solution to God. Fine. If that's what they want to believe, then fine. Whatever. I've even heard of some engineers getting together and praying for the solution. Again, fine. Whatever floats their boat.

But that's where the line must be drawn, because when the dialysis machines go to production, the designs must be 100% right, because *lives* are at stake. Imagine what would happen if instead the engineers only finished 50% of the designs and left the rest to God. They couldn't finish it, so they build only half the parts and leave the rest to *faith*. They then build hundreds of these only partially-functioning dialysis machines and let God control the last 50%. They then ship these half-functioning machines to hospitals across the country, hoping they'll magically start working, believing that God will see to it that they work.

Would each and every dialysis machine suddenly start operating fully and perfectly? Of course not. Would *you* want to be put on one of those dialysis machines? Would you really want hundreds of sick people to be attached to these dialysis machines instead of, say, ones that the engineers built completely and correctly?

Clearly, the engineers can't finish only half the machine and let God do the rest. They have to do the whole thing. But the way these Creationists want to transform our science classes, soon students are going to have no idea what real science and engineering is all about, and they will not be able to continue advancing our society and they just might want to see hospitals filled with faith-based medical equipment. Personally, I find that extremely frightening.

So yes, it's fine if a scientist wants to believe in God and go to church every Sunday, so long as they separate their religious views from their scientific research.

Supposed Flaws in Evolution

People who reject modern science and refuse to let go of old, outdated, superstitious beliefs such as Intelligent Design like to try to point out what they see as flaws in evolution. Earlier I spoke of how these people claim to debunk science. One topic they fail miserably at is the notion of the *Second Law of Thermodynamics*, something they claim proves evolution can't happen.

The laws of thermodynamics are a set of laws that are known to be true dictating how energy operates and is transferred between objects. The second law of thermodynamics deals with what is known as *entropy*. Entropy is often described as disorder, and a popular but incorrect notion is that entropy cannot decrease, that it can only increase. (But it can decrease, in fact.)

Here's a popular little story that people use to try to describe entropy (again, incorrectly): Suppose you have a working, functioning watch and you smash it. You then put it into a box and shake it. How much shaking will it take to get the watch to go back together and start functioning again? The idea is that no amount of shaking will do: You need to have a designer who puts together the watch. (Remember, I mentioned the watchmaker argument earlier.)

People make the claim that disorder can only increase without the help of an outside designer. Humans can design and build watches, but left on their own, the disorder will increase; watches will fall apart and stop functioning. Indeed, they say, the whole universe is really moving towards disorder.

To a certain extent, that is correct. The overall entropy of the universe does increase. But always equating entropy to disorder is wrong. Some teachers use the concept of disorder to introduce the concept of entropy. That's fine, but it only works early on, because to understand entropy and thermodynamics in full, soon you must leave behind the trivial notion of disorder and actually consider the mathematical formulas.

Entropy refers to the dispersal of energy, and the dispersal of energy follows very precise mathematical formulas. A good example of entropy in action (and to see how disorder does play a role) is when you drop something fragile and it hits the ground and falls apart, with pieces going every which way. The energy is spreading the parts out as the object breaks and becomes more disordered. The entropy increases.

But that's only an example where the entropy is obvious to the eyes. Entropy is really a value that exists everywhere as chemical reactions take place. And once you start to understand entropy, it's easy to see that entropy *can* decrease under totally natural situations. When water freezes into ice, the entropy decreases. That happens all the time in nature; something we experience as winter comes and the lake freezes.

A decrease in entropy happens in many other situations as well. Chemical reactions take place automatically without the need for some external hand making them happen. All they need is energy going into them, and here on Earth we have an abundance of energy for just that purpose: The energy from the Sun. The Sun's energy feeds into the chemical reactions here on Earth, resulting in decreases of entropy. That's how life goes on here on Earth, thanks to the energy feeding us from the Sun.

But what about The Second Law of Thermodynamics? Creationists like to bring that up. This law simply states that the *overall* entropy of a system must increase over time. There can be local decreases, and such decreases can happen naturally and automatically for many types of chemical reactions, provided the reactions have a source of energy from which to draw. And that's the case with our bodies; we have energy coming into us, and reactions take place that can result in a decrease in entropy. (It takes energy to build muscle mass, for example, as every serious body builder at the gym understands.)

In sum, then, the Second Law recognizes that entropy can decrease. But overall the entropy must go up. Where do we see the entropy increasing? In the sun itself. Eventually the sun will run out of energy. As the sun operates, it slowly runs out of energy, and its entropy increases. The sun won't run out of energy for a very long time, but it will happen eventually. And that increase in entropy greatly outnumbers the small decreases we see here on Earth when the ice freezes or the body builder's muscles grow; the difference when combined, then, is an overall net increase in entropy, even though we see a decrease in the ice and in the muscles. But let's not forget, entropy can and does decrease.

So what does this have to do with evolution? *Creationists claim evolution violates the Second Law of Thermodynamics.* They claim that as species become more complex and sophisticated, more order is coming out of disorder and that entropy is decreasing, which, they claim, isn't possible.

Armed with what we know about Thermodynamics, we can easily see why the Creationists are intentionally ignorant here. (I say "intentionally" because it's terribly easy to see why the argument is wrong, and yet, so many refuse to accept the facts. Thus I feel it is an intentional act on their part to ignore reality, an act of ignorance and stubbornness.)

Evolution does *not* violate the Second Law of Thermodynamics. Thermodynamics is not just a simple matter of increasing "disorder". Entropy is about the spreading of energy, and further, entropy certainly can decrease. Claiming evolution violates the Second Law is, first, incorrectly equating entropy with disorder, and second, ignoring the fact that entropy can and does decrease.*

Remember, evolution is about traits changing as they are inherited from ancestors. My body is a system and is a totally separate system and body from that of my ancestors. My parents are my ancestors, and I'm a totally separate body from them. How their body uses energy has no bearing on how my body uses energy. My father goes about his daily life with the chemical processes functioning in his body as he eats and (presumably) exercises, and as his metabolism runs and as his body digests fat and burns energy and runs the mechanisms of his body. My body is separate from his and also runs all the chemical processes to function. Why would traits changing as they are inherited violate the Second Law? They don't. Evolution doesn't break the Second Law.

And even still, if we humor the example people incorrectly give stating that the Second Law pertains only to disorder, consider a human embryo growing into a baby and then into an adult. This is an example of order coming from disorder, and the very fact that it happens means that the Second Law is not being broken (since it *can't* be broken). Yet Creationists don't have a problem with this cycle. So why do they have a problem with evolution?

The answer, as it turns out, is very clear. Creationists who use the Thermodynamics argument are dead-set on disproving a scientific fact using other science (albeit incorrectly). But at the same time they make outrageous claims that themselves violate science. (You would think they would accept evolution and brush off any *perceived* problems—that is, parts they don't actually understand—as simply "God did it"—even though the problems are only perceived and not real. That is, after all, how they conduct their day-to-day lives anyway.) Just look at some of the outrageous claims these people make, things that simply are not scientifically possible, which they just claim as being miracles performed by God. "God did it."

* In fact, recent research shows that evolution is an *example* of the Second Law of Thermodynamics. For a fascinating look at how evolution fits together with the Second Law, check out Into the Cool by Eric D. Schneider and Dorion Sagan (University of Chicago Press, ISBN 0226739376).

The first that comes to mind for me is the parting of the Red Sea. As the story goes, Moses freed the Jewish slaves from the hands of the Egyptians, and at one point had to help the former slaves cross the Red Sea. In order to get across, Moses stuck his staff into the sea, at which point the sea spread and provided dry land for the people to walk across. (I'm not sure what became of the massive amount of underwater vegetation that would have been a veritable forest for them to get through when the water cleared, but that's beside the point I suppose.) Once across, the sea closed up, drowning their pursuers.

If the Creationists claim evolution couldn't have happened because it supposedly violates the Second Law of Thermodynamics (which it doesn't), then why don't they also discount this little parting-of-the-sea number, because it certainly *does* violate the Second Law. Unless Moses knew more about physics and how to transform matter into energy than what modern scientists do, there is no possible way he could have accomplished this. Einstein's law tells us that if the staff were turned into energy, then there would be a huge amount of energy, perhaps enough to blow away the water of the sea (but that would have been an explosion big enough to kill Moses and all the people around). But Moses did not have any such technology back then. The whole story is attributed to God. God did it.

But either way you cut it, the story absolutely violates the Second Law of Thermodynamics. If the Creationists are so bent on making sure the universe abides by the Second Law, why don't they also point to little problems such as this?

The answer, of course, is obvious. They really don't care about whether the Second Law is violated. They're not just trying to behave as the Science Police, running around looking for flaws in the interest of bettering science and humanity. They don't *care* about thermodynamics (or even understand it, obviously). And they're certainly not about to embrace evolution, simply attributing the parts they don't understand to God. Instead, they care about disproving evolution simply because they don't want it to be real. Evolution conflicts with their own silly little Creation myth, an ancient, superstitious fairy tale that is hardly different from the other creation myths of the time.

Evolution and Morality

One logical fallacy I hear people making against evolution is that if evolution is true, all sorts of immoral behavior will happen. And to try to defend this argument, people will refer to Nazi Germany under Hitler, claiming that the atrocities that they committed were the result of studies in evolution.

But that's logically flawed. Any science has the potential for abuse, and that in no way makes the science incorrect or false. It amounts to saying a particular science is false because people don't like it. The pharmaceutical industry has used scientific research to create some amazing medicines to help us stay healthy, but at the same time, the science of pharmacology has been used to create illicit, addictive drugs that can be abused and cause severe health, emotional, and family problems. But do these problems mean the whole pharmaceutical industry is bad, and even scientifically *incorrect*? Of course not. The logic that the science of evolution might have been abused does not make it incorrect and untrue.

This gets to the heart of the evolution "debate" as people try to disprove it. They can argue against the moral aspects of it until they're blue in the face, and they can try to find flaws in it (which they won't), but all their work will be in vain, because it misses the real reason they object to evolution: They don't *like* it.

Facts are stubborn things; and whatever may be our wishes, our inclinations, or the dictates of our passion, they cannot alter the state of facts and evidence.

-John Adams (1735 - 1826)

But disliking it doesn't make it false.

Just because somebody doesn't happen to like a science doesn't mean the science is incorrect. Sorry. Deal with it. There are plenty of older people who don't like computers and don't like the idea of having so many areas of our lives run on computers. But you don't see these people trying to prove that computers *don't work*.

But that's exactly what Creationists do! They don't like a particular branch of science, and so they spend their time tying to disprove it, to say it's wrong and that it doesn't work. And remember what I said earlier, that further, they want to teach children in schools this is scientific, that scientists pick and choose which ideas they like better!

The idea of disproving computers because one doesn't like computers might seem like a stretch, but it really is no different. Evolution is real, and it happened and is happening. The existence of evolution isn't as blatantly obvious as computers are (you can just show somebody a working computer to prove they exist). But it's just as real, and biologists and other scientists and researchers are very aware of it and to them it is obviously real.

Why don't people *like* evolution? Easy: It goes against their religious beliefs which stem from the Bible. You can't have both a God who created the universe in six 24-hour periods (resting on the seventh) and simultaneously have a planet that evolved over millions of years. One of them *must* be incorrect.

And that's why these people don't like evolution, because it has the potential of proving that the first couple of chapters of the Book of Genesis are wrong. And if these chapters are wrong, what would that say about the Bible? The implications are severe for such people, to say the least.

Of course, there are plenty of Christians who do not buy into a literal seven-day creation. I dismantle this fallacy in Chapter 5 in the section "The myth of creation". For now, suffice to say that there are far too many items in the first few chapter of Genesis that, even when we adjust a "day" in the seven days of Creation to millions of years, the story still can't work. (In the story, the Earth and its plants are created before the sun, which isn't possible; plants can't exist without sunlight.)

And as for evolution being real, I couldn't possibly describe it all in this chapter. Fully understanding evolution requires advanced knowledge of many fields of science. Having a basic understanding of it and, more importantly, why it's correct, is possible for everyone. If you're interested in exploring this more, check out the books in the Bibliography at the back of this book.

Science is a Religion?

Too often people who wholeheartedly accept the Bible and all its inaccuracies like to claim that science is just a religion, and people such as myself blindly follow it. If the scientists say it, they claim, then I blindly believe it. But if you've read this chapter up until now, you should see clearly why science is not a religion at all. Science is built on facts and data, and solid conclusions based on those facts and data.

This then turns away from "faith" and into the area of "trust". I do not have "faith" in science the way a fundamentalist Christian might have "faith" in a faith healer. Rather, scientists have demonstrated to me that science as a whole can be trusted. Because this is such a big issue, I take this up shortly, devoting an entire chapter—Chapter 7—to it.

My Personal Journey: No Choice in the Matter

To conclude this chapter, I'd like to discuss the mindset of where I was and how I got through it.

In his book *The God Delusion*, Richard Dawkins speaks of a man named Dr. Kurt Wise, a Harvard-trained paleontologist who was both a scientist and a Christian. This man determined without a doubt that Science and what's written in the Bible do not fit together, that they can't *both* be right. This is a man with a doctorate in a scientific field, and with science, he knows his stuff. He's also a devout Christian and knows the Bible very well. And he said it himself, that the two disagree.

Like so many of us, he had a choice to make. Believe it or not, his choice, as Dawkins explained, was to ditch science and go with the literal, Young-Earth view of the Bible. Yikes.

Dr. Wise has made a choice to turn his back on the facts and data that are indisputable because they don't agree with the Bible.

I cannot do that. A Harvard-trained Paleontologist and devout Christian who was a prodigy of the great Stephen J. Gould has said himself that science and the Bible do not fit together and he chose the Bible.

I choose Science. How can I not? I simply cannot understand how somebody could turn against sound logic and reason.

Imagine if the Bible said that two plus two equals five. People of sound reason would have no choice but to turn on the Bible. I can't know what is going on inside Dr. Wise's mind, so I can't know what he would do if such a claim were made. But to many of us with science backgrounds, turning on evolution and embracing the Bible is as ridiculous as the idea of embracing 2+2=5 if the Bible were to say so.

There are, however, Christians who embrace all of science, every aspect of it. I did, before abandoning Christianity outright. The problem is that once you embrace all of science, you start to realize there's no *need* for divine intervention. Atoms can interact with other atoms without some God telling them to. Planets can revolve around the sun without God controlling them.

But recognizing that there's no need for divine control of the atoms and planets wasn't enough to make me walk away from Christianity. It was only after I started to analyze what Christianity is really all about did I finally break loose and realize I simply couldn't believe in it any longer. In the next chapter I'll take a more detailed look at Christianity, followed by, what I consider one of the most important chapters of this book, a chapter on how Christianity is built on myths.

Science teaches us to think rationally and objectively and to analyze data with an open mind. That's what I did with Christianity, and I found it simply wasn't possible to believe in it while remaining rational. Let's proceed.

five

Creating a Deity: Lies, Fears, Threats

If you live in the United States and you drive a car, you've undoubt-edly seen the billboards beside the highways that are just large black signs with white letters, along with a quote supposedly attributed to God. Then in the lower-right hand side is the name God. These billboards were originally developed and paid for by an anonymous person in South Florida. (Apparently he wanted the attention to be on God, not himself, thus the anonymity.) But after a run in South Florida, the Outdoor Advertising Association of America paid for them to appear across the country.

The billboards featured phrases like, "You think it's hot here?" and "What part of 'Thou shalt not' didn't you understand?" and "Big Bang Theory? You've got to be kidding."

When these signs appeared the first time, I was still a practicing Christian, but even then they bothered me. The reason was simple: They were quotes attributed to God, but they were *not* in the Bible. In other words, some guy just dreamed them up and decided to claim that God said them. Since the person is anonymous, we can't ask him if he really believes God spoke to him and that these are transcriptions of the quotes, or if he feels he just invented them and claimed God said them. But as a Christian, I was appalled that somebody would make up a quote and claim God said it, quotes that were certainly *not* in the Bible.

Now that I've managed to escape the brain-shackles of Christianity, I can look more objectively on the culture of Christianity, and I see this kind of thing happening quite regularly: People making it up as they go, claiming God said this and God said that, when there is absolutely no Biblical basis for their claims. Although that bothered me when I was a Christian, the reasons it bothers me now are different. Today, I couldn't care less if people are making it up, because that's what the Bible is anyway—a bunch of made-up stories.

Today, the problem I have is the deception and the lies. If the guy who made these billboards really believes God spoke to him, then fine; he's not lying (perhaps delusional, but not lying). But if he doesn't really believe it, then in my opinion he's lying: He's saying God said something when he knows God didn't. And in fact, Christians should also be bothered by this. But most don't seem to be.

And I see this all the time. Christianity has been filled with lies, and it's only getting worse. In this chapter, I cover this deception in more detail and go into the psychological and social implications associated with it.

Let's start with the lie of God being just.

God is Unjust

So often Christianity teaches us that *God is just*. Christians proclaim that God is the ultimate in justice, and justice will be served. The good will go to Heaven, and the bad will go to Hell.

Indeed, Christianity teaches of Judgment Day, when we will all be judged. Many people critical of Christianity have pointed out some issues here, and I'll repeat them. If God is so just, why would he send us to Hell for thought crimes (such as not believing in him), and why would he punish us for all eternity even when the sin is trivial (such as not liking your neighbor)? If somebody lives a good life and treats everyone with respect, but has a jerk living next door and just can't find it in his or her heart to "love thy neighbor" and refuses to repent for this, the Bible teaches us that this person will burn in Hell for all eternity. After all, that person broke one of Jesus' greatest commandments, and that person didn't ask for forgiveness. In Christian theology, that action (or inaction) leads to a punishable offense.

Today, punishments typically fit the crime, at least in Western societies. There's a huge difference between, say, going into your neighbor's garage and stealing a screwdriver and, say, breaking into somebody's house and raping and killing the occupant.

If you've never committed a crime and the offense is minor (like stealing a screwdriver), you will unlikely land in jail. But raping and killing will likely end in a life sentence, possibly even execution.

But *both* crimes, should you not repent, could land you in Hell, where you will be tortured in fire for all eternity.

Now come on. Is that really reasonable?

The Christians argue it is. If you are the type of person who would go to your neighbor's house and take his screwdriver when he's not home, then, so they teach, you clearly have evil in your heart, and you deserve no place in Heaven.

Now personally, I prefer not to steal, and I wouldn't go into my neighbor's garage and take something. But there are people who live good lives, but occasionally do something minor—maybe not stealing a screwdriver, but something that equally constitutes stealing such as taking a few pens from work, or not saying anything if the cashier at a grocery store charges you a couple bucks less than he or she was supposed to. I'm talking *very* minor things here.

Still, stealing is stealing. Most of us agree it's wrong. But what about other sins? What about drinking and partying? I grew up in a Lutheran church that had deep German roots, and beer was by no means seen as a sin. Every year in October, we would have a beer tent set up in the back parking lot of the church and have our own little Octoberfest. I'm not kidding.

But the church next door was an extremely fundamentalist Assembly of God church, and they viewed our acts as sins. To them, we were sinning by putting up that beer tent.

Do you think any of us confessed what we did? Of course not. To us, there was nothing wrong with it. But there certainly was something wrong with it in the eyes of the people next door. And to them, that was a sin, and if we didn't confess, we would wind up in Hell for all eternity along with the people who raped and murdered. We were just as evil in their eyes.

In today's society, we consider ourselves much more modern and civilized than ancient societies. In an earlier chapter I told the story of how a man in the Old Testament was picking up sticks to build a fire. Unfortunately, he picked the sticks up on the Sabbath, and that was considered a sin. The people took him to Moses, and Moses went to God about it, and God said the man must be *killed*. So what did these people do? They followed the orders, and all grabbed rocks and smashed the guy's head in and killed him, as instructed by this "just" God.

Today we would never do such a thing. We see such acts as barbaric.

Now if there is a God, would that God really demand people do something so barbaric and then send the man to Hell over such trivial matters? Certainly in today's world, most of our societies have learned not to be so barbaric. (Not all—people are still stoned to death in the Middle East, just as their barbaric religion taught them to do in the past. And I'm not referring just to Islam. Islam is a derivative of the religion of Abraham, as is modern Christianity and Judaism. Many Islamic countries still hold onto these ridiculous, barbaric beliefs, but all three come from a religion that taught such beliefs in the first place.)

Societies grow and mature over time and become more progressive. (Remember, "progressive" comes from the word "progress.") Countries are electing female leaders. The United States is finally letting people of color run for office. (Although interestingly the United States is far behind many other countries in having women win elected offices.)

As societies grow, we move to more equality and understanding, and we don't just kill people for silly little things. We believe in fair trials and we believe in human rights. Indeed, if we still held onto archaic and barbaric beliefs, we wouldn't even bother with DNA testing. DNA testing has helped many prisoners prove their innocence, and helped them get released from prison after our courts discovered they were innocent. But if we still held on to the ancient beliefs we would instead just kill the prisoners the moment they were found guilty and be done with it, and later DNA testing would be of no use since the convicted is already dead!

Thankfully, we've moved on from such ancient practices and now have modern systems of justice—*better* systems of justice. We now understand more what it means to be "just", which is the root word of "justice". Sure, even the most modern countries still might not yet be perfect, but the justice systems are much better, and more reasonable, than they used to be.

By comparison the God that is described in the Bible, particularly the old testament, is anything *but* just. Ruthlessly killing a man for gathering sticks so he can build a fire so his family can stay warm just because he did it on the wrong day is pathetic. Is that the work of a "just" God?

Now personally, I don't believe that story happened verbatim. The stories of the Old Testament have very little correlation with history. However, I don't doubt for a minute that similar stories did happen, where some delusional people got it into their superstitious—perhaps even psychotic—brains that God wanted them to kill somebody for some absurd reason, and that they beat the person with rocks and killed him. I don't doubt that it has happened millions of times, considering it still happens today. You still read stories in the news about a mother who decided her children were possessed by Satan, leading her to believe that God commanded her to kill them, or a man who killed his roommate for the same reason. This happens today, and I'm sure it happened back then. People believed God told them to kill others, so they did.

When the story appears in today's news, people are appalled. When the story appears in the Bible, people consider it the action of a just God.

But what about the afterlife? Even if the people had not stoned the man gathering sticks, Christianity teaches us that he must repent for his sins, or he will still go to Hell for continued punishment after he's dead. To me, it's sad and obscene for us to recognize modern systems of justice here in the physical world, but still hold on to an ancient barbaric system of justice for the supposed afterlife.

It's a double standard: Americans are appalled when they see modern tribes and communities in third-world countries enacting mob rule to kill a 16-year-old girl who had sex with a married man, yet these same people seem to think God holds onto the same horrible justice system. "We'll just throw them in jail," we say, "and let God deal with them in the afterlife." We put them in jail for their crimes, but God, we believe, will enact the ultimate barbaric punishment, one that is far worse than stoning, that of eternal damnation in a pit of fire—regardless of how severe the crime is. Yes, that is truly a double standard.

Surely, *if* there's a God (a big *if* indeed), then that God would be even more advanced and modern than we are and wouldn't use such ancient methods like those outlined by the superstitious people of ancient times, such as the example of the brutal killing of the man who was picking up sticks. Seriously: Does it really make sense that an all-knowing, omnipotent God who supposedly has the power of creating an entire universe would have such a horrible justice system, one that is *remarkably similar to what primitive tribes would come up with?*

Consider this, a point I brought up in earlier chapters. Look at it in reverse: What is more likely, that a perfect God would create a justice system and ask his people to enact it, one that is shockingly primitive and barbaric;

or, on the other hand, that a primitive, tribal people would come up with a story of a God, and that story would include the only kind of primitive and barbaric justice system the people know of? To me, it's a strong indication of the "who invented whom" idea: Did God create us, or did the people of ancient times create God based on their own culture and ideas? After all, if there is a God, why would his characteristics be so identical to the culture and times that the Bible was written, when today we're aware of many other possibilities?

In the next chapter, I talk about how the Bible is founded on myths that evolved over time from even earlier cultures. When you finally are able to step aside and look at the Bible objectively, it becomes incredibly obvious that the character and personality of God was nothing more than a god-version of extreme human characteristics, and that these characteristics were nothing more than the fruits of highly imaginative (and somewhat twisted) human minds.

The system of justice in the Hell theology of Christianity suffers from the same problem. The supposed Judgment that takes place after we die, as taught by Christianity, is suspiciously similar to the primitive system of justice which people employed two thousand years ago.

Why is that? If for just a moment we consider the idea that Judgment Day was invented by the people of 2000 years ago, is it any surprise that when these people came up with this idea, that they would draw on what they knew at the time? Indeed it's no surprise at all. Just look at it: The whole Judgment Day scenario is nothing more than a wildly embellished version of the same barbaric judgment system that was in place at the time. Those that commit even the most minor offense are tortured by God for all eternity.

It should, therefore, be painfully obvious that the system was completely fabricated and invented by humans and is in no way reasonable.

Lies, I Tell You! Lies!

There's a popular legend floating around the Internet that tells a story of how a young man in a classroom gets into a dispute with an "atheist professor" over whether God exists. The story says that the student quickly puts the atheist professor in his place through logic and reason, leaving the professor unable to continue. The story then says the young man's name was Albert Einstein.

The story is false. *It never happened.* It was made up. Somebody took time to carefully *fabricate* a story to push forward their religious agenda.

In the book The God Delusion, Richard Dawkins discusses the moral issues of abortion and mentions a popular story used by people who are opposed to abortion (people who, as Dawkins observed, are pretty much always religious). The story makes the claim that Beethoven came from a family of a bunch of blind and deaf and retarded individuals, and that if the parents had chosen to end their pregnancy based on the likelihood of the next child having birth defects, they would have killed Beethoven before he had a chance to provide the world with his wonderful music.

Dawkins explains the story is a lie and never happened, although he kind of brushes off that aspect and goes on with whether this is a viable method for determining whether to have an abortion. I'd like to approach the story from a different perspective and focus on the fact that the story is an urban legend.

Just as somebody made up the story about Einstein as a child quieting an "atheist" professor, somebody took the time to invent this story about Beethoven. Somebody fabricated a story. He or she *lied*.

Both stories are lies. If people are so strong in their conviction that God and Jesus are real, why couldn't they draw on real life experiences rather than make up stories and tell lies?

And it does make me wonder: Christianity as a whole prides itself on truth and honesty. So why do so many Christians put up with such lies? In my own journey, this just added fuel to the whole problem that really got me thinking and questioning everything.

Of course, Christians could jump on this and say that I'm singling out individuals and unfairly pinning it on all of Christianity, trying to make the religion as a whole look bad. Indeed. So let's take that up next.

That Doesn't Mean God and Jesus Are Lies, Does it?

A legitimate gripe here, however, is that *just because there are liars who are Christians, that doesn't imply that Christianity is wrong, a lie.*

I'll grant that much. People have used lies to forward causes that I agree with, and that doesn't mean I start disagreeing with the cause. (I disagree with using the lies, however.)

Many times I've heard Christians simply point out that there have always been some "bad" Christians, and they feel ashamed that these people behaved as they did, giving Christianity a bad name. They'll use this argument when faced with the different atrocities committed by Christians, such as the Crusades and slavery, to name a few. (Another such atrocity is the Holocaust committed by Hitler, a Christian, although very few Christians at the time agreed with him.*)

My answer to this is simple: If Jesus existed, was the Son of an all-knowing, all-powerful, universe-creating, perfect God, and was himself perfect, then any religion he would have started would have been perfect. It's as simple as that. The supposed Son of God created Christianity, and so Christianity would have to be perfect. But it isn't perfect. Many of the world's more horrible atrocities have been committed by Christianity as an institution. I'll allow that a few people have run rampant with their own silly ideas and have done things that are horrible (like bombing abortion clinics and killing doctors working at these clinics), and that these are bad people who did things separate from the religion as a whole. But as a single culture or institution, Christianity has also committed many atrocities as a result of official policy that have resulted in the deaths of millions of people, and has demonstrated it is anything but perfect. And such an imperfect religion could not have been created by a supposedly perfect deity.

Most Christians accept that Christianity has not been perfect. But they don't seem to realize that they're implying that Jesus, the man they claim founded their religion, screwed up. Aren't they, under the surface, by admitting Christianity is imperfect, thus claiming Jesus failed? To me they are.

Now they certainly wouldn't agree with that statement, but that is what they must be logically implying. They might even make the claim that Jesus didn't start Christianity, but rather Peter, the favorite apostle, started it. But that's a moot point, because Christianity is supposedly the result of Jesus, the Messiah, coming to Earth.

I've made arguments like this before towards Christians, and the response that perhaps disappoints me the most is when they claim that I obviously believe Christianity was started by Jesus, so clearly I believe in Jesus.

---

* Hitler was a Christian and drew on the writings of Martin Luther as a basis for his hatred towards Jews; Martin Luther wrote a hate-filled article called *On the Jews and Their Lies*. Christianity has spawned enormous anti-Semitism over the centuries, partly because Christians like to blame the Jews for "killing Jesus" at the crucifixion, which really doesn't make sense considering they look at Jesus' death as a good thing. But such are the contradictions of Christianity.

That is not what I'm saying, however. I'm simply saying that if they claim their religion was started by the Son of God, then their claim isn't very believable considering their religion is so imperfect.*

Now ultimately, this book is about my journey of leaving Christianity, and a theme that I've brought up before is this: Just because I don't like the system doesn't mean it's not real. And similarly, just because I don't like what the Christian church has done doesn't mean Jesus didn't exist. But don't worry; I take up the myths in the next chapter, where all the pieces will start to fit together: Clearly, Christianity has done some awful things, and clearly the religion is built on a myth. Ultimately, given the facts, a reasonable person would have no choice but to recognize that the beliefs of the religion are false.

Religion and Politics

Here's a realistic question: Why should I care if people continue to believe in the Bible?

The reason I care is it affects society and individuals on multiple levels. Children are the most receptive to this, because if they see people making up stories to defend their ideas, then they are likely to learn to follow suit, and

How convenient for our leaders who want to manipulate people: Get the people to be blind to truths, yet accept untruths blindly.

- me

ultimately rationalize their own stories, and likely even to become delusional themselves as they believe their own stories. This is dangerous for society in that it becomes filled with people (including leaders such as the President) who base their decision-making on nothing more than whims that they are convinced came from God.† Indeed, George W. Bush, has claimed that God spoke to him and told him to end the tyranny in Iraq.‡

Look at it this way: If two world leaders with different faiths both believe

---

* The Mormons are especially in trouble here. They claim that God sent a latter-day Prophet named Joseph Smith because the church was failing. But the same implication applies here: They're indirectly (and, I suppose, unintentionally) claiming that Jesus failed in his mission and God had to send another person, Joseph Smith, to clean up the mess.

† Presidents aren't immune to making up stories and believing them. Ronald Reagan told an elaborate story of a "welfare queen" in South Chicago who defrauded the welfare system. Later it was found he completely fabicated the story. Google "welfare queen" and you'll find many pages about it.

‡ This news story is available in multiple locations. For a version written outside of the US, see http://www.guardian.co.uk/world/2005/oct/07/iraq.usa.

to be hearing from God and they both come up with conflicting plans, then the messages can't possibly both come from God, now can they? And further, how are we to know that our leader is really hearing from God and is not just making it up? And if he's making it up, then he only thinks he heard it from God (in which case he's delusional). Otherwise, he is actually lying. Do we really want a President who is delusional or lying?

For a leader to claim he is taking his orders from God through a voice in his own head is dangerous to society. The leader can easily do whatever he wants—invade whatever country he wants, or take away whatever rights he wants from the people, or even randomly arrest people—and followers of such a leader will not dare question him because they believe the orders are coming directly from God!

In fact, if the followers have been raised in the religion, it's very easy for them to accept that their leader is hearing God talk. And that's where the real danger begins, because it means the leader can easily control the people by simply stating that his ability to rule comes from God.

Of course, this should be no surprise to anyone who has noticed the connection between politics and religion. In the US in recent times, the Republican Party has been the most closely tied to Christianity. I've met a lot of Christians who are liberals and Democrats, but many Christians vote Republican, even though the Republicans do very little for the common people and build their policies more around what the corporate leaders want. And further, in recent times the Republicans have been far more supportive of the wars in Iraq and Afghanistan than the Democrats.

Consider that for a moment. I find it interesting that so many Christians like to use the phrase "What would Jesus do?" to try to answer life's questions. And I find it ironic that by and large such people tend to be incredibly pro-war. While I agree there's nothing wrong with being patriotic (face it, the US does have a lot of good things about it), I just don't understand how people can claim to follow the teachings of Jesus, a character who was clearly a pacifist, yet at the same time support the mass killings of foreign citizens.

And what's especially sad is that the majority of these people are not receiving the benefits of the Republican policies. Rather, they are no more than human tools providing *votes*.

But should this be any surprise? Of course not. Leaders have, since the beginning of human history, been using various means (usually religion) to manipulate and to control their citizens for their own selfish purposes.

Consider the demographics of the extremely patriotic, war-loving, Christian people. By and large, they tend to be poor and not very educated, and it's very clear to many of us that the politicians consider these people *expendable*. To such politicians, these people are nothing more than uneducated tools that are supporting the needs of the people who really count—the rich.

This should disgust everybody in this country. So why don't so many people see it? Why aren't the common people rising up and rebelling? Because they truly believe that they, and the wealthy leaders, are *on the same side*. The leaders have easily convinced them of that by siding with them on religion. And once people realize their leaders share the same religion, and that their leaders are getting their orders from God—as Bush has claimed—then it's no question that these people will continue to vote for them.

Think about it: How many times do you see an expensive car covered with bumper stickers of flags and pro-war messages? Almost never. Usually when you see these bumper stickers they're on beat up old vehicles owned by people with little if any education beyond high school, people who are clearly not reaping the benefits of our economic system and the policies that our leaders create.

But while the policies do not help the poor, uneducated people, they do benefit the rich people. Consider the Bush family, which has spawned two presidents. They are a long line of oil tycoons with deep connections throughout the oil and energy industry. Who did the second President Bush pick for his Vice President? A man who at the time was working as the CEO of an energy company (the same energy company that—big surprise—landed numerous contracts overseas during the Iraq war). And what does Iraq have that any oil tycoon would want? Why oil, of course.

Compare the Iraq situation to North Korea. North Korea was claiming to have created a nuclear weapon. The "official" reason we invaded Iraq was because they had weapons of mass destruction. The leaders of North Korea even admitted to having such weapons, yet did we invade their country? No. Does North Korea have any natural resources that would benefit us? No.

But why don't the majority of Americans see something that is so painfully obvious and simple? Because they have a religious camaraderie with the president. They feel that God has chosen him to be their leader, and they feel that God speaks to him (and possibly even through him) and so they simply do not question him *any more* than they question the authenticity of the story of Adam and Eve and the talking snake. They are trained not to question and to simply accept whatever they are told by the leaders, whether truth or lies. And worse, when truths are presented to them, such as evolution, they are trained to reject these truths. How convenient for our leaders who want to manipulate people: Get the people to be blind to truths, yet accept untruths blindly.

When leaders use propaganda to promote their message, they resort to what is known as demagoguery. A demagogue is a leader who appeals to the emotions and prejudices of the people, without regard for facts and reason. Political talk radio hosts use these techniques.

Demagoguery techniques result in an extreme trust from the listener to the point that the radio host can say pretty much anything whatsoever, and listeners will believe him or her. (Sound familiar, much like a preacher in a church?) Once total trust is reached, the radio host then uses a technique called self-inoculation. This is where the host will say something like, "The Democrats will lie, but I'm here to tell you the truth." Then the radio host will follow this with a lie. But because the listener has total trust, the listener will not only believe the radio host, but when confronted with the *actual truth*, the listener will balk and not accept it as truth.

The fallout from these techniques is severe and widespread, resulting in millions of people voting for a politician who does not act in the interest of said voters. And it reaches elsewhere, too. A perfect example here is with science versus religion. On one hand you have some preachers teaching a literal seven-day creation. On the other hand you have science presenting facts and numbers which show that the literal seven-day creation is not only impossible, but absurd. Who will people believe? The scientist or the preacher?

Unfortunately, even though the scientist has data and proof, many people will blindly agree with the preacher, even though the facts to the contrary are so clear. Often, people have been trained to doubt facts and accept untruths. This is nothing short of mind control. Why do you think politicians are so eager to declare their faith? Religion is an incredibly powerful tool that can be used to control the minds of people.

And now let's take the argument one step further. Earlier in this book, I talked about how religion is holding back science classes. Indeed, which party wants to limit spending on public education? It's the party that claims to have the closest ties to religion.

Why is that? Easy. By keeping the masses religious, and keeping them "dumbed down," they won't question authority.

This might be bordering on the level of conspiracy theory, but it really does have a certain merit to it. President George W. Bush specifically stated that he believes in Intelligent Design, and doesn't accept evolution.* He and his party have also created many policies that will take money out of public education. Further, they support the notion of vouchers.

Who benefits from vouchers? Well, the story is that the children do because vouchers allow the parents to move their kids out of "failing schools" and into private schools using the money obtained through the voucher program. And where does that money ultimately end up? Well, in the hands of the people who own the private schools. Who typically owns private schools? Bingo. Churches. See how it has gone full circle here? (Consider this: Vouchers are hardly different from welfare, yet, from my own observation, most people who support vouchers are opposed to welfare. That's a double standard; however, the difference is that the people themselves are the beneficiaries because they don't have to pay tuition to send their kids to private schools. Suddenly welfare is okay when they're the recipients.)

Now how many schools run by churches are going to teach true science such as evolution and the correct age of the Earth and universe? Very few.

So perhaps this is not just conspiracy theory. This is a very dangerous reality. Schools are suffering. The people are remaining highly religious and are happily voting for a party whose policies do not benefit them (except for the one about helping them send their kids to church schools). And the cycle continues because their children are not getting the education they need.

I've seen the problems first-hand. I remember a high school friend hearing about a rather simple scientific fact (one from physics dealing with how things fall towards the Earth, a known fact easily demonstrated through simple, obvious experiments), and brushing it off with, "I don't buy that." Yet he would absolutely "buy" everything the priest taught him at his Catholic church as indisputable truth, even if there was scientific evidence to the contrary.

Yet, why should we take the words of the priests and ministers as absolute truth? After all, they're just humans offering their own interpretations to the Bible. And even if they quote right from the Bible, why should we accept it as literal truth over some other piece of writing, whether ancient or not? Remember, the Bible doesn't say anything about itself. There aren't parts of the New Testament that says the Old Testament is the literal truth, and that

* This happened in April of 2005. Again, there are many news articles about it; one is at http://www.washingtonpost.com/wp-dyn/content/article/2005/08/02/AR2005080201686.html.

the creation story should be taken literally. It is today's preachers who say so. And the people believe them—blindly and without question.

Of course, this doesn't mean that I'm saying the Bible is filled with stories that we should accept as being figurative, metaphorical, and inspired by God, even though they're allegorical. That's an issue I take up in the next chapter. For now, let's continue with the social implications of the Bible.

Who is Working for Whom?

Recently a video has been circulating on the Web that uses a common shock theme to try to convert people to Christianity and to get people to try to spread (infect?) their religion to other people.

This particular video is about a high school boy who grew up in Suburban USA, died, and ended up going to Hell because he had not *heard* of Jesus. And the video tries to put the blame on his friend, a boy who is still alive who is a Christian but chose not to teach the poor condemned dead boy about Jesus.

Before I attack the theological nonsense in this, I want to point out something that puts this video over the edge and into the realm of absolute absurdity: How could anyone possibly believe that this condemned boy never heard of Jesus? That's ridiculous. Are the people who created this video so delusional that they honestly believe that the majority of Americans have never even heard of Jesus?

But aside from that, let's look at the issues with this video that prove to me that the God and Jesus described in it are not real. Supposedly the boy still alive consciously decided not to share the "Good News" with this friend. But it was the friend who was punished for all eternity! The friend that's still kicking was apparently "saved" and will therefore still go to Heaven, I suppose, although it's not made clear in the video. Yet, at the same time, the authors of the video are trying to suggest that it's his fault that his friend went to Hell, apparently trying to appeal to the conscience of young Christian Americans, hoping they'll try to spread the word of Jesus to their unsaved friends so they won't go to Hell.

But what kind of God would do such a thing, sending the friend to Hell for never *hearing* of Jesus? There is no possible way that a deity who supposedly has the ability to create an entire universe would be so morally bankrupt. It's just unthinkable.

But what makes this kind of teaching despicable and disgusting is that the target audience consists of *children* and *teens*. To fundamentalists, it's vital to teach this kind of nonsense to kids. It's vital to scare the living *bejesus* out of them to get them to buy into their nonsense. And to me, that's appalling.

And what's also sickening about all this is the emphasis on Satan and eternal damnation. Even when I was a practicing Christian, a video like this would have disgusted me. It doesn't teach children to be *good*. It doesn't teach children to be *loving*. All it does is teaches people to proselytize, and now we're back to the old fear problem.

This video is only an example. So often I hear fundamentalists focusing on Satan and eternal damnation. But does the theology of a Satan even make sense?

Think about this for a moment: In the US court system, the judge and the prison warden work on the same side. The judge presides over the trial, and if somebody is found guilty, sends the person to jail. The jail is run by the prison warden, and the warden is not on the side of the inmate.

Now compare that to God and Satan, where God is the judge, and Satan is the prison warden. In the God vs. Satan myth, however, God is the judge, and Satan runs and oversees Hell, the prison of eternal damnation, but is on the opposite side of God—at least sometimes. When God determines that somebody must go to Hell, he hands the poor sap off to Satan, who happily accepts. The poor condemned soul then goes to live with Satan forever.

But Hell is described as eternal torture, and *not* a fun place. So clearly Satan's job is to carry out the punishment. Satan is the prison warden, and working for God.

It doesn't make sense. And if Satan really wants to tempt us to join up, wouldn't he make Hell the most amazing, enticing place?

The truth is, it doesn't make sense at all, no matter how you twist it. Are God and Satan supposedly on the same side or not?

Now one thing that I've been told by so many people is that Satan deceives us. Okay, let's go with that for a moment: Satan deceives us and tempts us to think that it would be great to join up with him. But then once we do, after we die, we get cast into hell forever, which is a punishment. But now where is Satan? He supposedly runs Hell, so now we're back to the previous argument I made. If he tricked us into going to a bad place, why does he make it a bad place? The whole theology of God vs. Satan is just absurd and nothing more than a man-made story.

At some point, somebody created these stories. They told a story—a lie. And people believed it and still do. I cover the history of this topic in more detail in the next chapter. The whole Satan story has an interesting history, one that is clearly based in myth. But with the present chapter's social theme, let's look at Satan a bit more and where he fits in.

Whose Side are THEY on?

The more I argue with fundamentalists, the more I see a common theme. These people claim to be good, God-fearing people who are filled with love and joy, yet when faced with people like me, they suddenly turn into the most hate-filled, awful people I've ever met. The things they say to me are horrible. Why is that?

One of them cleared it up for me: They believe I'm doing Satan's work. They believe that I am a demon! And they believe that Satan and his demons deserve no respect whatsoever. And so these people who claim to be loving, good people become the most rotten creatures I've ever encountered to the point that I feel compelled to protect my location for fear of my personal safety. That is sad indeed.

Many Christians believe they have been tasked with "planting a seed" as described in the 4th chapter of Mark. This means that if they suggest just a few tidbits about Christianity to people, the tidbits will germinate and grow inside the person until the person understands Christianity and becomes a full-fledged, reborn Christian; that is, the Holy Spirit will have been planted as just a seed and grow in the person. Further, they believe they are tasked with spreading God's word and growing the membership of the Church. They feel this is a job that God has tasked them with.

So I have to wonder: By verbally attacking me and pushing me away even further, are they really planting a seed? Is that really going to make me change my mind and suddenly start believing in their pretend friend and make me want to join up? Of course not. Indeed, in the past few months alone, I have seen many people chased off by Christians in online communities that consisted of both Christians and non-believers. When the non-believers were presenting scientific facts to back up their claims in areas such as evolution, the people who weren't sure (the "fence-sitters" as they're often called) were often swayed by the simple scientific facts. And what happened? The Christians in the forum became angry and would fight with the fence-sitters, giving them one more reason not to side with the Christians. And in the end, those of us with science on our side would easily sway the fence-sitters, while the Christians chased them off.

But I do have a question for them: If you believe in God and Satan, and God wants you to convert people to Christianity, and all you're doing is pushing me and others even further away, are you doing what God tasked you with? And if not, then who are you working for? Think about it. The Christians who do this are pushing people away, which is not what God wants, but more likely what this Satan character wants.

Letting Go of the Lies

In my own personal journey of leaving Christianity, I had to embrace the facts around me. I had to recognize that so much of what I was seeing was a lie. Interestingly, I had to become more open-minded.

So many times I've heard fundamentalist Christians claim that scientists are closed-minded. They truly believe it, too. They see scientists as blindly believing in evolution and refusing to consider any other possibilities, such as the possibility of this universe having been created by a loving God in the manner specifically detailed in the Bible. I've heard Christians make claims that they are more open-minded to the idea that the Bible is literally true.

But in my own journey, it was the opposite: In order to walk away from Christianity, I had to become more open-minded. People can make the claim that they are more open-minded, but only until they've actually allowed their minds to question what they believe and to consider the possibility that what they've always believed may not be real will they become more open-minded. And to the people struggling, I offer this suggestion: Question everything. Open your mind. Is it real? Is what the church has been telling you real?

I had to open my mind to the idea that what I was taught was a lie. I had to open my mind to the idea that there were truths out there that I've been turning my back on, scientific facts and truths.

I had to open my mind to the idea that the stories in the Bible were fabricated stories based on earlier myths—yes, *earlier* myths that long pre-dated the stories in Genesis.

But throughout the journey there was this nagging fear: *What if I'm wrong.* Virtually every person I've met who managed to escape Christianity has said the same thing: There was a period of total fear—that same fear that I described in the opening sections of this book. But in this case, the fear becomes even worse, because if what the Christians have taught us is real, then by proclaiming it to be wrong, we're really in trouble, condemning ourselves to Hell. That's fricking scary, frankly.

But how can it be real? So far through this book I've presented many ideas that seriously challenge Christianity, both in the flaws of its theology as well as its resistance to scientific facts—facts that we know are facts through tests and experiments.

But still: What if I'm wrong? What if Jesus and God are real, even though the ideas seem flawed? And what if they're going to be very mad at me? To get past this fear, I had to open my mind to the idea that humans existed long before the Bible claims humans did. I had to open my mind to the idea that the Bible was a lie and filled with myths. What myths? Let's tackle that in the next chapter. After all, if the Bible is just a mythical story, then we can easily see that not only is the theology flawed, but it's based on made-up stories, and ultimately not even real. The next chapter presents perhaps the biggest facts that helped me escape, facts that undeniably prove that the Bible is myth. Today I know there's no Hell, that the Bible is just a collection of myths, and there's no reason to be afraid.

six

Bible Facts and Myths

In the beginning, the gods created the heavens and the earth.

otice anything odd there? The word gods is plural. Why did I write it that way? Because that's how the original Hebrew has it in Genesis 1:1. Not "God" but "gods" as plural.

That's just one more piece of the puzzle where the whole Christian religion came caving in for me. But it is only one small piece of many.

I've spent a great deal of time talking to many other people who consider themselves "former Christians." Although they all have very different stories on why they found they could no longer believe in the Bible and what Christianity teaches, many say the same thing: They stopped believing only *after they read the Bible*—often several times over.

> *I've often thought the Bible should have a disclaimer in the front saying this is fiction.*
>
> *- Sir Ian McKellen, in an interview in 2006*

Why the change of heart? Because they found the stories in the Bible to be completely unbelievable.

In my case, it wasn't so clear-cut. It was more gradual, as I reviewed the stories I had been taught and believed since childhood. At first I tried to believe the parts that didn't set well with me. In other words, I was trying to figure out the deeper meaning; I was trying to interpret the Bible.

Just Interpret it... Or Replace it?

Churches have built an entire culture on interpreting the Bible's hidden meanings. Over the centuries, people have started to figure out that certain parts of the Bible just don't make sense or seem to portray God in a particularly negative light. But fortunately for Christians, that's where the preachers and ministers come in. To this day, every Sunday, millions of churches present the weekly sermon. Different churches have different ways of presenting it, but most churches base the weekly sermon on a passage from the Bible; the preacher then goes to lengths to explain what the passage *really* means.

Of course, the root psychology here is that the people already know in their minds without any doubt whatsoever that the Bible is correct and true. In Chapter 3, I spoke of presuppositions. The presupposition here is that the Bible is absolutely true. That's the fundamental basis. But when faced with some part of the Bible that seems absolutely unbelievable, the natural thing to do is to "dig deeper" and, possibly with the help of a trained theologian or minister, find the "real meaning" of the strange verse.

To a rational person, this alone should be a sign of trouble. If the Bible is written by God, then why does it need to be explained by humans using *other* words and sentences? And why should we believe that those humans' words are also inspired by God? Why should we believe them at all? And more troubling, what if two different preachers give different explanations and interpretations of the same Bible passage, something that happens quite regularly? Who should we believe?

This type of "interpretation" issue comes up often in the legal industry. Lawyers arguing a case will suggest that somebody claimed something that was written in a document, and the opposing lawyer will state that the document speaks on its own. Simply put: The words of a particular document are the words of the document and nothing more. For example, on election day a few years ago, a state amendment was on the ballot regarding marriage being strictly between a man and a woman. The wording was somewhat cryptic. An older man was standing in line in front of me at the polling booths. He was reading the ballot and was confused about what this amendment meant. He asked the guy working there what it meant; the employee responded, "Oh you only vote no on that if you support lesbians and that kind of thing."

I was appalled. I stood there in shock, and said nothing. I called a newspaper reporter to complain, and he informed me that he had heard of many similar complaints. He asked what I felt the employee should have said when explaining what it meant. Here's how I responded: *"The employee should have simply read the amendment to the man and said nothing else, because anything additional that he said would have been his own interpretation of it."* And that is true: Any additional words whatsoever would have been the employee's own words, not words from the amendment.

The same is true with the Bible:

Any words that somebody gives to describe the Bible are the words of the person doing the describing, and are not in the Bible.

What's probably a fascinating study in delusional psychology is that many people who interpret the Bible claim that they don't actually interpret it. I saw a web page that explains that unlike other Christians, they aren't "interpreting" the Bible, but rather, are "explaining" it. Come on. Same difference. Because if they're offering any words whatsoever other than just a straight read of the Bible, then they're explaining their own understanding of the Bible in their own words, which means they are interpreting it. They can rationalize it and argue it and manipulate the meanings of "interpret" all they want and use other words like "explaining" but the fact is, they're doing the same thing that everybody else does: Adding their own words.

Besides, if the Bible needs "explaining" as these people say it does, then why didn't God do a better job of writing it in a way that needs no explanation? As a writer, I would be appalled if somebody felt the need to break down my books and offer additional explanation, because it means I did a poor job of writing them.

If the Bible was really written by God, why should it need interpretation and replacement? If the Bible was truly written by an all-knowing, all-powerful deity, it should be perfect in every regard, and should need no interpretation. It should stand on its own when taken literally, as-is. The fact that it can't be taken so proves beyond any doubt that it was not written by an all-powerful deity, that it was written by humans[*].

---

[*] And that's why I now take a literalist approach to the Bible. Although I don't believe in the Bible, I feel that those that think the Bible is the literal truth are far more honest about their religion than other Christians who consider it allegory.

This interpretation happens everywhere you look. Go to virtually any website that tries to teach about specific Bible verses, and you'll find a description of what the seemingly hard-to-understand verse *really* means.

What it "really" means? To me, that translates to "What the author of the website thinks it means." And all too often, these interpretations are really just feel-good interpretations where somebody didn't particularly like what the Bible said and replaced it with something that felt better to them.

Case in point: The book of Revelation talks about 144,000 people going to Heaven. The people described are all men (no women!), and having come from the 12 tribes of Israel. This, of course, doesn't set right with Christians in America who would really like to go to Heaven. And so what do they do? They don't believe they can just disregard it (it is to them, after all, the Bible and word of God), and so they "interpret" it and try to explain what it "really" means. I'm not kidding: If you Google

Revelation "144,000"

you will find sites that explain that 144,000 doesn't *really mean* 144,000 at all! I won't bother with the details, except to say people go to great lengths to explain what the number really means to them. (But one has to wonder: If the Bible means something other than it says, doesn't that constitute a lie?)

Indeed, as I spent enormous amounts of time researching this book, one highly annoying thing happened repeatedly. I wanted to locate a particular story in the Bible, but I couldn't remember the book and chapter where I could find it. So I would Google for it. And instead of finding pages that told me the book and chapter, I would find somebody's own description of the story without any mention of where the story could actually be found in the Bible. For example, I wanted to re-read the story about Joseph, the son of Jacob in the Old Testament. With the help of Google, I found many web pages that described Joseph, but these were all somebody's own version of the story, their own original writing, with no mention of the exact book and chapter! But I wasn't interested in somebody's own, personal account of the story; I wanted to read the actual Bible verses.

When I was a Christian, I was just as guilty as everybody else. This culture of interpretation had an interesting effect on me. As I went through my teens and 20's, I started to do the same thing as many other readers of the Bible. I would find myself interpreting the Bible, especially the parts that didn't sit right with me. Instead of taking such passages at face value and believing them as the literal truth, I would replace them with my own interpretation, ultimately changing them into something better—something that was different from the original passage.

For example, the Bible is rather harsh on women, and being rather progressive, that always bothered me. Look at these verses, which are from letters supposedly written by Paul:

For the man is not of the woman: but the woman of the man. Neither was the man created for the woman; but the woman for the man. (1 Corinthians 11:8-9)

Let your women keep silence in the churches: for it is not permitted unto them to speak; but they are commanded to be under obedience as also saith the law. (1 Corinthians 14:34)

Verses like this bothered me, and so I conveniently "fixed it" like so: Somewhere I had heard that the rules Paul set forward for women were, in fact, far less severe than previous laws. With his rules for women, Paul was advancing women from *mere property* to a *slightly* higher level, and that only by today's standards does it seem like Paul was trying to degrade women. In fact, so the explanation goes, Paul was a feminist for his time.

By buying into that line, I effectively replaced the *existing* passages with a *new interpretation*, something that sounded right to me, something that was better, something I could actually accept—because I sure couldn't accept what was really said. What was really in the Bible was demeaning to women and simply not acceptable, not by this generation, not by today's society, and not by me.

But the problem is, Paul didn't actually say what my interpretation claimed he did! Never did Paul say anything like, "In the past women were just property. But I'd like to advance their cause by providing the following rules which give them new freedoms and rights."

Of course, upon realizing that, my head started spinning, and I modified it again. I put it into "cultural context." Cultural context seems to be the approach a lot of mainstream Christians take today. They'll say something like, "You have to understand the culture and times."

In fact, that's probably the most accurate and realistic approach. The truth is, Paul *was* writing for his culture and time, and that's all there is to it. At the time, women were property, and Paul was writing rules for the women, and such rules really have no bearing in today's society.

Fine. But if that's the case, then this story can't be a timeless lesson that is useful two millennia later. Because by saying such a thing, the Christians are *admitting* that certain parts of the Bible are *outdated* and *don't apply in today's world*. Further, whether they realize it or not, they're implying that those parts of the Bible couldn't have been written by God, because if God had written them, he would have done a much better job of creating a lesson that lasts forever, not just during a limited time period. (Of course, most people would likely deny that that's what they're saying.) And finally, they're presenting a very weak argument for why such passages should even be present in the Bible at all.

Most Christians today lie somewhere on a spectrum which interprets how literal the Bible is. Some say the Bible is the absolute, literal truth, and that everything in it is historically accurate. Other people say the Bible is mostly just allegory with some important life lessons. Most Christians are somewhere in the middle. I don't have any cold hard figures, but from my own experience, I would estimate that most Christians, while not on the absolute literal truth end of the spectrum, are at least close, accepting the majority of the Bible as absolute truth, but some parts as simply important lessons that require some interpretation or contextual understanding.

In other words, most Christians are replacing parts of the Bible with their own versions, just as I always did. They probably wouldn't agree that that's what they're doing, and they probably wouldn't be happy with me saying so. But that is, in fact, what they're doing, and looking back, I can see that that's what I was doing as well.

This is why I must respond to people who have criticized me and others for stereotyping all Christians as fundamentalists and literalists. There are a good number of Christians out there who consider themselves liberal. They vote liberal and think liberally, and agree with me on many political and social issues. And they're also disgusted by the fundamentalists.

Regardless of how much of the Bible is to be taken literally or not, the Bible is still there with messages that simply cannot work in today's time, and cannot possibly have been written—or even inspired—by a deity.

But if many Christians agree that certain parts of the Bible do not apply to today's world, then how did we end up with the Bible we have?

This is one area that never ceases to amaze me, because the Bible has gone through many changes over time, and ultimately Christians are putting their faith in the men (pretty much all men—no women) who have chosen the books of the Bible and who have removed books on their whims. Let's take that up next.

Who Compiled the Bible?

I'm shocked at how little many Christians know about the history of their church and their Bible. I recall a woman online making the statement that the Bible is the "oldest book we have." That's not true at all! But having lived that life, I remember as a child thinking exactly that. I imagined going back in time and there's the Bible, go back farther and farther until the first people, and there's the Bible being written, telling the story of the first people. I equated the Bible with the first people, and since they were first, it wasn't possible to have anything older.

Of course, most Christians don't quite believe that the book of Genesis was written as it was happening. A common belief is that Moses wrote the first five books (the *Pentateuch*) of the Old Testament. That, of course, is an assumption for which there is absolutely no evidence whatsoever. Moses (assuming he even existed) did *not* write the first five books of the Old Testament.

The first five books of the Old Testament are certainly ancient, but they do not make up the oldest book that ever existed. Other cultures outside of the ancient Jewish world have produced older books, which include their own myths, including Creation myths.

And further, the Bible as we know it today is not the same as it has always been. People are delusional if they think that 3000 years ago people carried around copies of the Old Testament exactly as it exists today, and then 2000 years ago the New Testament came to be and from then on people carried the entire Bible around in the same form as is currently used. That is simply not the case, no matter how many American Christians think otherwise.

Also, many Christians mistakenly think that the first five books of the Old Testament were written by Moses. This is categorically, undeniably false.* (Although many Christians believe Moses wrote these books, there are also many Christians who recognize that he did not. My take is that I'm

---

* I've seen some pretty absurd "proofs" that Moses wrote the Pentateuch. These "proofs" simply refer to other parts of the Bible that state Moses wrote it. That's circular reasoning: The Bible is true because it's written in the Bible. Unfortunately, they also claim Jesus stated that Moses wrote the Pentateuch, and to accept that Moses did not write it is to deny the divine nature of Jesus. Oh well.

not convinced Moses even existed so that pretty much discounts the whole issue altogether.)

Consider this fact alone: Today, the Catholic Bible and the Protestant Bible are different. The Catholic Bible has several books the Protestant Bible does not. This is the direct result of Martin Luther*, the man who lived in the late 1500s who spawned the Protestant Reformation. He was a Catholic monk who tried to improve the Catholic Church, only to be met with resistance. He finally had no choice but to leave the Catholic Church and start his own version of the Christian Church, a version that still lives on today and carries his name with it—the Lutheran Church.

There's not enough room here for me to detail all the changes the Bible has experienced. But here's the short version. The original Hebrew Scriptures consisted of several separate books and writings that were brought together most likely between 200BC and 200AD. Meanwhile, a group of about 70 scholars translated much of the ancient Hebrew books into Greek, creating what became known as the Septuagint. Ultimately, the Septuagint ended up including a few books that didn't get included in the Hebrew collection. Today, the Jewish people still use the Hebrew collection, which is called the Tanakh.

Today, the Catholics and the Protestants base their Old Testaments on the Septuagint, but with a few slight changes. In the 16th Century, after Martin Luther left the Catholic Church and created the Protestant churches, he rearranged the Bible. Luther felt several books of the Old Testament were not legitimate, in particular those books included in the Septuagint but not included in the Tanakh. He felt they weren't inspired or written by God. He moved some of these books out of the Old Testament and created a new section called the *Apocrypha*, and three of the books he simply tossed out altogether. (Today most Protestant translations of the Bible do not include the Apocrypha at all.)

Shortly after Luther made the changes, the Catholic Pope Clement VIII took the three books that Luther removed and placed them into an appendix while maintaining the rest of the Bible as it was prior to Luther's changes (and as such, there was no Apocrypha).

Then in the early 17th Century, the Church of England created the King

* I'm amazed how many Christians I've met who don't know who Martin Luther was, and they think I'm talking about Martin Luther King, Jr. Sorry, that's somebody totally different. Do these people not even know the history of their own church? In fact, most don't.

James Version (KJV, also called the Authorized Version) of the Bible. It used the same ordering and layout as Luther's Bible, except it also had the three books that Luther had tossed; these books were added to the Apocrypha that Luther had assembled. (Today's printings of the KJV typically do not include the Apocrypha at all.)

This is basically how the Old Testament was created. But where did the individual books and the stories they contain originate? That's something I cover throughout this chapter. As for the New Testament, it's gone through similar changes, the details of which I won't bore you with here.

There have been many more changes to the Bible throughout history (such as an additional Psalm, 151 that was added by some and removed by others). This very fact forces me to ask: How can this be the writing of a god if it has changed so many times over the centuries and today different branches of Christianity use Bibles containing different books?

But the confusion only worsens. One thing a lot of people don't realize is there are books in the Bible that make reference to verses in books that aren't officially part of the Bible, at least not officially according to, for example, the Protestants.

Here's a case in point: Jude 1:14 (found in the New Testament) mentions a certain prophecy as having come true. But the prophecy is in the Book of Enoch, which is not considered by many people to be the word of God, as the book is part of the Apocrypha. It's not considered divinely inspired, and as such isn't considered *true*. This should raise concerns for Christians. Why would a book that is considered a fairy tale by many be mentioned as fact in the Bible? The same thing also happens earlier in the same chapter of Jude. Jude 1:9 mentions a book called the Assumption of Moses, which again, was removed from the Bible because it wasn't considered to be inspired or written by God.

In addition to all the changes in the books of the Bible, there are many different versions of the Bible that are different translations from different sources. This is where things get very interesting indeed. These discrepancies have created huge differences and disagreements within the various Christian churches, although much of the difference today comes down to a point of contention over the translation of *one single verse of the entire Bible*, a verse that has great ramifications involving whether Mary, the mother of Jesus, was made pregnant by God or not! That's what I'll take up next.

Which Bible? Depends on How You Say "Virgin"

As you certainly know, there are many different translations of the Bible. In English alone, there are dozens, including the King James Version, the New International Version, the Revised Standard Version, and many others.

Each one was translated from ancient Greek documents. But they're all very different, and different Christians feel different versions are the true versions that were written by God.

A rather large share of Christians feel the King James Version is the only English version that was inspired by God, and that the others are mistranslations put into place by none other than Satan himself.

This always confused me as a Christian, because in the Lutheran church that I attended we were quite happy with the Revised Standard Version (RSV). But what also confused me was that various Bible Verse lookup sites that included many different versions often left out the RSV.

I didn't particularly care to investigate this, and so I brushed it off, figuring it had to do with some copyright issue. But then one day I stumbled upon the reason while researching for this book.

It turns out the release of the Revised Standard Version created a rather tense time for Christianity, and it all came down to one verse: Isaiah 7:14.

The RSV was released in parts; the New Testament was first released in 1946, and the Old Testament (containing the verse in question) came out in 1952. And that's when all hell broke loose.

The King James Version of the Bible (which came out way back in 1611) contains a verse in the Old Testament that supposedly predicts the birth of Jesus long before Jesus was born:

Therefore the Lord himself shall give you a sign; Behold, a virgin shall conceive, and bear a son, and shall call his name Immanuel. (Isaiah 7:14)

Notice the word "virgin" in there. Mary, of course, was a virgin in the New Testament stories of the birth of Jesus*, and this verse was referred to

---

* Really, of the four New Testament gospels, only two of them describe a virgin birth. The oldest, Mark, which was arguably the source for the other three, does not mention a virgin birth at all.

in the book of Matthew:

> *Now all this was done, that it might be fulfilled which was spoken of the Lord by the prophet, saying, Behold, a virgin shall be with child, and shall bring forth a son, and they shall call his name Emmanuel, which being interpreted is, God with us. (Matthew 1: 22-23)*

But when the Revised Standard Version came out, the Old Testament verse in Isaiah was different! Instead of saying virgin it simply had *young woman*. Yet at the same time, the story in the book of Matthew in the RSV still had the word *virgin*.

The Old Testament is often translated from ancient Hebrew, while the New Testament is often translated from ancient Greek. When the Revised Standard Version came out, the New Testament verse was clear, as the ancient Greek word easily translated to *virgin*. Thus, the book of Matthew has the word *virgin*. But the verse from Isaiah came from ancient Hebrew. And the word in that case was used several times in the Old Testament, and in context always meant *young woman*. However, specifically in the case of Isaiah 7:14, most Christian versions of the Old Testament have the translation as *virgin*.

Clearly the people doing such translations were biased and wanted to make the Isaiah passage "fit" with the Matthew passage and the story of the virgin birth, and so they deliberately translated it as "virgin". I'm probably being harsh here, but to me it seems quite likely that it was intentionally mistranslated. Indeed, modern Jewish scholars and rabbis agree that it should be translated as "young woman."

Regardless of how it really should be translated, this single verse in the RSV furthered a great divide that pretty much already existed between fundamentalist Christians and mainstream Christians. The fundamentalists made all sorts of accusations of conspiracy and what-not, and insisted that the King James Version of the Bible is the *only* translation that is inspired by God. (And some have personally told me that Satan inspired the others!) They claimed that other translations are trying to undermine the virgin birth of Jesus.

Many mainstream churches, however, preferred the Revised Standard Version and continue to use it to this day (or they use the revised version of the revised version, which is called the New Revised Standard Version).

But what's troubling to me about all this is that the whole notion of the virgin birth is not real anyway. Like so many of the stories in the Bible, it's a rehash of earlier myths. As you'll see in the sections to come, that's the case with much of the Bible. But let's start with the virgin birth.

Immaculate Conception

The idea of the virgin birth has come under intense scrutiny in the past decade or so. I haven't been active in a church during that time, but I'm told that many more progressive churches are abandoning this belief. Personally, I find that hard to imagine, as the virgin birth is one of the foundations of Christian belief.

However, Christians would be wise to let go of it for many reasons, especially considering the virgin birth was clearly a later addition to Christianity, as I'll explain shortly.

Recently there have been many books written about the myth of the virgin birth and about the myth of Jesus himself. One book that I reference in the bibliography is the book *The Jesus Mysteries*, by Timothy Freke and Peter Gandy. Another author named D. M. Murdok, who used to go by the pseudonym Acharya S, has written several books.

These works have come under intense attack from many different directions, which should be no surprise. These books put into question the existence of the man upon whom the entire Christian religion is built. Angry Christians have tried to discredit the books, the work and research put into them, and even the authors themselves (which is difficult to do, considering Acharya S is highly educated in classics, Greek civilization, archeology, and numerous languages, and Peter Gandy has a graduate degree in classical civilization and is highly trained in ancient religions).

I don't have room to cover the whole issue of the myth of the virgin birth, considering entire books have been written on the subject. However, in the book *The Jesus Mysteries*, the authors make a pretty good case that the story of Jesus was essentially a fusing of the ancient Jewish idea of a future messiah coming to save the world and of pagan beliefs of a hybrid godman who was born from a human woman who was impregnated by a god. The idea put forth in this book (which is well defended) is that when Christianity was extremely new, in order to make it more appealing to Greeks, people took the existing Greek gods and mixed them with the Jewish religion.

The Jewish people had their stories of a future Messiah. The Old Testament is pretty clear about what the Messiah would be responsible for, including a specific set of events that would include things like returning the Jewish people to Israel and rebuilding the temple. But the biggest thing is that the Messiah is portrayed in the Old Testament as a king, and that all nations would then be at peace with each other:

And he shall judge among the nations, and shall rebuke many people: and they shall beat their swords into plowshares, and their spears into pruninghooks: nation shall not lift up sword against nation, neither shall they learn war any more. (Isaiah 2:4)

The Jesus character of the Old Testament was certainly not a king, and we haven't seen an end to war. (Incidentally, it's easy to find a lot of references online that explain why Jesus doesn't fit the Old Testament description of the Messiah. Most Jews do not accept Jesus as the Messiah and have written a great deal on the topic. Google the words Jewish Messiah and you'll find a lot of pages.)

But the problem is, the Greek people were unwilling to accept this Jewish idea of a messiah. They had their own gods and goddesses, and their stories spoke of a hybrid godman being born to a virgin. The way to get people to accept a Jewish messiah, then, was to create a character that was a combination of a Jewish messiah and the pagan idea of a godman born of a virgin. The end result is the character known as Jesus.

Indeed, the earliest writings of the New Testament make no mention of the virgin birth, and are limited in supernatural acts. The book of Mark is the earliest of the four gospels in the New Testament, and it doesn't mention the virgin birth at all. Clearly, the idea of the virgin birth was added later, after the gospel of Mark was written. And the idea put forth in The Jesus Mysteries is that this addition was put in to make the story more acceptable to the Greeks. And then once the stories were more fully established, the longer gospels (Matthew and Luke) were written, which included the virgin birth. (Of course, most Jewish people saw through the story and didn't accept this Jesus man as the Messiah and still don't to this day.)

Acharya S has made a pretty strong case that many of the supernatural descriptions of Jesus (which were not prophesied in the Old Testament), such as the virgin birth, clearly had roots in one godman in particular named Mithra. Mithraism, as the religion is called, was a huge religion that was spread out geographically from Persia to Rome, long before Christianity, making its way into areas of India by around 1500 BC. Mithra was a sun god and was often depicted visually with a ring of light around his head, which is much like the way Jesus is often depicted in paintings. There were many parallels between Mithra and Jesus. Some were somewhat superficial (they shared birthdays in the Spring equinox, although realistically December 25 wasn't chosen as Jesus' birthday until many centuries after Jesus supposedly existed). But there are many other similarities that *are* important, especially the virgin birth, as well as others, such as having 12 followers who went on to start a huge church, being described as a divine savior and a good shepherd, performing baptisms and eucharist (communion) to remove sins, and even dying and rising again on the third day. Sound familiar?

I can't overemphasize just how big Mithraism was. Yet how many Christians have even heard of it? By around 250 AD, this religion was at least as big as Christianity and a definite competitor. It had its own savior, huge numbers of followers, was officially sanctioned by Rome, and stretched throughout Europe. Recently, in 1954, the ruins of a Mithraic temple were found in London, England!*

The parallels to Jesus are obvious. Of course, Christians don't like the suggestion that their savior was a ripoff from an earlier godman, and so they've gone to great lengths to try to prove that it went the other way, that the Mithra character was influenced by the stories of Jesus. But these arguments are weak and unconvincing.

In addition to Mithra, many other ancient religions spoke of virgin births. It's clear, then, that this mythical idea found its way into Christianity and is totally fabricated. The virgin birth is clearly mythical.

But the myths continue. That's just one of the biggies. What about the rest? Let's proceed.

History and Myth

I've heard all too often that the Bible must be true because it is backed with historical and archeological facts. While it's true that archeology has verified *certain parts* of the Bible, the claim is, in fact, misleading.

Remember, the Bible consists of two events that many people, in their minds, fuse into one:

---

* Google Temple of Mithras Walbrook and you'll find more about these ruins in London.

- The writing of the Bible,
- and the events told in the Bible.

These are two totally separate events that didn't occur at the same time. For example, the events described in Genesis were not written down during the time they are supposed to have occurred. Rather, they were written down several *centuries* later. Further, the stories in the Bible consist of both mythological or supernatural events that were clearly influenced by earlier myths, along with actual historical events that have been verified archeologically.

I am not therefore, claiming that the Old Testament was written after the time that Christ supposedly walked the Earth. Archeology and other history has proven that the people of Israel really existed and that the books of the Old Testament most likely did exist prior to the time of Jesus.

What I *am* disputing, however, is the claim that the ancient supernatural stories of the Bible are original. In fact, they are clearly based in earlier myths. Further, I'm disputing the notion that much of the Bible was written around the time that the stories supposedly took place.

It's easy to lose sight of the time span covered in the Bible. For example, people claim Moses existed around 1200 BC. Archeology has demonstrated— nearly proven—that much of the texts about Moses were written around 600 BC. That's a difference of 600 years. Think about our times today and what happened 600 years ago. That's a huge time span. Six-hundred years ago Christopher Columbus was a child and hadn't yet come to America. Six-hundred years ago, America was inhabited only by the indigenous people, and no settlers had yet arrived. And does anybody alive today remember that time? Of course not. And what do we know about from the time of Christopher Columbus? We know a great deal because of what was written about it at the time Columbus existed, and shortly thereafter.

Some people claim that many of the stories in the Old Testament were passed down orally, and somehow remained totally intact. Suppose some stories were passed down orally from the time of Christopher Columbus. Can we really believe that after all these years and generations the stories would be intact? Of course not. Here's a good comparison: Consider today's modern stories of George Washington, for example. Legend says that as a child, George Washington cut down a cherry tree. When confronted about it by his father, he admitted to doing it, saying he could not tell a lie. That story never actually happened. Historians know that for a fact. It's made up.

And it has been passed down orally, and there's no way to know just how it originated. It may have been based in some early story, and it was likely embellished greatly over decades.

Oral tradition simply isn't reliable. Of course, the Christians who talk about the oral history also like to say that God watched over it and made sure that the stories remained consistent until they were finally written down. And I've also heard claims that the ancient Hebrew people were incredibly careful and meticulous in their retellings, to make sure the stories didn't get modified over generations. But, as you'll see in the sections that follow, the stories couldn't have actually occurred, and they were clearly inspired by earlier myths, and embellished over time and formed into their own unique myths, oral tradition be damned.

I mentioned that the Old Testament stories cover a 4,000-year time span. However, the Old Testament was not written over the 4,000 years that its stories cover. Rather, it was written towards the end of that time span, as much as 3,000 years after the earliest events supposedly took place. And further, it was written over at least a couple hundred years. And during that time, the people recorded their spiritual and religious beliefs, along with what they perceived to be the history of the world, a history that included both historical fact as well as mythological and supposed supernatural events.

As for the separation between the historical events and the mythological events, archeology has verified that many of the kings mentioned in the Bible as having ruled over the ancient Israelites did indeed exist. But that fact alone does not imply that earlier people, such as Noah and Abraham existed. And so for people to claim the Bible is backed by historical fact is to deny logic and true facts.

Common Ancient Myths

Once you've been away from Christianity for awhile, you realize just how silly many of the stories in the Bible are. For me, I particularly notice the Old Testament's style is identical to all the other ancient myths that feature a deity with suspiciously mortal, human qualities who seeks revenge on the people.

Think about it. Start with the notion of a deity. That deity in turn creates humans, animals, and plants on a carbon-based planet. This planet has a circle of life that involves eating and procreating. The bodies are clearly "created" for such purposes. Humans and animals have genitalia for the purpose of procreation, as well as for expelling waste. The mouth exists to consume food and to communicate using sound waves which travel through air in the earth's atmosphere. If a deity created this whole ecosystem and its inhabitants, the deity would have no reason to make the inhabitants in his "own image" (as claimed in the book of Genesis) but rather in a manner that is uniquely suited to life on this planet.

If this deity is not on Earth but rather some spiritual being, would it need physical eyeballs to see light waves? Would this deity need a penis (assuming it's male) that is used for impregnating females and for expelling liquid waste? If it exists in a spiritual realm, would these types of things be necessary?

A myth is a religion in which no one any longer believes.

- James Feibleman

When we approach the stories in the Bible with a clear mind that is not stuck in a worshipful mindset, it is easy to see that, in fact, the deity was modeled in the image of humans, not the other way around. The deity described in the Old Testament is simply an anthropomorphic being that is almost 100% human. And that makes sense: The stories of the Old Testament were created by superstitious, tribal people of ancient times whose worldview extended hardly beyond their isolated, rough way of life. It made perfect sense for them to contrive stories whereby this deity was essentially human in nature but had a few supernatural abilities.

But what about those supernatural features of the deity that were not human? If you look closely, these extra-human abilities were limited to things that people needed to do but couldn't, things that people wished they could do. Moses' people were trapped at the river and had no boats to get across. The solution? Part the sea. People can't do that, so have the deity do it.

But wait! In the case of the parting of the Red Sea, who was doing the parting? God had apparently given Moses certain supernatural abilities—again, abilities that were extra-human but needed by humans.

And think about this: If the deity were real, he could certainly have transcended time and would be well aware of 20th and 21st century technology, and even beyond. Why didn't this deity simply make a helicopter materialize, or perhaps some futuristic machine that we 21st century beings haven't yet thought of?

If we step back and look at it rationally, the reason is clear: The people who wrote the stories were limited in their knowledge and worldview, and the deity they created was therefore similarly limited. Not only were these people unaware of 21st century or 30th century technology, but they could not even conceive of such technology. So it's simple: Such modern technology didn't appear in their stories. To me, this is perhaps one of the most compelling reasons not to accept the ancient stories as any more than that: just made up stories thought up by humans.

Of course, people will rationalize it. I myself did. I most often rationalized it by saying that it wouldn't have made sense for God to create a helicopter, as the people would have been totally confused by such a thing. I argued that God created miracles that would set most easily with the culture and the times. But that was nothing more than rationalization. There's absolutely no reason to suggest such a thing. Rather, it's a rationalization to explain to oneself something that one knows inherently makes no sense.

Growing up, I read a lot of the ancient myths from different cultures, and one thing struck me about the Bible: unlike the other myths, the Bible somehow seemed more "real" to me. It seemed like the stories weren't as fantastic as the other myths, and to me, that gave the Bible more credibility. Also, the Bible stories sounded more religious and holy in nature, whereas the other myths I was reading sounded more like old fables.

However, there was a missing element in my studies: I was primarily focusing on Greek mythology, and had not yet discovered the myths of the Sumerians, the Babylonians, the Canaanites, and the Hittites, which were all Middle Eastern. When you start reading these myths, you find that same tone of reverence that gives them a religious feeling much like the Hebrew stories that make up the Old Testament of the Bible. In fact, the stories are religious and spiritual in nature, in contrast to many of the supposed Greek myths children today study for fun.

And further, you find a lot of similarities to the Hebrew; yet these stories predated the Hebrew stories. For example, you'll find people having conversations with individual gods, and calling them reverent names that translate to *Lord*, just as with the ancient Hebrew stories. And people prayed to these other gods just as the Hebrews prayed to God, and occasionally people claimed that these gods spoke to them, just as Moses and others claimed God spoke to them.

For example, in the mid-19th century, a stone was discovered that dated to the 9th century BC. The stone is called the Mesha Stele, and carved into it is writing apparently by a Moab king named Mesha. Parts of it are broken off, but most of the writing is intact. And in this writing, Mesha describes how he went to his god Kemosh and Kemosh spoke to him and told him what to do—in the same way, for instance, that Abraham in the Old Testament went before God and God told him what to do. (Most Christians would likely discount Mesha's conversation with his god has simple fabrication or perhaps delusion, yet they wouldn't apply the same logic to Abraham, accepting the story of Abraham as literal fact.)

All this came as a bit of a shock to my system when I found this, because I thought that the Hebrew stories were supposed to be special and unique, and totally different from the other myths.

The Babylonian myths include several "wisdom" stories that are surprisingly similar in nature to the books of Proverbs and Job in the Old Testament. These stories deal with morality and human suffering and overcoming life's problems.

Indeed, if the Greek stories, for example, are written in a King James style English, they still sound like fables because the tone is still different. But these Middle Eastern myths, when written in King James English are virtually indistinguishable from the Old Testament stories in the King James Version of the Bible, because the tone, style, and spiritual nature is the same, regardless of which English dialect they're translated into.

Also with the other myths, you find some of the same characters present in the Old Testament, along with other gods and interactions between the gods and humans. In other words, when you read the ancient Hebrew myths alongside the other myths, you start to get a bigger picture of the mythology of an entire region of which today's Old Testament is only a small part. And in this bigger picture, there are many gods, not just the one god that today's Christians and Jews worship.

All of this is of particular interest because I suspect that most people have only compared Christianity to the more well-known myths of the ancient Greeks and their stories of Zeus and other gods. And so when pushed, you'll hear Christians make the same arguments that I always believed, that the ancient Hebrew stories were far superior and much more believable. But have these people even read anything about the various Middle Eastern myths? Doubtful. How many people have, for example, studied ancient Sumerian myths? How many people even know the names of the characters in the stories? In truth, most people know nothing of these myths. And so when they argue that the Hebrew stories are superior to other myths, they're doing so with serious ignorance.

The fact is, the ancient Hebrew stories that make up our Old Testament today are very similar to other stories of the ancient times. And the more you look at them critically and realistically, you start to realize just what they are: Myths.

Myths Predating the Old Testament

When considering the ancient stories of the Bible, it's important to remember three aspects:

- First is the supposed creation of the Earth, including the first man and woman, Adam and Eve.
- Then there's the beginning of the verbal stories conveying what happened in the beginning.
- Finally there's the actual writing down of these ancient stories.

When I was young, I felt this all happened simultaneously, that the stories in Genesis were written down as they occurred, making it a first-hand account. But even most people of the various Jewish/Christian/Muslim beliefs today recognize that the writing of these tales did not happen as the tales supposedly took place.

What really happened is that the ancient Hebrew people were a pastoral people who moved into the land of Canaan, which was already well-populated, and the primary work done by the people already there was agricultural.

During those times, agricultural and pastoral/nomadic economies did not fit well together, and were seen as threats to each other. Thus, there was certainly an inherent conflict between the Hebrew people moving into Canaan and the people who already inhabited the area.

And what modern research has shown us is that the Canaanites already had established religious ideas and myths (today called Ugaritic myths) that were *gradually* absorbed by the Hebrew people.

And these Canaanite myths were influenced by yet an earlier group of people, the Sumerians. This we know as *fact*. The Sumerian people had the most ancient of the myths; all the myths from the Sumerians predate the stories in the Book of Genesis. (I should point out that up until about 100 years ago, little was known about the early Canaanites. In 1928, the Ras Shamra Tablets were discovered, which were painstakingly translated, finally providing much detail for what I'm describing here, much to the chagrin of the Christian Church.)

Remember, the myths were passed on orally, and as people conveyed the stories, they were influenced by other stories they had heard. The stories *gradually* morphed and changed over generations. And as the Hebrew people heard the stories of the Canaanites, their stories gradually included various features of the Canaanites' stories.

This explains a problem I used to have: When I finally started reading some of the other ancient myths that were supposed to have influenced the Hebrews, I thought they were too different. There might have been a few similarities here and there, but they seemed too different to possibly have been an "earlier version."

But what I was missing was that the stories gradually morphed and changed over generations, and it was a *long* time after the influences took place before people finally started writing these stories down, both the original ones and the influenced ones. And so that gradual influence wasn't apparent.

Further—and this is important—was that I was missing one of the biggest points of influence: The theme of the stories. While the stories may have looked very different and contained different characters, they had themes that were nearly identical. And that's where the biggest influence was.

Understanding this, the following became clear to me: The stories in the Old Testament were, indeed, re-hashes of earlier myths, and were not original. Further, the earlier myths were from other religions featuring multiple gods, gods that most people today write off as having been fake and made-up—or, in the case of Christians, people believe those other gods are actually demons. (I say more about that in "The myth of monotheism," later in this chapter.)

This can only mean one thing: If a fake, made-up myth morphed into another myth that is used today as the basis of a worldwide faith, clearly that new myth is also fake. That's not good news for the Christians all across the planet, now is it? And it certainly was an eye-opener for me.

Before looking at these myths, however, I want to share what is one of the oddest, most ridiculous explanations I've heard for the existence of earlier myths that were clearly influences for the Hebrew myths in the Old Testament. I am not kidding, there are actually people who insist that the reason for the earlier myths is that Satan knew what was going to happen and purposely planted these myths based on the later Hebrew stories, so that it would appear that they came earlier. I'm not going to tackle that other than to say it's a bunch of total nonsense created by delusional people who are in denial of the historical facts.

Overlapping Tidbits

I hesitate to bring this up, because I predict that when people set out to "debunk" this book, they'll single out this section and point to it as being trivial and nonsensical. So I'll attack that right on: In this section I'm going to show that the Bible is filled with tiny little pieces of stories that overlap with other myths. This is rather minor to the point, as the several sections in the rest of this chapter show. But before I get to those sections, I want to show the setting in which these myths were all created and with the setting, the numerous common elements.

Although these are small and somewhat trivial individually, as a whole they start to add up to show that there is definite influence between the Old Testament Hebrew myths and the earlier myths. This is just a foundation, and in the next sections I'll show many even bigger overlaps.

For starters, in the Old Testament there are many mentions of places. Now certainly the other tribes in the region would be familiar with the same places—mountains, valleys, and so on. But where the overlap becomes apparent is when these places are used by various gods for the same rituals.

For example, in the Ugaritic myths, the god Baal has a palace on Mt. Zaphon. In the Old Testament, Mt. Zaphon is mentioned in Psalm 48 as being God's holy mountain. (In the Hebrew, the word was Zaphon, often spelled Tsaphon, which translates to the "north side". This refers to the mountain to the north of Mount Zion, and is referenced in many ancient myths.) The similarity here is that this location was considered a holy abode by the gods, first by the Canaanites and their god, Baal, and later by the Hebrews and their god.

Also in the Ugaritic myths, Baal has an adversary named Mot who he fights and must defeat. Mot is the god of the underworld, as well as god of sterility. Baal wants to bring rains so crops can grow, while Mot wants the opposite. The ancient Hebrew texts make reference to Mot in that there's a connection between Mot and their own word for death, which is mot.

There are also similar descriptions of how God behaves compared to how other gods behave. For example, Psalm 104 talks about the creation, and describes some of the things God did:

Who layeth the beams of his chambers in the waters: who maketh
the clouds his chariot: who walketh upon the wings of the wind.
(Psalms 104:3)

The process of laying beams in the waters and riding the chariots are highly similar to the acts of two gods in Ugaritic myths, Ea and Baal.

There are also many instances in the Bible where angels all sing for joy and celebrate God, and there are similar stories in the earlier myths where other gods sing and celebrate another god.

And there are other common themes that appear in the Old Testament that clearly had influences in earlier myths. For example, I already mentioned the issue of pastoral versus agricultural cultures. This tension influenced many of the stories not only in the Bible, but in other ancient myths, such as the Ugaritic myths. Usually tensions such as this and others were personified in both Ugaritic myths (as battles between gods) and in Hebrew myths (as battles between god and demons, or between heroes of the Bible).

I know these are all minor examples, but they serve to show the foundation from which many similarities in how the stories are told are derived. So let's move on to the big similarities, and why I have no choice but to accept these big stories—the creation, Adam and Eve, Satan and Hell, Noah's ark, and the Tower of Babel—as nothing but myth.

The Myth of Creation

Virtually every culture has had a creation myth. Indeed the ancient Middle East had its share of creation myths beyond what we read in the Christian Bible.

The myth given in the book of Genesis consists of the pretty well-known seven-day account of Creation. But guess what: It turns out that this seven-day account, in fact, closely parallels an earlier story that was used in Babylon.

This is particularly interesting, because the Babylonians celebrated the new year each year, and it included a seven-day festival. To the Babylonians, this was the time that the world was recreated each year. And that's where their story likely came from. And remember, this story predated the book of Genesis, and was likely an influence.

In addition to the well-known portions of the Book of Genesis, the creation story is also described further in other parts of the Bible, something a lot of Christians (who haven't actually studied much of the Bible) probably don't even realize.

Psalm 74 speaks of the Creation, and includes a story of how prior to creating the world, God had to first slay a dragon called Leviathan. This is a direct copy of a Canaanite myth where the god Baal killed the dragon of the same name prior to creating the world.

There can be no doubt that the Hebrew story was influenced by the Ugaritic myth. It was not original. And further, this myth was itself influenced by an even earlier Babylonian myth whereby the god named Marduk slew the dragon and split him into two parts. The dragon represented chaos, and slaying chaos and dividing it into two resulted in order. In other words, order was created out of chaos. This is also echoed in the Old Testament story as God split the universe by creating the firmament.

The fact is, the story just wasn't real. Therefore, in my own studies, I was *forced* to decide:

1. This part of the Bible wasn't real, but the religion was still real.
2. This part of the Bible was not real, thus providing a rather blunt blow to the idea that the entire Bible was written by God.

This is a thought that had already been haunting me since I began to question the story of the Tower of Babel, and it would continue to haunt me as I attempted to work through all this.

I had no other choice than to eventually make a decision, for to not decide would be to just ignore the facts and to blindly and mindlessly accept my faith, something I refused to do.

But could the ancient creation myths in Genesis be considered allegory and, therefore, not literal at all? I've heard many people say that each day in the seven-day creation story represented thousands or millions of years. In my later days as a Christian I tried to embrace this idea, that the story was just allegorical (but still real) and that each of the seven days could have represented great lengths of time. (That still wouldn't be enough time to fit the known age of the universe, but bear with me.)

This still doesn't work. Through today's science, we know the Earth is far younger than the age of the universe. And even so, as I mentioned at the start of this chapter, in the Bible account, plants existed and thrived before the sun was created, something that is scientifically impossible. It just doesn't work even if you try to assume each day of the seven is a huge length of time. It's still *wrong*.

And so again I was faced with a problem: There was something *wrong* in the Bible. Should I—or more so, *could* I—keep believing something as the word of God when it had things in it that were incorrect?

Let's look at another myth.

The Garden of Eden story was almost an identical copy of an earlier Sumerian myth involving a place where people did not get sick or grow old and animals were not eaten. To ignore the fact that the story in Genesis came from earlier stories in other religions is nothing but denial*. Accepting the Adam and Eve story as real and literal is nothing but blind, irrational faith. It was an ancient story that originated by superstitious people with no understanding about science, and it was passed down by tribes and eventually found its way into Hebrew mythology, and into the Christian Old Testament (and the Hebrew and Muslim scriptures).

The Myths of Satan and Hell

The idea of Hell is of particular interest, because so much of today's Christian theology depends on it. At the beginning of this book I spoke of the threats of Hell that are used to convert people and keep people shackled to the faith.

But where did the concept of Hell and eternal damnation even come from? Is it even real? And if not, what does that say about the faith?

This is of vital importance to many of us who are walking away from the faith. We have had fears forced into our heads since we were children, and for many of us, the fear occasionally comes back: What if I'm wrong? What if there really is a Hell and God is going to send me there for all this? And what if I did something so bad as to write an entire book about why I'm not a Christian!

But it just isn't true. There is no eternal punishment. How could there be? Let's break this down into several levels to see that it is categorically false, a lie, a made-up threat that serves one purpose: To scare people into submission.

* See, for example, Hooke's book, *Middle Eastern Mythology*, mentioned in this book's appendix. In particular note the chapter on Hebrew Mythology in the section on Creation myths.

I've already made a pretty strong case in the first two chapters of this book that the threat of Hell serves as a means to control people. Without this threat, people could easily slip away from the religion, which would cause the church to lose its power (and money from the collection plates). Therefore, it is in the best interest of the church to keep the myth alive that there's an underworld filled with terror and torture just waiting for you if you even think about straying.

This grip on the people is surprisingly easy for the church to maintain, because the people themselves perpetuate the myth. The church certainly keeps the myth alive, but the people take it and let it grow in their minds into something that's absolutely terrifying. People read books and see movies that perpetuate the myth. People talk about it to each other, and remind each other of these horrible things that happen in Hell.

What is the usual picture of Hell? A dark place filled with red and orange flames, and people screaming and howling, and this big red guy with horns—the Devil—overseeing the whole operation.

The whole notion of Satan makes little sense. I already talked about the comparison to a judge and warden (God is the judge; Satan is the warden) and how they would be on the same side and why the Christian idea is absurd in this regard.

Certainly, Satan is very real to most Christians, and perhaps the most frightening guy that ever existed. Christians are terrified of him. But why should they be? He's nothing but a myth. Let's explore that a moment.

In the Bible, there are a couple different names which today Christians all equate to the Devil. One, of course, is Satan. Another is Lucifer. Then there are some strange connections with a few other individuals, such as the King of Tyre. And finally, there's the somewhat familiar name Beelzebub that many people have seen mentioned in the Bible.

First let's explore Lucifer. The name Lucifer itself is actually only mentioned once in the Bible, and that's in the book of Isaiah. (And many modern translations don't even use the name Lucifer in that chapter.) The chapter that mentions Lucifer is used by most Christians as the basis for the story of how the Devil fell from grace, and was effectively booted out of Heaven:

How art thou fallen from heaven, O Lucifer, son of the morning! how art thou cut down to the ground, which didst weaken the nations! For thou hast said in thine heart, I will ascend into heaven, I will exalt my throne above the stars of God: I will sit

also upon the mount of the congregation, in the sides of the north:
I will ascend above the heights of the clouds; I will be like the most
High. Yet thou shalt be brought down to hell, to the sides of the
pit. (Isaiah 14:12-15)

But the name Lucifer technically didn't even appear in the original Hebrew version of Isaiah. It couldn't have, because the word isn't Hebrew. It's Latin. And it refers to a morning star (which is typically considered to be not a star at all, but Venus).

But the "morning star" has its roots, like so much of the Old Testament, in Babylonian ideas. "Morning Star" was a title applied to Babylonian kings. And so Lucifer is really just a placeholder for the idea of a word that refers to an unnamed Babylonian king.

Knowing this translation, we can then find other instances in the Old Testament where a Babylonian king is referred to as a morning star. One important place is Ezekial 28, because this also provides a description that is typically equated to the Devil. This is kind of long, but it's worth reading to gain an insight into the mind of the Christian:

Moreover the word of the LORD came unto me, saying,
Son of man, take up a lamentation upon the king of Tyrus, and
say unto him, Thus saith the Lord GOD; Thou sealest up the sum,
full of wisdom, and perfect in beauty. Thou hast been in Eden
the garden of God; every precious stone was thy covering, the
sardius, topaz, and the diamond, the beryl, the onyx, and the
jasper, the sapphire, the emerald, and the carbuncle, and gold:
the workmanship of thy tabrets and of thy pipes was prepared in
thee in the day that thou wast created. Thou art the anointed
cherub that covereth; and I have set thee so: thou wast upon the
holy mountain of God; thou hast walked up and down in the
midst of the stones of fire. Thou wast perfect in thy ways from the
day that thou wast created, till iniquity was found in thee. By the
multitude of thy merchandise they have filled the midst of thee
with violence, and thou hast sinned: therefore I will cast thee as
profane out of the mountain of God: and I will destroy thee, O
covering cherub, from the midst of the stones of fire. Thine heart
was lifted up because of thy beauty, thou hast corrupted thy wisdom

by reason of thy brightness: I will cast thee to the ground, I will lay
thee before kings, that they may behold thee. Thou hast defiled thy
sanctuaries by the multitude of thine iniquities, by the iniquity
of thy traffick; therefore will I bring forth a fire from the midst of
thee, it shall devour thee, and I will bring thee to ashes upon the
earth in the sight of all them that behold thee. All they that know
thee among the people shall be astonished at thee: thou shalt be a
terror, and never shalt thou be any more. (Ezekial 28:11-19)

Even though this passage clearly states that it's a Babylonian king (the king over the region called Tyrus), Christians have long equated this to the Devil. And they use this passage as further description of the Devil, and how he was a beautiful angel who was booted out of Heaven.

But it isn't the Devil. It's referring to a Babylonian king; it clearly states so. And it's important to remember that back in those days, people were not allowed to speak out against the kings, lest they be punished. (Today we have freedom of speech, something not granted to the people back then, which is just one more piece of evidence that our laws today were *not* inspired by the Bible.) And so instead of mentioning a king by name, the writers would use metaphors. (I mention this again later when I discuss the Book of Revelation.)

People combine these two chapters—the one from Isaiah and the one from Ezekiel—into a single portrayal of the Devil as having been a beautiful angel who was high in rank (a member of the Cherubim, which are second in rank just under the Seraphim) who decided he was better than God and who was ultimately kicked out of Heaven. But look at who these two passages actually refer to: One is Lucifer, which meant a morning star, a title for a Babylonian king, and the other is from somebody called the *King of Tyre*, another Babylonian king. So both were talking about Babylonian kings, not some Devil character at all.

That pretty much dismantles the common conception Christians have about this character who they call the Devil, a conception of a beautiful angel who decided he was better than God, and was ultimately kicked out of Heaven.

Think of it! This is the background people use to describe the Devil. And without this, what's left? Not much, but let's continue, because the book of Job offers more insight into a character who is also equated to the Devil.

This is where we finally come upon the name Satan. I won't quote the whole thing here, as it appears throughout the first two chapters and is kind of long. But I will quote the first appearance:

> *Now there was a day when the sons of God came to present themselves before the LORD, and Satan came also among them. And the LORD said unto Satan, Whence comest thou? Then Satan answered the LORD, and said, From going to and fro in the earth, and from walking up and down in it. (Job 1:6-7)*

But interestingly, the word that has become Satan in English actually has roots of a common noun, not a name at all. In the original Hebrew, the word that was used translates literally to "the adversary." And as such, the name Satan isn't a name at all, but a description of sorts, of an adversary to God. But in these cases, the adversary character is some kind of supernatural being. (Remember, just to clarify my own stance, I'm not saying I believe that this supernatural being exists, but rather I'm saying that the made-up character in the made-up story is supernatural.)

What all this means is there are two different aspects to this character that people now consider the Devil: A human—a Babylonian king—and an angel that represents an adversary to God.

We can ignore the aspect representing different Babylonian kings, since they are representative of a human, and I'm not interested in trying to explain how that could symbolically represent the Devil, since the Devil doesn't exist. I'll leave such arguments to the theologians, as they seem to have plenty of time to waste on this matter.

By removing the Babylonian king verses, we remove the parts that are just a story about a human. And we're left with a characterization of an angel that tempts and tests people. And that aspect can be traced back to earlier mythologies, demonstrating again that the supernatural aspects of the Bible are nothing more than re-hashes of earlier myths.

In other words, what's left of the supernatural aspect of a Satan character in the Bible originated from earlier myths. These earlier myths involved gods fighting other gods, some representing good, and some representing evil. And those stories were nothing more than myths. So what's left? Nothing. There is no Devil, no Satan. He's completely fabricated, and his character has grown and evolved over the centuries.

What's perhaps even more absurd about the whole idea of Satan is that most of the ideas people have about Satan and Hell don't even originate in the Bible, the document that Christians consider the word of God. Rather, much of it comes from a story that even Christians would consider fiction, a story called Inferno, which is a chapter in a book by Dante Alighier; the book is called *The Divine Comedy* and was written—in Italian—between 1308 and 1321.

You have to wonder how many people even know that their perceptions and ideas about this Satan character aren't even of Biblical background.

The story is about a guy who dies at the age of 35. With the help of a guide, he makes his way through Hell. (He eventually moves up to Heaven.) The author, Dante, gives an incredibly elaborate and detailed description of Hell, as well as the Devil.

His description of the Devil is rather frightening, to say the least. I imagine when Christians read this book, if they believe every word of it, they are absolutely terrified, even though the information in it is not in the Bible—again a case of people adding to the Bible on their own whims to fit their needs and then passing this information on down to others.

The book was originally written in Italian in verse form, and there have been several translations. The famous 19th-century writer Henry Wadsworth Longfellow gave us one English translation. Here are some tidbits from the English version where Dante describes what the Devil, which was bigger than a giant, looks like:

> *O, what a marvel it appeared to me, When I beheld three faces on his head! The one in front, and that vermilion was;*
> *Two were the others, that were joined with this; Above the middle part of either shoulder, And they were joined together at the crest;*
> *And the right-hand one seemed 'twixt white and yellow; The left was such to look upon as those; Who come from where the Nile falls valley-ward.*
> *Underneath each came forth two mighty wings, Such as befitting were so great a bird; Sails of the sea I never saw so large.*
> *No feathers had they, but as of a bat; Their fashion was; and he was waving them, So that three winds proceeded forth therefrom.*
> *Thereby Cocytus wholly was congealed. With six eyes did he weep, and down three chins, Trickled the tear-drops and the bloody drivel.*

At every mouth he with his teeth was crunching; A sinner, in the manner of a brake, So that he three of them tormented thus. To him in front the biting was as naught; Unto the clawing, for sometimes the spine; Utterly stripped of all the skin remained. (Inferno: 34:37-60)

Yes, the Devil has two enormous bat wings and six eyes with blood gushing out of them. Next is where we get to see Judas, of the 12 disciples, the only one who turned against Jesus:

That soul up there which has the greatest pain, The Master said, is Judas Iscariot; With head inside, he plies his legs without. (Inferno: 34:61-63)

And yes, Judas is being eternally tortured inside Satan's jaws. In the verses that follow, we find that Brutus (you know, the guy who killed Julius Caesar) and Cassius (one of Brutus' helpers) are in the other two mouths, also being chewed on and tortured for all eternity. I can only guess why Dante singled out these two guys for eternal punishment in addition to Judas.

The description of Hell is pretty terrifying as well, but I won't bore you with the details. You can look it up online and read it if you're so inclined.

But remember: None of this is in the Bible! What is in the Bible is a small set of vague references and nothing more. And that, frankly, is quite ironic: Even Christians, who so wholeheartedly believe in a Satan character, have little basis in their own scriptures. You would think that they would easily agree with us non-believers about the non-existence of their beloved Satan character.

Before leaving the idea of the Devil, I want to cover another name that comes up in the Bible, which provides characterizations that many people apply to the creature they call Satan.

This character is Beelzebub. The New Testament doesn't suggest that Beelzebub is real; rather, Beelzebub is a demon that people during the New Testament believed in. People accused Jesus of getting his powers from Beelzebub. Here's a verse from Matthew; Jesus had just healed somebody, and in this verse the Pharisees accused him of summoning Beelzebub to accomplish the task:

But when the Pharisees heard it, they said, This fellow doth not cast out devils, but by Beelzebub the prince of the devils. (Matthew 12:24)

The Old Testament also mentions Beelzebub, although it's harder to find in searches, because it's often written Baal-Zebub (more on this shortly). In all of these cases, however, the word is used as the name of a god who was worshipped by the people in nearby Ekron, and there's really no mention that this is somehow the Devil. However, the name is clearly the same as Beelzebub, and we can surmise that by the time of the New Testament, the Hebrew people had adopted this god into their own mythology, but identified him as a demon rather than a god.

That, in fact, brings me to a central point about the myth of monotheism, which I take up next.

The Myth of Monotheism

One defense people make of Christianity is that it is based on monotheism, meaning it recognizes only one god, the "One true God." The claim is that other religions are polytheistic, and as such, can't be true.

First, the logic here is absurd: Why does monotheistic imply truth? There's no rationale for it.

Second, it's not exactly true that Christianity is based on a monotheistic religion. In the early days of Judaism, before Christianity, the people worshipped a god they called Yahweh. People today consider this to be the same god that Christians worship. But in ancient times, long before the time Jesus supposedly existed, the Hebrew people, the Yahwists (people who worshipped Yahweh) recognized many other gods, and their different gods were absorbed from other cultures, especially those of the Ugaritic religion.

These gods are mentioned many times in the Bible, but always as either untrue gods or as demons, and in both instances the people were forced by the leaders to stop worshipping these other gods. In other words, while the leaders wanted it their way (worship only Yahweh), in practice, the people were taking a different approach (worshipping multiple gods).

For example, there is a god named Asherah who appears in the Old Testament. (Interestingly, the name is removed in most translations, but the New International Version keeps the name Asherah.) Asherah was a female god, and many women worshipped her, and many Hebrews viewed her as the Queen of Heaven. Of course, being a male-dominated culture, the worship of a female god wasn't appreciated, so the leaders demanded the practice stop. Exodus 34:13 speaks of the shrines people built towards this goddess, and how Yahweh wants them torn down.

Of course, many Christians would be fine with this: The people were worshipping a false god and were told to stop. But the situation is a bit more complex than that, because when you factor in other practices, it becomes clear that Yahweh was just one of many gods that the people of this time worshipped, and for political reasons, the leaders managed to squash the worshipping of the other gods and maintain a single god.

One technique to get people to stop worshipping these other gods was to "demote" the character from god to demon. In cases like this, the gods weren't even declared fake or non-existent. Rather, they were declared true but demonic!

I already mentioned Baal in the Ugaritic mythology. Baal was a Ugaritic god and was easily absorbed by the Yahwists as a demon, and he persisted right into the New Testament, as people continued to believe he was a demon. Indeed, if you refer to him by the modified name, Beelzebub, most Christians to this day believe in him.

In other words, they believe in a supernatural being but play the word game and don't technically call him a "god" even though, by all regards, he is a god in their eyes.

And of course there's the whole complicated issue of Satan. Earlier I talked about how Satan is barely even represented in the Bible. But regardless, to most Christians, Satan is very real and very powerful.

Again, by all regards, Satan is a god to these people. They don't *call* him a god, but he is.

Although the history of the ancient people in the Middle East during the beginnings of the Hebrew religion is vague, since we're on the edge of when writing began, there are many indications that the Hebrew people simply absorbed the religions around them. And as I've said, it wasn't all at once, but gradual. And over time the people gradually pushed away the other gods, removing them or demoting them to demons. And as such, it's clear that the Hebrew religion, on which Christianity is built, was initially not a monotheistic religion. Only over time has it come to be considered one, but even still, that's debatable when you factor in all the lesser gods and demons that Christians still believe in.

Further, the Bible occasionally makes reference to other gods, but it's easy to write these off by suggesting that God in the Bible was saying these other gods were made-up pretend gods that people worshipped, but that didn't really exist. For example, Exodus 15:11 could easily be interpreted as meaning that the other gods don't exist:

Who is like unto thee, O LORD, among the gods? (Exodus 15:11)

There are plenty of other such verses where, as a Christian, I was simply taught to believe that the "other gods" were fake gods living in the minds of the people, or inanimate objects like a cow made out of gold, or even something like money. Indeed, often people refer to the worshipping of these other gods as idolatry, which in turn is usually used to mean the worship of man-made objects.

This made good sense to me, as we have all met people who worship money, and verses like the Exodus one I just quoted could easily refer to man-made objects that are like gods to some.

Here are two more verses that can be interpreted in this same way:

Among the gods there is none like unto thee, O Lord. (Psalms 86:8)
For the Lord ... is to be feared above all gods. (Psalms 96:4)

Unfortunately, however, this doesn't work with all the verses that refer to other gods. Here's a verse some people might not be aware of:

Thou shalt not revile the gods, nor curse the ruler of thy people. (Exodus 22:28)

This particular verse seems to have caused some problems. The King James Version, which I used for this verse, is considered by many to be the most perfect version ever. Yet why is "gods" written in plural?

As usual, this doesn't set well with people, so they search out alternate meanings. Instead of taking it at face value, many commentators I've studied go against their notion of "literal truth" and instead replace "gods" with another word: *judges.*

Other modern translations simply *change* it to singular: "Do not revile

God…" And probably the oddest interpretation I found was a page online that explained that it does mean "gods" in plural and does refer to other "false" gods, and that it means we should respect the other religions without actually subscribing to them!

Indeed, the original Greek (the Septuagint) has the word as plural. The Greek word used is θεους which translates to "gods".

But perhaps the single biggest proof that the Hebrew religion was not built on monotheism is in the very first verse of the Bible, Genesis 1:1. Most American Christians have this verse memorized as, "In the beginning, God created the heavens and the Earth."

But that's wrong. The original Hebrew uses the word Elohim for God. But the problem is, Elohim doesn't translate to God. It translates to gods, plural. The Hebrew word is םיהלא. Hebrew goes from right to left, and the left-most letter is ם, which is the Hebrew m. The singular word would be written הולא, which in English is written Eloah. The difference is in the ending, with the m in this case denoting plural.

Thus, the literal translation is, in fact, "In the beginning, the gods created the heavens and the earth." Yes, plural, the *gods*.

But that's not all. The word Elohim itself has an interesting history. Turns out it comes from the Ugaritic myths! The word El is the name of the supreme Canaanite God. The word Elohim actually appears in the Ugaritic texts, and refers to the entire family of gods!*

Look at this verse from Psalms:

God standeth in the congregation of the mighty; he judgeth among the gods. (Psalms 82:1)

The phrase "congregation of the mighty" is not what the original Hebrew says. Rather, the original Hebrew refers to the company of "gods". In other words, they're saying that this supposed "only" God has stood among other gods. Then this comes up again in a later Psalm:

For who in the heaven can be compared unto the LORD? who among the sons of the mighty can be likened unto the LORD? (Psalms 89:6)

---

* Readers who want to explore this further are encouraged to read Chapter 8 of Did God Have a Wife? by William G. Dever (ISBN 0802828523).

In this case, the Hebrew word again refers to the Gods. And since it's talking about "sons" it implies a family of gods.

The name El appears in many places in the Old Testament, always with a title after it, to refer to God. When God spoke to Abraham, he told him his name was El Shadday. This is another place where there's some confusion. Many Christians are taught that El Shadday means "God Almighty."

It doesn't.

Shadday means Mountain. And so El Shadday means God of the Mountain. And again, El is the Ugaritic God, so this is referring, once again, to the supreme Canaanite god.

Later on in the Old Testament, God appears to Moses and reveals his real name, Yahweh. This is where that name finally appears in the Bible. This is the name that has been used throughout history. The word is written in Hebrew as יהוה which translates to the English letters YHWH, with no vowels present. People have added vowels in different ways to come up with Jehova and Yahweh. (The German language used J for the letter Y; thus the name Jehova came from the German translation of Yahweh.)

As it happens, the name Yahweh may even have roots in the Ugaritic text. This isn't totally clear to modern scholars, but there's indication that the Hebrew name YHWH came from the Ugaritic god YW, who was a son of the supreme god El. (Not all scholars agree, however, that YHWH came from YW. However, the evidence is strong in that many of the words and names in ancient Hebrew were almost identical to words of the same meaning in ancient Ugaritic, but with a couple letters added. The case, then, is strong.)

Whether or not the name Yahweh has roots in the religion of the Canaanite people, it's clear that the stories and other names in the ancient Hebrew Bible do. Add to this the fact that the first chapter of Genesis refers to gods in the plural, and it's pretty hard to deny that the religion of the people in the Old Testament was a derivative of the polytheistic religion of the Canaanites.

To close this section, I want to share with you something Richard Dawkins says in his excellent book, *The God Delusion*, which I've mentioned in earlier chapters. (If you haven't read it, I strongly encourage you to. It really gets people thinking.) The argument he makes won't mean much to a totally defensive Christian, but it's still fun. Dawkins points out that although Catholics don't consider dead saints "gods" as such, for all intents and purposes they are when you factor in that these saints can be prayed to just like any other god, for problems the particular saint specializes in helping. Dawkins writes in his usual delightful elegance:

> *The pantheon is further swollen by an army of saints, whose intercessory power make them, if not demigods, well worth approaching on their own specialist subjects. The Catholic Community Forum helpfully lists 5,120 saints, together with their areas of expertise, which include abdominal pains, abuse victims, anorexia, arms dealers, blacksmiths, broken bones, bomb technicians and bowel disorders, to venture no further than the Bs.*

Of course, a strict Catholic would be unmoved by this argument, claiming that they're not gods but rather angels of the one single God. But is that really a valid argument? They're still supernatural beings, and one can manipulate the words all they want, but the fact remains that there are many beings in this supposed world that could easily qualify as gods.

Mythical Creatures in the Bible

I saw a video online of a talk given by a guy named Kent Hovind, a Young Earth Creationist, who is currently in prison for tax-related charges. Prior to his imprisonment, he had written many books and videos forwarding his cause of Young Earth Creationism.

In the video I recently saw, Hovind mentions that dragons used to exist. Why does he say this? I suspect it's because:

The Bible says dragons exist.

I don't know how mainstream Christians react to the Bible's claim of dragons existing, but I have seen how several vocal, fundamentalist Christians such as Kent Hovind take the Bible literally and therefore seem to believe such outrageous claims.

The claim of dragons is in the Book of Job, chapter 41. The word is usually translated as Leviathan, which I briefly mentioned earlier when talking about the myth of creation. It's not clear what exactly a leviathan is, but we do know it comes from earlier myths. And we do know that the 41st chapter of Job gives a pretty detailed description, which sounds exactly like what

most people think of as a dragon. The chapter mentions Leviathan in the
first verse:

*Canst thou draw out leviathan with an hook? or his tongue with
a cord which thou lettest down? (Job 41:1)*

And then goes on to describe Leviathan in several ways. Here are a
couple of gems:

*Who can open the doors of his face? his teeth are terrible round
about. His scales are his pride, shut up together as with a close
seal. One is so near to another, that no air can come between them.
They are joined one to another, they stick together, that they cannot
be sundered. (Job 41:15-17)*

And he's described as being rather powerful and frightening:

*His heart is as firm as a stone; yea, as hard as a piece of the nether
millstone. When he raiseth up himself, the mighty are afraid: by
reason of breakings they purify themselves. (Job 41:24-25)*

*The arrow cannot make him flee: slingstones are turned with
him into stubble. Darts are counted as stubble: he laugheth at
the shaking of a spear. Sharp stones are under him: he spreadeth
sharp pointed things upon the mire. (Job 41:28-30)*

But why do people think he's a dragon? Because he breaths fire! No, I'm
not kidding. It's right in the Bible. See for yourself:

*Out of his mouth go burning lamps, and sparks of fire leap out.
Out of his nostrils goeth smoke, as out of a seething pot or caldron.
His breath kindleth coals, and a flame goeth out of his mouth.
(Job 41:19-21)*

It's right there in the Bible. The Bible speaks of a fire-breathing dragon.
Faced with this verse, then, a Christian is forced to decide:

Is this literal, which means dragons once existed?
Or is this not literal and does it represent something else?

If one takes the stand that the Bible is literal, then one must believe that this is referring to a fire-breathing dragon. And that's exactly the stand some people have taken. On the other hand, one might try to do as I've been saying, interpret the Bible and change it into something other than what it says so it *feels* better. Perhaps the Leviathan represents some sea creature. Or perhaps it represents the Devil. I did find some web pages making the claim that this dragon-thing represents Satan. But the Bible doesn't *say* it represents Satan. That's something people are adding to the Bible to turn something unbelievable—the claim of a dragon—into something they can believe exists—Satan.

But the fact is, these verses are present in the Bible. And further, the verses in Job 41 are supposedly spoken by God himself to the man named Job. God himself spoke of the Leviathan. It's pretty hard for a Christian to discount it if the words were supposedly spoken by God.

And so we have at least one mythological creature that the Bible claims existed: The fire-breathing dragon. What does this say about the accuracy of the Bible? Very little, in my opinion.

Before moving to another mythological creature, I should mention that the book of Revelation, the final book in the Bible, also mentions dragons several times (such as in Revelation 12:3). I haven't said much about Revelation yet, because it's so bizarre and nutty, and has been the source of much separation within the Christian Church, that I'm devoting two sections to it, one later in this chapter, and one in the next chapter. But if you want to include its mention of a dragon as a count towards made-up creatures being in the Bible, be my guest. (Incidentally, the word *dragon* originated from an early Greek word δρακων, or *drakon* in English characters, and that word is what appears in the early Greek manuscripts of the book of Revelation.)

It turns out that the book of Job is a lovely source for mythological characters. Also present in that book are unicorns! The unicorn, in fact, is mentioned several times in the Old Testament, at least in the King James Version. You can see for yourself; it's in Numbers 23 and 24, Deuteronomy 33, Job 39, Psalms 22, 29, 92, and Isaiah 34. Many times the verses don't actually say unicorns exist; rather they reference it in such phrases as "the strength of a unicorn." But the books of Job and Isaiah use the word as if these creatures actually do exist.

The mention of unicorns is raised often by atheists and agnostics to show that the Bible isn't real (as I'm doing here). But there are, of course, plenty of Christians who will come up with all sorts of the same, usual excuses about why such arguments against the Bible are unfair.

Some fundamentalist Christians will go the route of Kent Hovind's claims about dragons and simply say that unicorns really do exist. But many don't. Even many of the literalists will default to their favorite old standby, mistranslation. In the case of unicorns, I found several web sites claiming that the word unicorn is simply mistranslated. In fact, if you search the different versions of the Bible, while the King James Version shows nine instances of unicorn, the New International Version, for example, shows no instances. The word unicorn has been replaced in those translations with other words, typically *wild ox*. (Of course, that presents a bit of a problem, I suppose, for the people who feel the King James Version is the only true, literal version.)

When you look at the path of translation, however, it does start to appear that the word was mistranslated. The King James Version of the Bible was translated from early Greek versions of the Bible. The Old Testament, however, wasn't originally in Greek; it was translated from the early Hebrew documents to Greek. The Greeks who did the translation could easily have just been confused about what creature was being referred to, because in the Greek translation, the word is monoceros (mono=one, ceros=horn). In the English translation, a single-horned animal could be a unicorn. But indeed, virtually all other English translations of the Bible do not use the word unicorn, opting for words like ox, as I mentioned.

That scenario seems feasible and forgivable. But there's a problem, because it gets even stranger when you explore what on Earth this creature was in the original Hebrew; that's when it truly begins to take on a mythological feel and becomes rather bizarre.

The original Hebrew word, written in English characters with vowels included, is re'em, sometimes spelled just reem without the apostrophe.

What exactly is a re'em? A re'em is a mythological creature that appears in ancient Hebrew writings, both in the Old Testament, as well as in other rabbinic literature of the ancient Hebrews. It's the rabbinic literature that provides some insight, particularly a story in a section of literature known as the *Midrash Tehillim*. Now admittedly, this story is outside of the Bible, and so virtually all Christians reject it as being truly the word of God, and as such, not likely to be taken seriously by many Christians, if any at all. However, this does provide some insight as to what the ancient Hebrew people were referring to.

This particular story in the *Midrash Tehillim* tells us more about King David. King David is credited by Christians as having written many of the Psalms. One verse in Psalms 22 refers to how David was rescued from the re'em (or unicorn in King James Version, wild oxen in most other translations).

But in the *Midrash Tehillim*, there's a story that seems to explain this verse. Now I have to be fully truthful here: I have not read the story directly. I have not found an English translation of the story, and have to instead rely on secondary sources and tertiary sources. But all these sources seem to agree on the general nature of the story. King David was traveling in the wilderness and happened upon a re'em. Again, the story doesn't say what a re'em was, but it describes it as being so huge that David thought it was a mountain, and he began to climb it. This woke the creature, who then lifted David high into the sky with his horns. (Note the plural here. More on that shortly.) God came and rescued David by sending a lion. The lion is the king of the beasts, and so the re'em quickly submitted to its king. And the story goes on to tell how David was rescued in turn from the lion, and so on. And David then vows to build a temple as high as the re'em's horns, which was 100 ells high. (An ell is an ancient form of measurement, although it doesn't appear in the Bible; it's hard to say when this measurement crept into the story.)

It's not clear to scholars when this story was written. Some scholars say it was written as early as 100BC. That's long after the Psalms were written, and that could be why the story never made it into the Old Testament. But it is apparently based on a much more ancient tradition of stories which date way back. Regardless, it provides us a bit of clue into the mind of the ancient Hebrews and what exactly a re'em is. And one thing is clear; the description is of a creature that doesn't really exist; it's mythical.

Indeed, some Christians today acknowledge it as a creature that doesn't exist today. (This isn't true of all Christians, but more so of the literalists.) I've seen some accounts where people go to great lengths to explain that the re'em was a huge creature much like we think of a unicorn and that the creature died in Noah's flood. Of course, that is not in the Bible, and is just one more example of people embellishing the Bible to fit their needs. But as you'll see in the next section on Noah, that story in particular has had loads of embellishments to make an absurdly impossible story work in the minds of believers. In some stories of Noah and the re'ems, claims are made that the re'ems (and other large creatures) were put on the boat as babies so they would fit, but the re'ems later died after the flood. And probably the most bizarre story I encountered was where the re'ems were too big to fit so Noah tied them to a rope and dragged them behind the boat, and they swam as long as they could but eventually drowned. (Where do people come up with this stuff!)

Of course, I want to be absolutely clear: These are stories outside of the Bible and clearly outside mainstream Christianity. Most mainstream Christians would not buy into them any more than I do. And so I'm not using this as reasoning for why I no longer accept Christianity. Rather, I'm using it as one more example of how mythology overlaps the Bible; noting such is unavoidable.

Before I leave the re'ems and unicorns behind, I want to say something about the number of horns. If you search the web to get the low-down on the word unicorn appearing in the Bible, many people claim it was just an accident by the early scholars who translated the Old Testament into Greek. And they'll point out that the creature couldn't be a *monoceros* (single-horned animal) because the Bible clearly states the creature had multiple horns. This is true. Deuteronomy 33:17 mentions a re'em, translated as unicorn in the King James Version, and refers to it as having multiple horns. The same is true for Psalms 22, a verse I mentioned earlier. But Psalms 92 uses singular:

> *But my horn shalt thou exalt like the horn of an unicorn: I shall*
> *be anointed with fresh oil. (Psalms 92:10)*

Again, this could be referring to only one of multiple horns; it's hard to say.

Regardless, there's definitely a mythological bent here. A creature called a re'em, which nobody seems to be able to describe, appears in the Bible, a creature that seems to exhibit mythological characteristics.

So let's move on to the next mythological creature. In the King James Version of the book of Isaiah, the word *satyr* appears twice:

> *But wild beasts of the desert shall lie there; and their houses shall*
> *be full of doleful creatures; and owls shall dwell there, and satyrs*
> *shall dance there. (Isaiah 13:21)*
> *The wild beasts of the desert shall also meet with the wild beasts of*

*the island, and the satyr shall cry to his fellow; the screech owl also
shall rest there, and find for herself a place of rest. (Isaiah 34:14)*

A satyr was a creature in ancient Greek and Roman mythology; it was
half man, and half goat.

Just as the re'em is translated as *wild ox* in most English versions, satyr
is translated as *wild goat*. Some even translate it as *shaggy goat*. But some,
however, go so far as to change the meaning altogether from some kind of
animal to a demon. A translation called *Bible in Basic English* translates it
as *evil spirits*. But I should qualify that one a bit: This particular translation
was compiled by S.H. Hooke. S.H. Hooke was a 20th-century mythology
expert (1874-1968), and wrote a book called *Middle Eastern Mythology* that
I've drawn on from time to time in researching this book, and mention in
the bibliography. It's doubtful that most Christians today would consider his
translation authentic and inspired by God. And from all the translations I
checked, his is the only one that translates the satyrs to *evil spirits*.

However, there is some merit to Hooke's translation. The original Hebrew word that was translated in the King James Version to satyr is שעירים,
which simply means a hairy creature. But in Isaiah 13:21, it's accompanied by
the word ורקדו, which means to dance. Thus in this case, it's talking about a
dancing hairy creature.

But what dancing hairy creatures are these? The Old Testament was
translated to Greek in the first century BC by Hebrew scholars, resulting in
a version of the Old Testament called the Septuagint, as I explained at the
beginning of this chapter. And what word does the Septuagint use here? It
uses the Greek word σατυροι, or, in English letters, satyroi, which means
satyr. And it's accompanied by the word χορευει (horeyei in English letters),
which means dancing. So we have a dancing satyr.

This explains a great deal. Today, many Christians think of the goat as
being a Satanic symbol. In ancient times, the Hebrews adopted many of the
gods and mythical creatures of those cultures around them, and felt they
really existed, but demoted them to demon status. The satyr is likely one
such creature. The satyr was a mythical goat-like creature. And in the Bible
we have two references to such a creature. Some translations call it a goat;
at least one calls it a dancing demon. Now we can see one place where this
symbol comes from.

In fact, the symbol of the goat representing a demon appears elsewhere,
just not translated as a hairy, dancing satyr, but rather, simply as a goat.

Leviticus 17:7 speaks of people sacrificing to devils. The New International Version calls them devils, but includes a footnote that says "O demons." Young's Literal Translation, which is basically a word-for-word translation into English, calls them neither devils or demons, but goats! And interestingly, a version used by some Jews called the Jewish Publication Society Tanakh reverts back to the word satyr.

And thus we once again have an instance of a creature that is mythological appearing in the Bible, and indeed, one that has evolved further into a symbol of evil. And this connects us back to my earlier discussion about Satan, and provides one more piece of evidence that Satan, and now the symbols representing Satan, are nothing more than elements of mythology.

Most mainstream Christians simply write off these mythological creatures as mistranslations and consider the new and revised translations (jackal, etc.) as the correct word.

But you do have to wonder, how did these words end up in the Bible at all? How could a deity who is all-knowing and all-power allow blatantly fake, pretend animals to make it into a book that is supposed to be holy and right?

Of Nephilim and Giants

Although this is a topic I could have discussed in the previous section, I wanted to devote an entire section to it to draw special attention to it. I suspect this section will catch the eye of some perusing this book, as a lot of speculation has been made in recent years on what exactly the Nephilim are.

The word Nephilim appears twice in the Bible, but only in some versions. It doesn't appear at all in the King James Version. Here are the verses used in the NIV. The first comes from Genesis. (Note that the NIV is filled with footnotes given by letters in brackets, and I provided the ones for this passage at the end of the passage. The small raised numbers are the verse numbers.)

> [1] *When men began to increase in number on the earth and daughters were born to them,* [2] *the sons of God saw that the daughters of men were beautiful, and they married any of them they chose.* [3] *Then the LORD said, "My Spirit will not contend*

with [a] man forever, for he is mortal [b] ; his days will be a hundred and twenty years."

⁴ The Nephilim were on the earth in those days—and also afterward—when the sons of God went to the daughters of men and had children by them. They were the heroes of old, men of renown. (Genesis 6: 1-4, NIV. Footnote [a] is "Or My spirit will not remain in". Footnote [b] is "Or corrupt".)

And now from the book of Numbers:

³¹ But the men who had gone up with him said, "We can't attack those people; they are stronger than we are." ³² And they spread among the Israelites a bad report about the land they had explored. They said, "The land we explored devours those living in it. All the people we saw there are of great size. ³³ We saw the Nephilim there (the descendants of Anak come from the Nephilim). We seemed like grasshoppers in our own eyes, and we looked the same to them." (Numbers 13:31-33, NIV)

The mention in Genesis is strange, to say the least. It's saying that the "sons of God" bred with the "daughters of men." This seems like it's implying that some kind of deities procreated with humans, who gave birth to hybrid creatures called Nephilim. The passage in Numbers is part of a story where Moses sent some people ahead into a new land to explore it. (The land was Canaan.) The explorers came back and reported that the land was inhabited by huge people, the Nephilim.

Before explaining what's going on here, I want to show you what the King James Version says for the two verses mentioning Nephilim (the emphasis is my own):

*There were **giants** in the earth in those days… (Genesis 6:4, first part)*
*And there we saw the **giants**, the sons of Anak … (Numbers 13:33, first part)*

In both places, the word used is giants instead of Nephilim. And the Young's Literal Translation is interesting for the Genesis passage:

*The **fallen ones** were in the earth in those days... (Genesis 6:4, first part)*

(However, the Numbers passage in Young's Literal Translation says Nephilim.)

So in the different translations, we have Nephilim, giants, and fallen ones. (The Hebrew texts use a word that roughly translates to fallen; the Greek texts use a word that translates to giants.) And in the book of Numbers we have that these people were descendents of somebody named Anak.

It's not clear who Anak is supposed to be. Recently, some people have tried to relate the name to gods of other area religions, but I'm not going to go that route because it's purely speculative. Instead, I'll leave it that we don't know who this character is supposed to refer to. (The name does appear a few more times in the Bible, but who he is isn't very clear in those verses either.)

Earlier in this chapter I mentioned the Book of Enoch. This book presents a bit of a problem for Christianity, as it's not considered part of the Bible, and as such, not considered to be inspired by God. But the book is referenced in the book of Jude, which *is* canonical (that is, part of the official Bible). This should force most Christians to decide: If Jude is real and inspired by God, shouldn't Enoch be as well, since Jude mentions Enoch? And why isn't Enoch canonical?

The reason I bring up the book of Enoch is it has some bizarre things in it, one of which is a fairly detailed description of what the Nephilim are. This section of Enoch is called The Book of the Watchers. Here we have 200 fallen angels who came to Earth and impregnated human women, who in turn gave birth to giants. These giants were evil and ate people and sinned against the animals (whatever that means), and they even started eating each other and drinking each other's blood.

Another non-canonical book called the Book of Jubilee provides a similar story. In this version, the fallen angels were supposedly descendents of Seth, Adam's third son, and the human women were daughters of Cain (Adam's other surviving son). And here we find out that the hybrid children that were born, the giant Nephilim, were destroyed during the flood.

This is interesting when you consider where the mention of Nephilim occurs in the Old Testament. It's right at the beginning of the story of Noah. Genesis 6 talks about how the Nephilim were present, and then it immediately seems to change the topic in a rather abrupt, disjointed manner, talking about how wicked man had become on Earth. The Nephilim are in verses 1 through 4, and then verse 5 starts the story of Noah, beginning with the wickedness of men. The two seem unrelated, until you start reading some of the other literature such as Enoch and Jubilee. Then it all fits together as a horribly strange, obviously mythological story where fallen angels or deities had sex with human women and produced a breed of hybrid man-gods who were enormous giants and who were ultimately killed off by God through the Great Flood.

This story is obviously mythological and there is no way it could possibly be taken seriously. But as is usual with so much of Christianity, when faced with something that is obviously fake, Christians come up with a replacement version in their minds to fix it. The replacement version is not in the Bible. But to the devout Christian, the story itself, since it's in the Bible, *is absolutely true.* But since this creates an obvious dilemma in the Christian's mind (Giants? The Bible says Giants used to exist?), the Christian is forced to come up with a replacement version that works in his or her mind.

The idea of the Nephilim was problematic to St. Augustine, a man I briefly mentioned in Chapter 2, and who I describe in more detail in "Cult of Sin" in Chapter 7.

St. Augustine lived several centuries after the stories of the Nephilim were written. Therefore, any interpretation he has of the stories is just that: His own personal interpretation to make the story work for him, since the original story is quite obviously unbelievable and mythological.

The interpretation given by St. Augustine and others is that there were two separate lines of descendents from Adam: One line was evil and descended from Adam's son Cain, the one who killed his brother Abel. The other line descended from Adam's third son, Seth, and that line consisted of good people. The claim is that the Nephilim descended from Cain, and the two lines were mixing and marrying.

Of course, that's just another instance of a feel-good replacement to what's in the Bible, because, as-is, the story is unbelievable and obviously fabricated.

St. Augustine lived from 354AD to 430AD. But even much later theologians were still arguing for the literal story that fallen angels were procreating with human women.

What's strange about Augustine's idea, however, is that whereas the original verses seem to suggest that the angels in the story are evil fallen angels,

Augustine felt that the "Sons of God" were the good ones, descended from Seth, and that the men from this line married the women from the evil line who descended from Cain. In other words, as is so often done in the Church, women are associated with evil.

Of course, it doesn't matter what Augustine believed, because this story is obviously yet one more myth included in a Bible that is so filled with myths, and Augustine simply did what everybody else did; he attempted to fix it and make it into something real—when it isn't. Indeed, I found a Catholic priest online who had written a commentary about this story, and he said he finds Augustine's version more "satisfying." I can't help but wonder if he really means to suggest that people are free to manipulate the Bible as they see fit to transform it into whatever is most "satisfying."

Just Plain Nuttiness

One person who has helped many of us escape the shackles of Christianity is a man named Dan Barker. Dan Barker has lived a rather fascinating life, going from one extreme to the other. He started out his life as a fundamentalist preacher, traveling from church to church, giving powerful sermons. At first he believed every word of his sermons, but over time he started to question what he was saying. Then one day it suddenly hit him: God doesn't exist. It's all untrue. At that moment he accepted he was an atheist. After that he started writing books and giving talks about how he managed to break free from Christianity. Today he's co-president, along with his wife, of the Freedom from Religion Foundation.

Having lived the life of a fundamentalist preacher, Dan Barker has been able to provide a unique perspective on Christianity. Many of us have lived the life of a Christian, but he has lived it at an extreme level, as a traveling fundamentalist preacher.

As a result, he probably knows the Bible better than most Christians do. And in an article he wrote*, he talked about an organized debate he had back in 1997 with a well-known, respected theologian. The title of this debate was *God and the Bible: Fact or Fable.*

In preparing for the debate, Dan Barker started out where most people might start: He got out the dictionary and looked up the word *fable*. And he was surprised to find out that one fundamental requirement for a story to

* For the article, see http://www.theskepticalreview.com/tsrmag/976serp.html.

be considered a fable is that it must be a moral tale involve *talking animals*. Surprised by this, Barker looked up the word in several other dictionaries and found that this requirement was common. Thus, a story with talking animals that is supposed to teach something moral is a *fable*.

Well, the Bible is certainly supposed to teach some morals. But talking animals?

In researching this book, I found several instances of just plain nuttiness in the Bible. And, of course, one of the most well-known "nuttinesses" is the story of the snake that talked to Eve in the beginning of Genesis. And as Dan Barker cleverly points out, this tidbit implies that, by definition, the Bible is a fable!

And it turns out there are several instances of talking animals in the Bible. One particularly bizarre example is in the book of Numbers, where a man gets upset at his donkey (or his ass, if you will) and beats the donkey. He does this three times and then the donkey talks! Look it up for yourself; it's in Numbers chapter 22.

Of course, the Bible makes the claim that it's God's voice coming through the donkey. Yes, God needs to speak to this man, and instead of opting for a snake as the devil did, he makes use of the next best thing: talking out this man's ass. (Okay, although I just made a joke, the story *does* say that God talked through the man's donkey, and that, frankly, deserves to be made fun of just a bit.)

In addition to talking animals, I did encounter some additional nuttiness. Somebody put together an excellent web page that runs down what he considers the nuttiest things in the Bible. You can find the page at http://www.infidels.org/library/modern/donald_morgan/absurd.html.

One item that I found in addition to this fine list was in Daniel 4. In this chapter, King Nebuchadnezzar was sent to the desert and ate "grass like cattle" while his hair "grew like the feathers of an eagle." And we're supposed to take this literally? And if not, we're supposed to consider it inspired by God?

The Myth of Noah and of "Kind"

The sheer absurdity of the story of Noah's Ark has been covered in great detail elsewhere outside of this book. The best breakdown and dismantling of the story I've seen is written by Adrian Barnett and can be found at

http://www.abarnett.demon.co.uk/atheism/noahs_ark.html

(If the page ever comes down, Google the four words **"Adrian Barnett"** **"Noah's Ark"** with double-quotes as I have here and you'll probably find a copy somewhere.)

What I'd like to do here is tackle the issue of whether the story is allegorical, and whether it was influenced by earlier myths.

I'll get right to it: It's not allegory. It's myth; it never happened, whether literally or allegorically. Some people have suggested that maybe the flood happened but didn't cover the whole world, only the "known" world.

But that's not what the Bible says. It says, "all the high hills, that were under the whole heaven, were covered," (Genesis 7:19) and "the mountains were covered" (verse 20).

And verses 21 through 23 make it pretty clear that all land-life died, not just that around the "known" world:

> *And all flesh died that moved upon the earth, both of fowl, and of cattle, and of beast, and of every creeping thing that creepeth upon the earth, and every man:*
> *All in whose nostrils was the breath of life, of all that was in the dry land, died.*
> *And every living substance was destroyed which was upon the face of the ground, both man, and cattle, and the creeping things, and the fowl of the heaven; and they were destroyed from the earth: and Noah only remained alive, and they that were with him in the ark. (Genesis 7:21-23)*

If somebody were to suggest that "every living substance was destroyed" really means only those in the known area around Noah, then they're being dishonest. They're changing it to fit their fancy. And if we're free to modify it to fit our fancy, then where do we stop?

We must decide: Either it's true or it isn't. Yes or no. And I say no. There is no possible way this story actually happened, and I'm not about to try to modify it until it feels right for me so I can continue believing it. It didn't happen. Period.

Besides, there are some immediate questions: How could Noah have picked up the marsupials which live in Australia? (Or, even if they didn't supposedly originate in Australia, how could he have dropped them off there after the flood?) And seriously, how could Noah have possibly carried the tens of millions of species currently known?

I've mentioned Ken Ham earlier in this book, the man who built the Creation Museum in Northern Kentucky outside of Cincinnati. Ken Ham has created a rather complex, sophisticated explanation of how the animals dispersed after being let off the ark—animals which, I should add, included dinosaurs!—and how the animals morphed and changed quite rapidly. In fact, many Creationists I've heard who reject evolution have tried to point out that Noah didn't take individual *species*, but rather he took *kinds* of animals. Apparently to these people, the word kind is a classification of animal. But it isn't. It's a made-up classification created by Creationists to justify a mythological story that otherwise isn't realistic by any rational means.

In addition to the obvious absurdities, the myth has been found to be directly influenced by older myths—including a Babylonian myth, which in turn was influenced by an even older Sumerian myth.

The older, the Sumerian myth, involves a story whereby the gods decide to wipe out all of mankind, except for one rather good man and his family. The Sumerian god Enki is the one who helps the man build a boat so he can be safe from the rising waters.

In the Babylonian form of the myth, which came after the Sumerian one and served as a heavy influence to the Hebrew Noah story, the gods decide to flood the planet. A god named Ea helps a man named Utnapishtim build a ship. The man is to gather every type of animal and bring them all onto the ship. (In this version, he's instructed to bring "the seed of all living things.") And just like the Noah version, this version describes the exact dimensions of the ship. The man builds the ship, and the storm comes for six nights. On the seventh day the storm ends. (See the parallels also to the creation story? However, the Noah version has it raining for 40 days and 40 nights.) In this Babylonian version of the story, like the Noah version, the ship finally lands on the top of a mountain, in this case one called Mt. Nisar (as opposed to Mt. Ararat where Noah's ship lands).

And also just like the Noah story, this man sends out a dove to find dry land other than just the mountain top. The dove returns with no indication of dry land, just like in the Noah story. Next he sends out a different type of bird. (In the Noah story, the second time he sends another dove.) The bird again finds no indication of dry land. (The Noah story is slightly different in that the bird returns with an olive leaf.) He then sends out a third bird, which does not return, just like in the Noah story (except the types of birds differ again in the two stories.)*

Certainly there are some minor differences. But the similarities are too great to ignore. Remember, these stories were passed down orally, and absorbed from one culture to another, and were certainly modified to fit the local beliefs of the culture. The stories changed a little, but the fact that this story originated with earlier myths is clear and undeniable.

Now some people have suggested that there might have been a great flood that took place in ancient times. Even skeptics have suggested there's evidence of a flood. Maybe. Maybe not. But one thing is sure: If there was a flood, the story of Noah herding all the animals onto an ark that he built still didn't happen. It's an ancient myth that was copied from earlier myths, and scientifically we know it never occurred anyway, and therefore can safely be disregarded.

The Tower of Babel Myth

People refuse to accept the reality of evolution as they hold onto the myth of creation. But it's astounding that they also hold onto another ancient story that is obviously made up: The story of the Tower of Babel.

As I mentioned in the first chapter of this book, the Tower of Babel was pretty much what started it all toppling for me. I had mostly let go of the Creation myth, but I did hold on to certain aspects of it, and considered much of it just allegorical. But the Tower of Babel presented serious trouble for me, because I knew that history tells us that the languages of the world did *not* originate there.

The story itself is actually quite short in the Bible. Here it is, in its entirety:

> *And the whole earth was of one language, and of one speech. And it came to pass, as they journeyed from the east, that they found a plain in the land of Shinar; and they dwelt there. And they said one to another, Go to, let us make brick, and burn them thoroughly. And they had brick for stone, and slime had they for mortar. And they said, Go to, let us build us a city and a tower, whose top may reach unto heaven; and let us make us a name, lest we be scattered*

---

* This Babylonian myth comes from the Epic of Gilgamesh, Tablet 11. You can Google **Epic of Gilgamesh** to learn more about it.

abroad upon the face of the whole earth. And the LORD came down to see the city and the tower, which the children of men builded. And the LORD said, Behold, the people is one, and they have all one language; and this they begin to do: and now nothing will be restrained from them, which they have imagined to do. to, let us go down, and there confound their language, that they may not understand one another's speech. So the LORD scattered them abroad from thence upon the face of all the earth: and they left off to build the city. Therefore is the name of it called Babel; because the LORD did there confound the language of all the earth: and from thence did the LORD scatter them abroad upon the face of all the earth. (Genesis 11:1-9)

After being away from Christianity for some time, this story strikes me as shockingly mythical. First, there's the interesting little tidbit about the people discovering brick and mortar, which seems to be a separate story in itself. But it's the next part that's particularly bizarre. God comes down from Heaven and looks at the building and is frightened that the people will become unstoppable and able to do anything.

Let's get this straight: This is a god who supposedly created the entire universe and is supposedly capable of flooding the entire planet to "reboot" humanity, and yet he's frightened that if the people build this tower they'll become some kind of super-people, able to do anything imaginable? He feels threatened by them? Why would a powerful god feel threatened by his own people?

And then the myth turns into some kind of historical nonsense, suggesting that this is where the different languages of the world originated.

Now we know for a fact that the languages that were used in ancient China, for example, did *not* originate here. Yet the Bible says that prior to this the whole world was of one language. Clearly, the Bible is *wrong* here.

A more liberally-minded Christian could pull a cop-out and simply say it's allegorical. But that doesn't change the fact that it's a non-truth, a *lie*. And thus this book could not have been written by a god who is supposed to be morally perfect.

This is also a place where there's a contradiction in the Bible. The previous chapter of the Bible describes a totally different situation where people were dispersed into different languages! That's something most Christians

I've met have not even realized. (Partly because most Christians hear these stories in bits and pieces each Sunday throughout the year; most Christians don't read it straight through.) Look at the first five verses of the previous chapter, Chapter 10, which describes Noah's family going off and creating different nations:

> *Now these are the generations of the sons of Noah, Shem, Ham, and Japheth: and unto them were sons born after the flood. The sons of Japheth; Gomer, and Magog, and Madai, and Javan, and Tubal, and Meshech, and Tiras. And the sons of Gomer; Ashkenaz, and Riphath, and Togarmah. And the sons of Javan; Elishah, and Tarshish, Kittim, and Dodanim. By these were the isles of the Gentiles divided in their lands; every one after his tongue, after their families, in their nations. (Genesis 10:1-5)*

Chapter 10 states that different nations formed, each with their own language. Then Chapter 11 states that the people had all one language. Unless these stories are somehow in the wrong chronological order, they can't both be correct. Thus, a contradiction exists, and at least one is a falsehood. (Really, though, they're both false, having originated in nothing more than ancient myths.)

In fact, some mythologists such as S.H. Hooke suggest that the story of the Flood and the story of the Tower of Babel are two independent, separate, and certainly contradictory mythological legends of how the nations and languages formed, and that an ancient editor compiled the two stories together into a single book.

But aside from that, there are some really odd things about this story in the parts I called mythical—at least they seem odd, until you start reading other myths from the same region.

There's this character of God coming down from Heaven, just like some kind of superhuman might do. And he's talking to others, just as the gods in other ancient myths do. Clearly, this is a character straight in line with other myths, a god who is more of a superhuman who has others around him that he talks to, and a god who physically comes down to interact with people.

Now admittedly, the story doesn't say that God physically came down. And as such, most Christians would assume it means there was some kind of spiritual presence. But put into the context of all the other ancient, mythological stories, it's clearly nothing more than just another example of a god character coming down just as the gods in the other ancient myths did. And as such, this is nothing more than a myth.

In fact, this myth strongly resembles a myth from the earliest people of the region, the Sumerians. The myth is called Enmerkar and the Lord of Aratta. In this myth, the people are building a great big tower just like many towers that existed in Babylon—a *ziggurat*—and the gods come down and end up dispersing the languages. The translation, however, isn't clear; some people claim the people were combined into a single language. The story has many differences from the Tower of Babel story, such as the purpose for the building of the tower, as well as there being multiple gods involved. However, the fact that the story is about a tower being built and languages being formed is a pretty strong indication that it served as an influence on the Hebrew story.

The fact is, it's just myth. The story of the Tower of Babel simply didn't happen. It's a myth and there is no reason whatsoever to believe that it really happened.

The Myth of Revelation

During my later years as a Christian, I considered the final book of the Bible, Revelation, a major thorn in the side of Christianity. The reason was that I found it totally unbelievable. Remember, I was Lutheran, and indeed, Martin Luther, the founder of the Lutheran church (the first major breakaway from Catholicism) felt Revelation had little value. But he reluctantly chose to keep it in the Bible; however, to this day, the Lutheran church rarely talks about Revelation. (In the next chapter, Dissecting Christianity, I talk about opinions of Revelation in more detail and the impact on Christianity today.)

Revelation provides many stories that are supposedly going to happen in the future. And today many Fundamentalist Christians state as fact that the stories in Revelation *will* happen, probably sooner rather than later. And they point to many events that have already happened that are supposedly predicted by Revelation.

Unfortunately for them, there are scholars who actually study the form of writing used in Revelation, call *apocryphal* writing, a form that was used in many other writings outside the Bible. And such scholars warn us to use extreme caution when trying to interpret Revelation. (The book is written in a style used to convey information without saying anything treasonous.)

But what of the predictions in Revelation that already have supposedly come true? Look at Nostradamus. He was a writer who lived in the early 16th century and wrote books offering predictions. Many of his prophecies "seem" to come have come true when you take a modern event, and twist and turn and interpret his writings and find a potential match.

Yet most Christians don't believe what Nostradamus wrote. Why not? They consider the matching of events with the predictions mere coincidence, and rightly so. Anyone can write a book about what's going to happen in the future. Considering how many people are on the planet and what all goes on, if you look hard enough you'll find that some of your predictions will come true, provided they're not specific enough.

Nobody has ever used Nostradamus' writings to successfully predict a specific event and, if the event is a bad one, to prevent it. Only after the fact have people forced the issue by trying to fit his prophecies to an event after the event happened.

The talented Las Vegas magician Criss Angel even talked about something similar on the TV show *Phenomenon*, of which he was a judge. He said, "…if on 9/10 somebody could have predicted that 9/11 was going to happen, they could have saved millions of lives." Indeed, nobody, whether using Nostradamus' writings *or the Book of Revelation*, or any source whatsoever—had predicted 9/11.*

Now think about the Book of Revelation. Many times I have heard the claim made that the prophecies are coming true. But the only way anyone can make it appear that the prophecies are coming true is to point either to the incredibly vague ones, or to re-interpret the specific ones in a wildly imaginative manner, just as some people do with Nostradamus' predictions.

For example, 666, the supposed number of the Beast, simply refers to Nero Caesar, the Roman Emperor at the time of the writing (because it was considered treason to write negative commentary about the rulers back then). But using absurd imagination, people claim that 666 refers to the number of some modern world leader or one that will soon exist. But that claim has been made for centuries, and, I hate to be the one to break the news, the world is still here. Any time people have tried to apply the prophesies to modern times, they have been wrong.

---

* Some people claim Nostradamus predicted 9/11. But the paragraph they refer to was not even written by Nostradamus; it was a forgery. See http://www.snopes.com/rumors/nostradamus.asp.

Other people have used a great deal of creative imagination to make the prophecies "work". For example, there are some people who think Social Security numbers are the mark of the beast, which, according to Revelation, is a mark that will be placed on the forehead of people. Others think the new chip implants some people are pushing are the mark of the beast. None of these are real. (Plus, Social Security numbers couldn't be the mark, since they're only used in the United States.) At the time Revelation was written, people viewed the entire world as their own area and surrounding countries, and they couldn't fathom today's world spanning multiple continents with hundreds of separate countries, and they certainly couldn't imagine what the world would be like in 2000 years.

Going back and forcing a prophecy to fit into something that has already happened is often called *retroactive clairvoyance*. Try Googling that phrase and you'll find a lot of articles on it. You can also look up *postdiction* as well as *hindsight bias*, as these are other terms for similar ideas.

The fact is that Revelation was written referring to events of the time and has no bearing on events today.

No Evidence

One of the fundamental shortcomings of the Bible is the total lack of physical evidence mixed with the contradiction of other historical records.

Many times I've heard people say, "We have evidence in the form of ancient writings; these writings are now called *the Bible*." However, the Bible alone is not enough. As I already described, there are thousands of ancient writings that are just made-up stories. Indeed, most Christians agree that these other ancient stories, such as stories about Zeus, for example, are simply man-made and not to be taken seriously. So why single out the ancient Hebrew texts as being special? Of course, that challenge won't even be considered by Christians, because they'll just answer that the ancient Hebrew texts are special because they come from God. But that would prove my point: *Just because there's an ancient piece of writing doesn't mean it is to be taken as historically true.* And surely we are all in agreement on that.

And so what is left? Just a bunch of documents with no physical evidence. There is absolutely no archeological evidence to back up the outrageous claims made in the Old Testament. None. There are people who claim there are, but they are deluding themselves, because in the same way there are Creationists claiming scientific proof against all real evidence, there are rogue archeologists who likewise claim proof against all real evidence.

One thing people occasionally point out is the fact that the Bible mentions real, historical figures such as various kings and rulers. That is true. But all that proves is a timeframe in which the documents might have been written. But even that only provides a huge window, since technically that just points to an earliest point in time. A document that mentions Julius Caesar, for example, couldn't have been written before Julius Caesar existed, but it could have been written anytime after.

In fact, there are other things in the Bible that strongly imply they were written after the time they supposedly took place. Now certainly the books in the Old Testament are very old; nobody is disputing that, and they were written before the time that Jesus supposedly existed. That we agree on. But two issues that factor into their dating are when the various alphabets and written languages were developed, as well as the cultures described in the Bible.

Remember, archeology is a highly specialized field that requires years of training. Archeologists aren't just digging up old junk and talking about how pretty or unusual these artifacts are. Rather, when they perform a dig, they carefully note exactly where each item was found. Using many different techniques, they can start to piece together cultural information. And they can compare the information to that of the surrounding areas.

Babylon and Egypt in particular have very rich histories and a great deal is known about them, since they were far more advanced civilizations than surrounding areas such as Israel. And from those rich histories it's possible to figure out timeframes for the cultural and business activities that took place.

In the same way that a mention of a historical figure implies a document couldn't have been written prior to that historical figure, a mention of various technologies or customs imply the document couldn't pre-date those technologies and customs. For example, if somebody found a document that was supposedly written in the 19th century, and that document mentions an Intel dual-core microprocessor, then I think we would all agree the document could not have been written prior to the 21st century.

In the Bible we have that happening. People have found many such instances. The most commonly-mentioned example is in the following verse, from the story of how Joseph, son of Jacob (also called Israel) was sold into slavery by his brothers:

> *And they sat down to eat bread: and they lifted up their eyes and looked, and, behold, a company of Ishmeelites came from Gilead with their camels bearing spicery and balm and myrrh, going to carry it down to Egypt. (Genesis 37:25)*

But there's a problem here. The author of this story is speaking of the camels carrying various products for trade. But the problem is we know from other history and archeology that this trade with Egypt didn't begin until several centuries after this story supposedly took place.

This means that clearly the story was written much later than it supposedly happened.

In fact, speaking of camels, the archeological and historical records tell us that camels were domesticated and used starting about 1000 to 1500 BC, which is after many of the stories in Genesis are supposed to have taken place—yet, camels are mentioned throughout the Bible, as early as Genesis 12, when Abram acquired them (before his name was changed to Abraham).

Bible experts consider Abraham to have been born some three hundred years earlier than the absolute earliest date that camels were domesticated. So how could Abraham have had camels? Again, the obvious answer is that the author wrote the story long after Abraham supposedly existed. (Of course, I should point out that there is absolutely no proof, archeological or otherwise, that Abraham even existed.)

Now let's put this into perspective: It's clear that the stories in the Bible were written down *several hundred years* after they supposedly took place. The general assumption among Christians is that prior to the stories being written down, that they were passed on by word of mouth.

And realistically, how reliable could that possibly have been? Many Christians have claimed that in this case it's 100% reliable because God supposedly managed the stories and made sure they were passed down accurately before being written down.

But obviously that couldn't possibly be the case, because there were references to cultural items that didn't even exist at the time the story supposedly took place.

Clearly, then, a supposed deity—God—wasn't managing the stories. Combine that with the lack of any physical evidence that people like Moses or

Abraham or Noah even existed, and you're left with a rather empty plate.

But just to make matters worse for the state of Christianity, archeologists have found plenty of evidence of civilization in other parts of the world, which conflicts with the Biblical account. There is strong evidence that horses were domesticated in the Ukraine area around 4000 BC. This is about the time the Biblical account claims creation took place! And archeologists have located tools in Vietnam to date to this same period, or even earlier.

But that's nothing: Pottery dating to 10,000 BC has been found in Japan. And even farther away from ancient Israel, all the way in North America, plenty of evidence of early humans has been found. This evidence also dates back to 10,000 BC. (This, of course, has resulted in more science that Creationists feel obliged to try to debunk, by making outrageous claims about carbon dating not being accurate, and so on.) And if that's not good enough, DNA testing has shown that dogs were domesticated possibly as early as 12,000 BC. And these dogs, of course, weren't domesticated without humans being present. But care for more? Archeologists have uncovered sophisticated tools dating to around 50,000 BC. And through extensive scientific research, modern humans date back about 150,000 years.

So why should I believe the Old Testament account when it clearly couldn't have occurred as-is? There is no reason to. There's no evidence the stories took place. They are myths.

Is it Allegorical?

I've mentioned this before and I'll say it again here. People, especially more liberal and moderate Christians, have pointed out that just because the Bible might not be literally true in every one of its stories, it doesn't mean it's not real.

Sure, there are some good lessons in the Bible. Jesus' Golden Rule of "Do unto others as you would have them do unto you" is certainly a wonderful lesson, and one that I personally live by. So why can't I accept the allegorical nature of the Bible and accept that Christianity is real?

The reason I can no longer accept it is that once you start peeling away parts of the Bible that are supposed to be just allegorical, the Bible gets slimmer and slimmer. As you continue to peel it away, you're finally left with almost nothing at all. The Bible is almost completely myth, completely allegorical. What do you have then? You have a religion that is based on the philosophies of an ancient group of people from one tiny little region of the planet. That's it.

As soon as we recognize something in the Bible that clearly contradicts what science is telling us, something that seems mythological, we're forced into a decision:

- The Bible is 100% true and science *must be* wrong
- Science is right, and the Bible contains stories that are wrong.

But if the Bible has stories that are simply myths, then we are forced to ask how that could happen. Could the Bible truly have been written by an all-knowing, perfect God and contain errors and non-truths in it?

My answer is no. It couldn't be. And therefore, it is clear to me that the Bible is *not* inspired by a god.

The stories in the Bible were nothing more than re-hashes of similar myths from nearby regions. In my own journey, realizing that the stories I believed in were nothing but re-hashes of other myths I didn't believe in pretty much made the whole thing collapse.

It soon became clear to me that all this stuff I believed in was just a myth.

Why should I accept the ancient Hebrews' god as the one true deity? In Chapter 8, I talk about Faith versus Trust, and that factors in here. I have no reason to trust this ancient Middle Eastern tribe of people for my life's lessons and for a description of what happens after I die and for stories of how the universe was created.

Rather, I'd prefer to live my life as a good person and care about other people without wasting my time worrying about whether my actions are up to par based on ancient, archaic rules and laws. And I'm certainly not going to base my actions on whether I'll be rewarded or punished after I die. I'd prefer to focus on this world and making it a better place. And believe me, when you factor in the number of wars on this planet that have been the result of religious differences, then I can't say the religious people are doing a very good job of making the world a better place. Forget the ancient myths, because that's what they are. Today's people are just as capable of coming up with good ideas and philosophies as the ancient people were. In fact, I'd say we're better, because we know today's society and culture and can make our philosophies pertinent to today—not a backwards, superstitious tribal culture from several thousand years ago that invented myths based on older myths.

So let's face it together: The Bible is predominantly *myth*. There's no denying that, so why sit around worrying about what happens to our soul after we die and whether we'll burn in Hell?

Your Own Journey and Struggles

But for those of us who have struggled with our own religious beliefs, understanding that the Bible is based on myth doesn't quite help. We can accept the Bible as myth and still find some good lessons in it. But in the same way that not liking the Bible doesn't mean the Bible isn't real, does accepting that it has myths in it make Jesus and God not real?

Indeed, the questions of God being real and of Jesus being real are two very separate issues, and here's why: It's possible to believe in one and not the other. Specifically, one can believe there's a God of sorts, but not accept that Jesus ever existed, either real or spiritually. Such people, then, by definition, are not Christians: Christians believe in Jesus Christ. And this god of sorts that one could believe in could be very different from the God described in the Bible.

The issue of whether Jesus existed or not was one I struggled with for a long time with. On one hand, it would be easy to believe in a purely spiritual Jesus and write off the entire Bible. But is that sensible?

In one way, it does make sense. People have made some pretty strong arguments that Paul, who wrote a good chunk of the New Testament, didn't believe that Jesus existed physically. Rather, they make the argument that Paul more subscribed to a pagan approach based on the earlier Greek myths, with roots in what people call Mystery religions. There's been a great deal written on this matter, and if you're interested in exploring it, check out the Bibliography. But for now, suffice to say that Paul's writings, taken alone, nearly build a religion based strictly on a spiritual Jesus that need not have existed physically.

Even if one believes Jesus exists but only spiritually, then one still is essentially a Christian—albeit an extremely liberal one with many similarities to those who practiced an early form of Christianity called Gnosticism.

Ultimately, we must each make our own decision, of course. I can't sit here and force you to believe one way or another whether Jesus is real or not, either physically or spiritually. I can present strong evidence that the Bible is based on Myth. And if you're reading this book cover-to-cover, you may be where I was about midway through my transition. But ultimately our beliefs (or lack thereof) happen inside ourselves, and nobody else can answer this for us, not even a preacher.

For now, what I advise you to do is take it slowly, as I did. At this point, I hope that you'll see that the Bible, particularly the Old Testament, is based predominantly on myth, and much of it never actually happened. Ponder that, and ask yourself plenty of questions. Don't fear any question at all. Ask the tough ones. Was Jesus real? Why are there so many people who devoutly believe what they do but are not Christian? Why are there so many varieties of Christianity? Can they all be correct? What about the other religions; could they be correct? Will those people burn in Hell, even if they're good people? Does it make sense that the single most important thing God wants is that we believe in his existence, and that such belief should trump all the good and bad acts we commit? And finally, where do our own beliefs come from? Aren't they strongly influenced by what we were taught as children, particularly by the churches our parents chose for us? And do we really have reason to believe as we do? Think of the things we strongly believed but eventually found weren't true. Wasn't that just as real as what we're taught in church?

If you care to, you might try meditating and ask yourself these questions. On a subconscious level, by asking yourself questions, you are likely to search for answers. Over time, again on a subconscious level, you will be able to start to see whether or not there's more out there. Maybe there is, maybe there isn't. And meanwhile you'll start to come up with very real answers from within.

Remember, the heart of the matter is whether Jesus is real. Ponder it; question it. And don't be afraid. I think I've made a pretty strong case that Hell doesn't exist, so what do you have to worry about? Nothing. Question your religion, and focus on opening your mind. Consider what you've read in this chapter, as it's vital to recognizing the foundation of the entire culture of Christianity that has spread throughout the planet. Is it real—the foundation, the beliefs? Think about it and question it. And don't be afraid.

Of course, the answers won't come right away. And there's plenty of more exploring to do. In the next chapter, let's peel apart the Christian Church itself and see what we end up with. That will hopefully help you question things as well and provide some greater clues to the answers.

seven

Dissecting Christianity

There are Christians who believe that other Christians are destined for Hell because the other Christians don't believe exactly what they do. (Not all Christians believe this, but a good share do.) A quick search on Google reveals many web sites created by Christians explaining why other types of Christians are wrong. For example, I found several pages by Protestants giving long, detailed explanations (usually backed by Bible verses) why Catholicism is a "false religion," and even evil. At least one I found went so far as to say that Catholicism was created by Satan himself; this particular site had many pages devoted to dismantling Catholicism, including a huge list of things the Catholic church has done over the centuries that are, as this man claims, "anti-Christian," and, thus, "heretical."

That same site, in fact, also has pages explaining why many other beliefs (other than this guy's own breed of fundamentalist Christianity) are wrong. The list of false religions include the Church of Christ, the Episcopal Church, Greek Eastern Orthodox, Lutherans, Mormons, Pentecostals, Russian Orthodox, Seventh-Day Adventists, to name the Christian breeds, as well as others such as atheism (which isn't a religion at all), Baha'i, Freemasonry (that's hardly a religion), Hinduism, Humanism (that's also not a religion), Judaism, Moonies, Scientology, Unitarian Universalism, Witchcraft, Wicca, and, of course, Satanism. (But many of us non-believers would lump Satanism with Christianity, since Satan was invented by Christians, but I digress.)

Not surprisingly, many of the web sites which profess that theirs is the only true religion tell you that if you want to know the rest of the story, you can order plenty of books, brochures, and other junk from them. In other words, they want you to *send them money*. Imagine that.

Incidentally, this particular site that I was looking at also includes a page called "I used to be a Christian (No you didn't)" and it makes the claim that if one becomes a born-again believer, he or she can't "undo" it, and therefore people like me who left Christianity were never Christians to begin with. (Of course, I was Lutheran, and the author of this page says that the Lutheran Church is "straight from Satan himself," which doubles his reasoning for why I was never a Christian in his mind. C'est la vie.) And this isn't the first time I've heard this particular claim, either, that former Christians were never Christians. But I can say this: Until my late 20's, I completely believed that Jesus was a real man and that Jesus died on the cross for our sins, and that Jesus rose from the dead and went to Heaven. I believed that Jesus now exists as a spirit, as the son of God. I completely believed it to be true. Have I ever seen George W. Bush or Bill Clinton? No, but I believe they both exist, and I believed Jesus exists as much as I believe Bush and Clinton both exist. There was no doubt at all in my mind. So was I a Christian? Of course I was.

But believe me, more than once I've been told I will go to Hell. One Christian online made it very clear in no uncertain terms that Satan is my father and that it is too late for me and that I am guaranteed to burn in Hell forever. (But if you read Chapter 6, you realize by now that Hell does not exist, nor does Satan!)

The fact is, when you start grilling individual Christians on their beliefs, you rarely find two people with *exactly* the same set of beliefs. But "belief" is an interesting thing. If you consider the word at face value, by definition the person holding the belief is convinced the belief is true; otherwise he or she wouldn't hold onto it as a belief. As such, it would seem sensible to conclude that the majority of Christians, each having his or her own unique beliefs, would likely think other Christians—with slightly different beliefs—are wrong. And, based on the large number of Christian web sites explaining why other Christians are wrong, I'm compelled to feel this is indeed the case.

This conundrum presents many challenges for Christians. First, if some-body is new to Christianity and interested in becoming a Christian, how would he or she know which type of Christian to listen to? And considering the negative way so many Christians feel about the beliefs of other Christians, Christianity is more like a huge mass of separate ideas all under the single umbrella name Christianity, almost to the point that they aren't even the same religion at all. And further, doesn't it seem logical that if Christianity varies so much, that Christianity is likely not true? Consider this: if very few Christians have precisely the same belief, then at most only a few people on the planet *are right*—assuming any people at all have *exactly* the set of beliefs that their supposed God expects them to have. For me, that's a pretty strong indication that Christianity isn't true, along with all the other reasons I've explained in this book.

Indeed, the arguments various branches of Christianity use against other branches could probably be lumped together to debunk all of Christianity, now couldn't they? The fundamentalist Protestants give us some pretty good ammunition why Catholicism is wrong, and the Catholics give us some pretty good ammunition why Protestants are wrong. Sounds like they're both wrong to me.

Curious why Catholicism is wrong? Ask the Protestants. Curious why the Protestants are wrong? Ask the Catholics. Combine them and the case is closed. Christianity is wrong. It almost seems like they don't even need help from people like me.

But what are we to really make of all the breeds of Christianity? In this chapter, before closing the book, I explore some of the types of Christians and show that there really isn't a single religion called Christianity. And as such, if there is any single branch of Christianity that is correct and real (unlikely, of course), then the chances of somebody happening to land upon that particular branch are quite unlikely indeed.

Revelation or No Revelation

I already talked about the Book of Revelation in the previous chapter. But here's how it fits into Christianity, as well as how it factors into my breaking away. Later in my days as an active Christian, I started to notice there were a lot of Christians who seemed to subscribe to ideas that I didn't. The more I explored the beliefs of these people, the more I realized that they were basing almost their entire belief system on the book of Revelation.

As I dug more into what was going on, I put my finger on it. As I mentioned in the previous chapter, in the beginning of the Protestant Church, Martin Luther had gone through the Bible and threw away several books that were present in the Catholic Bible that he felt didn't belong in the Bible.

One book he had trouble with was the book of Revelation. This book struck him as almost certainly *not* inspired by God. He came very close to throwing it into the fire (literally; he tossed several books into his fireplace as sort of a symbolic move). But looking more carefully through it, he decided that it might have had at least a few good verses and so he reluctantly decided to keep it.

The Book of Revelation is where you find a story of the end times (supposedly anyway, according to a lot of people). This is where you find the story of Jesus taking people up to Heaven in the Rapture and other people being "left behind."

Since Luther had very little respect for this book, even today the Lutherans put little emphasis on it. The preachers in the Lutheran Church spend very little time teaching about the book.

In fact, I didn't even know what the Rapture was until I was in my mid 20's. I would see those bumper stickers that said, "In the event of Rapture, this car will be un-manned," and I thought it was a joke. Later I started to realize that the people sporting those stickers were very serious. (And I had the urge to ask them how they know the Rapture didn't already happen and they were left behind!)

In general, when you encounter the type of Christian who yells a lot about how the world is going to end and that Jesus is going to come down in a blinding light and take all good Christians away, you're probably dealing with a Fundamentalist Christian who bases his or her faith almost exclusively on Revelation.

This focus on Revelation has caused one of the many great divides among Christians. People think of Christianity as being divided up into Catholics and Protestants, but I definitely have noticed a more severe difference between those who focus on Revelation and those who don't. Usually, that's the same line between Fundamentalists and what I'll call Mainstream Christians.

There's a rather vocal anti-homosexual Christian group that I mentioned earlier in this book called American Family Association. On their web site, you can order anti-homosexual propaganda in various forms, including DVDs. One DVD is called *It's Not Gay*, and is supposed to be a documentary about "former homosexuals" and it claims to expose the reality behind the homosexual lifestyle. And somewhere online I saw an ad for it, encouraging people to buy it and show it to church Sunday school classes.

Now although I consider myself a former Christian, this was a shock even to me. In the more traditional churches I attended and was familiar with, they never would have shown such a video. The traditional, mainstream Lutheran and Methodist churches that I went to never even mentioned the word homosexual.

And so I can only wonder: Do the fundamentalist churches today actually have sermons that feature anti-homosexual, gay-hating messages on Sunday morning?

People have argued that folks like Richard Dawkins and other outspoken atheists are unfairly characterizing all Christians as homophobic, right-wing fundamentalist bigots. In fact, the churches I went to were quite liberal and at least one of the Lutheran pastors called himself a liberal. These people were not gay-haters at all.

And so I know firsthand that this characterization isn't accurate. Clearly there are at least two very separate, very distinct Christian churches, a separation that seems quite independent of a Protestant/Catholic division, and independent of any denominational lines. And this distinction I've alluded to throughout this book, referring to "fundamentalist" as opposed to "mainstream" or "traditional" Christians.

When I was a member of a mainstream Christian church, I was quite shocked at some of the things I would hear and see. I would be alarmed by people who had stickers on their cars loudly proclaiming their love for Jesus. I was shocked the time I saw an argument online that had nothing to do with religion, and a woman saying she couldn't believe "Christians would behave that way," when she didn't even know the religious backgrounds of the other people in the argument. I was stunned by the people on TV all decked out in expensive jewelry, crying on TV about how the Lord has changed their lives. This was clearly not my religion. It was completely different from the religion I was familiar with.

I soon discovered the writings of a man named John Shelby Spong. He had written several controversial books, such as one titled *Why Christianity Must Change or Die: A Bishop Speaks to Believers in Exile*[*]. John Shelby Spong is a retired Bishop in the Episcopal church, and has long been labeled by many as a heretic, and an extreme liberal because of his controversial beliefs about God and Jesus. (Apparently, he rejects both the virgin birth and the physical resurrection of Jesus. You can learn more about this interesting man on his official website at http://www.johnshelbyspong.com/.)

---

* Spong, John Shelby. *Why Christianity Must Change or Die: A Bishop Speaks to Believers in Exile*. HarperOne, 1999. ISBN 978-0060675363.

I was immediately intrigued by what Spong had to say. I picked up a couple of his books and read them. They were fascinating reads, and I still have respect for him. However, it was clear that his ideas were *not* mainstream by any means. Even though the churches I attended were more liberal, this man's ideas wouldn't sit well even with them.

But even though I was a member of one portion of Christianity that was radically different from the other, my beliefs were gradually moving more and more away from what the churches were teaching, even those of the mainstream, non-fundamentalist churches that I attended. And while Spong's ideas definitely made more sense to me, his beliefs were still Christianity, and still about Jesus. In fact, reading Spong's web site, he clearly believes that a man named Jesus really existed and really did preach to the people and really did have 12 disciples—even if Spong's beliefs pretty much end with the book of Mark, the shortest Gospel, that includes no mention of a virgin birth or a physical resurrection. And so his beliefs are still Christian, albeit an unusual form of Christianity.

But is this realistic? Is it sensible to believe in only part of the Bible and reject other parts and to call oneself a Christian? Believing the book of Mark but rejecting the other four gospels means not embracing so many of the ideas that most Christians hold onto, including the virgin birth and physical resurrection of Jesus.

In the final chapter of this book, I present my final perspective on Jesus. But for now I'll say that even the book of Mark is more than I'm able to believe, because it still has its roots in the ancient stories that clearly didn't happen; they were myths. I have no reason to believe a man named Jesus ever existed.

And so from my perspective, even though Spong rejects much of the New Testament and the associated long-held beliefs, in my mind, he is still a Christian. He's an odd one, to be sure, and his unusual belief represents a tiny minority of Christianity. But he does believe in the Lord Jesus Christ, and he believes he existed, and he is, therefore, a Christian.

As such, regardless of which side of the line people sit on—fundamentalist or mainstream (or even the extreme left such as Spong)—they are all, to me, peas in a single pod. They are different, but at heart they still rely on the Christian Bible, a book filled with reinterpreted myths. In the previous chapter I presented a great deal of evidence that Christianity is built on myth. But even without that, one has to wonder how "it" can be true if there isn't even a single Christianity but rather hundreds upon hundreds of drastically different Christianities that blatantly contradict each other.

So where does that leave me? Let's keep exploring this, as these two final chapters of the book pull it all together.

Peeling Away the Differences

In the previous chapter I mentioned that many Christians are unaware of their religion's history. But I've also met people who are blissfully unaware of all the varieties and branches of Christianity. How can they truly understand their beliefs if they don't know how the different theologies compare?

About ten years ago I had a neighbor who belonged to a small community church, and her pastor gave her the impression that Christians were a tiny, tiny minority of the American people. (In fact, various polls and estimates put the number anywhere from 80% to as high as 95% of Americans identifying themselves as Christians.)

When my neighbor found out I believed in God and was a Christian, she was shocked and excitedly said, "I didn't know you were a believer!" Now this was in Orlando, Florida. She asked what church I belonged to. I told her that we had recently moved there and hadn't found a church (which, on hindsight was a bad thing to say, because she would later invite me to her church). She asked where we came from. I said, "Atlanta." She said, "Who was the pastor of your church?"

I said, "Well, he was Lutheran, and that was in Atlanta, so you probably don't know him." She looked at me confused, apparently unfamiliar with the term "Lutheran." She said, "Well what was his name?" Did she have no idea how many ministers and pastors are in the country? I said his name and she thought for a moment, as if she felt she should know the name. She finally confessed, "Hmmm... I haven't heard of him."

Well of course she hadn't. She had lived in Orlando all her life. But she seriously thought that the Christian community was so tiny that certainly they all know each other!

Even though there are many different branches of Christianity, at heart they all share the Bible. (Although even that isn't quite true, since different branches include different books in the Bible.) But after you peel away all the denominations and variations in Christianity and look to the Bible itself, you start to encounter some problems. The Bible has some things in it that many people probably agree cannot possibly be morally and ethically good.

Already, in Chapter 6, I discussed how many verses gave me trouble, and so I would look for the "deeper meaning," to try and find out what it really means. In my mind, many troubling verses couldn't be taken at face value, of course, because no loving God who cares about his people could ever do or say such horrible things. In my own journey over time, my embellishing and re-interpreting only got worse and worse. And I saw how bad it gets with other people, too.

For example, I recently saw people defending the passages about slavery, saying it wasn't really slavery that was condoned by the Bible (even though it clearly says slavery). In fact, these people claimed, it was people voluntarily going to work for somebody to pay back a debt. But it doesn't say that at all! These people obviously didn't like the fact that the Bible condones something that we modern humans find morally repulsive:

> 'Your male and female slaves are to come from the nations around you; from them you may buy slaves. You may also buy some of the temporary residents living among you and members of their clans born in your country, and they will become your property. You can will them to your children as inherited property and can make them slaves for life, but you must not rule over your fellow Israelites ruthlessly. (Leviticus 25:44-46, New International Version)*

But by changing the meaning from slavery to indentured servitude, these people modified the verses into something that felt better, something that worked for them today. That is, they disagreed with the Bible so they changed it, just as I did.

But that's exactly the problem: If there's a God, then it is his religion, not theirs. Where do they get off modifying it into something other than what's laid out in the Bible and then demanding that they're correct? And why should I give their ideas even a moment's consideration? It's their own

---

* I purposely chose the New International Version here, because it uses the word slave. The King James Version, interestingly, translates the word as "bondman". However, the various dictionaries I checked give this word as a synonym to slave, and one can hardly argue that the word means a paid servant. Also, it's interesting to note that instead of the "nations around you," the King James Version has, "heathen that are round about you," which implies a certain level of bigotry towards other people, again an outdated, narrow-minded view. What God would be so focused on such an individual tribe and culture—unless, of course, that God were invented by the people of that tribe and culture.

invention and at that point becomes their own myth and legend, just like the ancient myths that they themselves reject, such as the ancient Egyptian and Greek myths that have long been disposed of.

What's interesting is that now that I've broken myself away mentally from the shackles of interpreting the Bible to my liking, I see the Bible in a different way. I see it as an ancient, archaic document written by backwards, tribal, superstitious, bigoted, narrow-minded people of ancient times. If today we stumbled upon an island in the middle of the ocean and found a primitive tribe of people who have never had any contact with the modern world, most likely they would have their own stories and superstitions that they've created to try to explain things about the world that they don't understand. Would we take their ideas seriously? Would we look at their ideas as the word of God and build an entire religion on these ideas? I doubt it, but that's exactly what we've done by creating Christianity and its sister religions, Judaism and Islam.

And so when I look at the Bible objectively, I see all these morally reprehensible ideas. And yet, there are some churches out there following the Bible verbatim. And unfortunately, the sermons and teachings of these churches are also morally reprehensible—not just in my mind, but in the minds of even most Christians today. For example, there is a very famous church in Kansas that pickets the funerals of homosexuals. These people are known for claiming that God hates homosexuals. They make the claim that God does not actually love everybody, and the idea that "God loves all of us" is a made-up idea. And you know what? Although their ideas disgust me and I really wish they could be stopped (but they're protected by the Bill of Rights), the fact is, much of what they say really *can* be found directly in the Bible before modifying it with one's own nice, feel-good interpretation.

So if you want to know what's *really* in the Bible, these awful, hate-filled groups are a pretty good indication. For example, they claim that the Bible says that God said it's an abomination for two men to have sex. And they claim that homosexuals should be put to death.

And you know what? The Bible indeed *does* say that. Those verses are actually present:

Thou shalt not lie with mankind, as with womankind: it is abomination. (Leviticus 18:22)[*]

---

[*] Interestingly, this verse seems directed at men. But that should be no surprise as women were considered hardly more than property at the time.

If a man also lie with mankind, as he lieth with a woman, both of them have committed an abomination: they shall surely be put to death; their blood shall be upon them. (Leviticus 20:13)

Or, for a version that's even more clear, check out the New International Version for the latter verse:

If a man lies with a man as one lies with a woman, both of them have done what is detestable. They must be put to death; their blood will be on their own heads. (Leviticus 20:13, New International Version)

A few years ago I attended a lecture by a theologian who was trying to make the case that the Bible really isn't opposed to homosexuality. He made quite a good case for it. He explained that the famous "Sodom and Gomorrah" scene where God destroyed a town filled with homosexuals wasn't actually an attack on homosexuals at all. He said that God destroyed the city not because of the homosexuality but because of the lack of hospitality.

At the time (I was still a Christian), having some relatives who are homosexual, I wholeheartedly agreed, and started taking on my Christian friends who were opposed to homosexuality. I defended the Bible and claimed the God is fine with homosexuals, and that everybody who says otherwise is simply misinterpreting the Bible.

But there's a problem here. The man who gave the lecture was wrong. The Bible *does* preach against homosexuality (I just quoted some verses!), and this interpretation that it doesn't was nothing more than that, an interpretation, and a nice, feel-good one at that. That lecturer (and I too) was chipping away at the Bible, taking the parts he didn't like (God hates homosexuality) and replacing it with something that felt better (God, being a good progressive liberal, is fine with homosexuality—naturally!).

Indeed, the Old Testament is filled with hate-filled, backwards laws, including those that outlaw Christianity. These laws I'm referring are mostly in the book of Leviticus. This book contains a series of arcane, highly specific laws that were supposedly given by God to Moses to give to his people to follow. The laws contain some very odd ones, such as what to do if you develop sores on your skin, or what food priests may eat compared to what other people may eat.

Today, many Christians ignore these laws, saying that Jesus said they no longer had to follow the old laws. (Indeed, most devout Jews today still follow many of these laws. That's why Jewish people eat food they consider kosher; the laws I'm speaking of describe such rules for eating.)

But the New Testament isn't even clear on whether these laws should be followed or not. On one hand, Jesus said he didn't intend for the laws to go away:

> *Think not that I am come to destroy the law, or the prophets: I am not come to destroy, but to fulfil*. *(Matthew 5:17)*

Yet, on the other hand, we have Jesus and the apostles saying the laws *are* going away:

> *For there is verily a disannulling of the commandment going before for the weakness and unprofitableness thereof. (Hebrews 7:18) In that he saith, A new covenant, he hath made the first old. Now that which decayeth and waxeth old is ready to vanish away. (Hebrews 8:13)*

Or, in modern English:

> *The former regulation is set aside because it was weak and useless. (Hebrews 7:18, New International Version)*
> *By calling this covenant "new," he has made the first one obsolete; and what is obsolete and aging will soon disappear. (Hebrews 8:13, New International Version)*

And so once again we're back to picking and choosing which parts of the Bible we like and don't like, only following those we like, and creating out own interpretations so that we can end up with a religion that feels good.

Of course, some people want to keep both verses, so again they'll offer their own interpretation to make them co-exist without contradiction. At least one web site I found tried to explain this discrepancy about the Old Testament laws by saying that when Jesus said he didn't come to destroy but to fulfill the law, that he didn't mean the old laws would stay the same. As

---

* The King James Version spells "fulfill" with one L at the end.

if that even makes sense! And that, of course, is just more interpretation to make it work in one's own mind.

Different people interpret the verses differently to suit their needs. Certainly the words are all there, spelled out for us. But my main thesis is that if the Bible is filled with so many inaccuracies, so many problems and contradictions, and so many moral abominations, and can be used for such hatred (such as hatred towards homosexuals), then clearly the Bible cannot have been written by an all-knowing, perfect God. It just isn't possible—especially when you consider that geneticists have isolated genes that cause homosexuality. Why would God create somebody with a gene that dictates whether they're gay or straight, and then discriminate against those people hardwired to be gay, and even proclaim that they are evil and should be put to death? It's senseless. I cannot accept it. In fact, when you add in my points in Chapter 6 about the religion being based on myth, then together there's no reason at all to accept it. Indeed just because one doesn't like a religion, that alone doesn't make it false. But when that religion is clearly based on myth, then it's easy to see why it's false.

(And back to the topic of homosexuality: I doubt any fundamentalists are reading this, but in the event that they are, don't give me that crap that homosexuality is a choice. I am straight and I am not *able* to become aroused by another man. If you believe you are making the choice to *not* be gay, and ultimately the choice to be straight, then you are lying to yourself about your true nature. Straight men cannot become aroused by other men. If you're capable of it, then you are dishonest to yourself, and you are a homosexual in denial; you need to start being honest with yourself and accept yourself for who you are—and stop attacking others for being honest with themselves and their true nature. And further, enough with calling people who oppose gay lifestyles or marriage as "pro-family" and those who support it "pro-homosexual," as the American Family Association calls them. Rather, call it like it is: Those who oppose homosexuality are anti-homosexual. The rest of us are *pro-everyone*, because we support equal rights for all and choose not to leave out certain people. Such hatred and discrimination is no different from stopping blacks from having equal rights.)

Even when Christians choose to ignore the laws of the Old Testament, often they'll still hold strongly to the Ten Commandments and even insist they should be displayed in the courthouses and public buildings in the United States. (I talked about why this is wrong in Chapter 2.) Yet, these same

Christians ignore other rules laid out in the New Testament as well, by Jesus himself. Here in the United States, when we are to give testimony in court, we put our hand on the Bible and swear by God to tell the truth. Yet, Jesus forbid this in the Book of Matthew:

> *"Again, you have heard that it was said to the people long ago, 'Do not break your oath, but keep the oaths you have made to the Lord.' But I tell you, Do not swear at all: either by heaven, for it is God's throne; or by the earth, for it is his footstool; or by Jerusalem, for it is the city of the Great King. And do not swear by your head, for you cannot make even one hair white or black. Simply let your 'Yes' be 'Yes,' and your 'No,' 'No'; anything beyond this comes from the evil one. (Matthew 5:33-37)*

So to the people who want the Ten Commandments in the courthouses, I ask: Why are you on one hand defending your religion, while on the other hand, turning your back on a rule spelled out by Jesus himself?

A Strange Obsession with Hell and Satan

Obviously, Hell is very important to Christians in order to perpetuate their religion. I've said it before: Without the threat of Hell, people would quickly pack up and leave the faith and never look back. Hell is required to keep people faithful to Christianity, out of sheer terror. I've met many people who are so close to letting go, but they maintain just a tiny shred of fear that Hell might be real, and just that tiny feeling is enough to keep them from leaving.

To pretty much every single Christian, Hell is a very real place. And oddly, even though Christianity is supposed to be about saving people so they can go to this eternal paradise called Heaven, in fact, many Christians spend the majority of their time talking about Hell, not Heaven. It's almost like they enjoy talking about it. Clearly, many Christians are obsessed with Hell.

Comedian Dana Carvey, during his tenure on Saturday Night Live, created the hilarious character known as The Church Lady. This was basically a caricature of the Christian everywoman in that she was completely obsessed with Satan and Hell. Clearly, Christianity has developed somewhat of a reputation for this odd obsession.

I'm not even going to attempt to explain why so many Christians obsess over Hell. I've noted why the church itself needs to perpetuate the myth of Hell as a necessity to continue its existence. Perhaps the individual people have fallen so far into the theology that they are fundamentally evil people, that the idea of Hell comes natural to them. (Just kidding.) But one can only wonder.

But here's the kicker: There's very little Biblical basis for Hell at all, especially the vivid descriptions of an underworld filled with red and orange fire and the Devil with horns. Some of it is in the Bible, but most people take it to an extreme far beyond what's actually in the Bible. And if it's not in the Bible, why are so many Christians perpetuating the idea?

I've already mentioned in Chapter 5 where many of the notions of Hell originate, both prior to the writing of Genesis, as well as after the writing of the New Testament. But what about Hell in the Bible itself? This might surprise you: *There's almost nothing.*

The Bible uses three different names that people have equated to Hell: Sheol, Hades, and Gehenna.

Sheol is primarily in the Old Testament, and is a Hebrew word. This word is translated in different ways in English Bibles, often simply as "grave," as in Genesis 37:35, shown here translated in the King James Version:

And all his sons and all his daughters rose up to comfort him; but he refused to be comforted; and he said, For I will go down into the grave unto my son mourning. Thus his father wept for him. (Genesis 37:35)

Sheol seems to just be a place that people believed souls go after death, but there's little indication of any kind of flames or suffering.

The next word is Hades. The term Hades actually comes from the Greek idea of the afterlife, and this term primarily occurs in the New Testament in the early Greek versions of the Bible. But just to complicate things, often in the early Greek translations of the Old Testament, Sheol was in turn translated into Hades. And indeed, just like Sheol, Hades is generally used in neither a positive or negative way, with no flames or suffering—except for one instance. This one instance occurs in Luke 16:23. Here, Jesus is telling a parable and mentions Hades, where a man who died was being tortured. The word used in the earliest Greek versions here is Hades, and some English versions translate the word to Hell, but many leave it as Hades. (The NIV uses hell with a lowercase H, and has a footnote that says, "Greek Hades". The Revised Standard Version and the New American Standard Bible, for example, leave it as Hades.)

In general, many theologians say both Sheol and Hades represent the same thing, and that the two words represent some kind of temporary place after death, although this temporary place does seem to be separate from a paradise (i.e. Heaven) of sorts. (But as usual, I feel compelled to point out that this is the interpretation of these theologians, and so not all Christians agree on it.) Still, there's little mention of any kind of bad things happening in Hades in the Bible, just that it's separate from a paradise (and interestingly, the paradise is usually depicted as an abode where Abraham is).

But this is where the cross-over from mythology comes in. The word Hades occurs multiple times in the Greek version of the Old and New Testaments. The idea of Hades already existed in the minds of the Greeks through their own mythologies. In Greek mythology, Hades was the underworld. Although the ancient Hebrew myths primarily came from Babylonian and Canaanite myths, there's clearly a common theme here, the idea of some kind of (literal) underworld where people go after they die. So it's interesting that when translating the Old and New Testaments into Greek, the early authors and editors readily adopted the existing Greek word Hades, even though most Christians today reject the Greek mythologies as nothing more than ancient fables. (Scholars figure the reason the early translators did that was so the people reading the translation would more easily believe it. Ancient Greeks were more inclined, for example, to believe a story if it incorporated ideas from their own religion and belief set.)

That covers the first two words, Sheol and Hades. Undoubtedly, the biggest ideas people have of Hell come from the third word, Gehenna. This is where the ideas of eternal fire come from.

The word appears several times in the New Testament, but is usually simply translated as Hell. Some English translations, however, do leave the word Gehenna intact. One such translation is Young's Literal Translation, which I've mentioned on occasion as an odd but useful translation, because it's pretty much a word-for-word translation from the Greek to Old English.

Here are a couple passages that mention Gehenna, along with some rather vivid imagery:

And if thy hand may cause thee to stumble, cut it off; it is better for thee maimed to enter into the life, than having the two hands, to go away to the gehenna, to the fire -- the unquenchable -- where there worm is not dying, and the fire is not being quenched. (Mark 9:43-44, Young's Literal Translation)

That's from Young's translation. The NIV and KJV both use the word hell (lowercase h).

And what was Gehenna really? It was a huge garbage dump outside of Jerusalem. This was where they threw their trash as well as the bodies of criminals who were executed. Fires burned in the garbage dump, often for days on end. The people in Jesus' time were quite familiar with the dump, and so the stories that mention Gehenna easily hit home with these people.

But I should probably clarify something here. I've said over and over that I no longer believe the stories in the Bible as anything more than myth. The New Testament is about the life of Jesus and the apostles, and the teachings of the apostles. The stories of Jesus show him mentioning things like Gehenna, which is a place that actually exists to this day. (Although today it's not a fiery dump.) Today, in English, the name of the place is the Valley of Hinnom.

It's easy to start with the assumption that Jesus was real, and then to see that Jesus made references to Gehenna, since that's something the people of the time could easily relate to, and then start applying my own interpretation— something I've preached against in this chapter.

However, because the stories were written by people other than Jesus (Christians agree on that) and meant to teach the people of the time, people who were quite familiar with Gehenna could easily relate to the stories. So whether Jesus existed or not doesn't change the point here: Gehenna really existed, without need for some interpretation, and was a fiery dump, and mentioning it in these stories made quite an impression on the people of the time.

Overall there's actually very little mention of Hell in its various forms. I've listed only a few verses, and there's not a lot beyond that. Young's Literal Translation is helpful here, along with one of many online Bible search tools. With this translation, you can easily search for specific words like Gehenna that haven't been translated into Hell. Here are the totals I've found:

- *Gehenna* is mentioned 12 times in the entire Bible, all of which are in the New Testament.
- *Hades* is mentioned 11 times in the entire Bible, four of which are in the Book of Revelation, and all of which are in the New Testament.

- *The Valley of Hinnom*, which was the same as Gehenna, is mentioned 11 times, all in the Old Testament (but only in the later books of the Old Testament).
- *Sheol* is mentioned the most, with 62 instances, all of which are in the Old Testament. (Remember, Sheol is the Hebrew word, and the New Testament didn't originate in Hebrew.)

In the King James Version, the 62 instances of Sheol are translated in different ways, sometimes simply as grave, other times as pit, and sometimes as hell (starting with a lowercase letter).

Now consider that in the King James Version of the Bible, the word Hell appears only 62 times in the entire Bible. Gehenna, Sheol, and Hades do not appear at all in the King James Version, although the 11 instances of Hinnom are left intact as Hinnom.

In short: *Out of the roughly 31,000 verses in the Bible, Hell only occurs in 62 of them.*

What does that tell us? It says that the huge notion of Hell, in all its gory detail, and with its heavy emphasis within much of the Christian church, has come from what adds up to about a single page of text, maybe two pages tops. How could people develop an entire theology with such vivid, frightening imagery, and an obsessive belief from so few sentences?

Realistically, they can't. As I described in Chapter 5, the concept of Hell has been embellished well outside of the text of the Bible into a place that is very real to almost all Christians. But it's all been created outside the Bible. You do have to wonder if these Christians even realize how little mention Hell is even given in the Bible, and that most of their twisted ideas came from elsewhere!

But it certainly works: The more the threats are piled on, the more people go to church, week after week, and the more money people drop in the collection plates.

And thus, the obsession with Hell continues.

Persecuted Christians?

"If I'm going to be persecuted for following my Lord Jesus, then that's just the way it's going to have to be."

I heard a former coworker say that several years back. But come on: Who is he fooling? Does he really feel persecuted for being a Christian?

With the popularity of such books as *The God Delusion* by Richard Dawkins and *Letter to a Christian Nation* by Sam Harris, people seem to believe that a huge, major war is brewing against Christianity, and that the massive number of atheists and agnostics are going to stomp on the few Christians.

But Christians make up nearly 90% of the US population. That is not a minority! Christianity is the dominant religion in the United States. Churches are on nearly every corner. People all over have stickers on their cars declaring their Christianity. People wear crosses on necklaces declaring their Christianity. And really: How often do non-Christians ever confront them for it? Have they really ever been assaulted—verbally or otherwise—for being a Christian?

Every once in a while you hear news stories about an atheist or non-believer who goes and shoots up a church and kills people. Recently, a young man by the name of Matthew Murray went on a shooting rampage and killed several Christians at two locations in Colorado. He allegedly posted messages on a web site prior to the act, saying he planned to do so because he hated Christianity.

These are horrible incidents, and they get huge news coverage. But in fact, they rarely happen in the US. How many people in the United States have been murdered for being a Christian? It's hard to locate an exact figure, but more people die of the flu each year.

In other countries, people do get killed for being Christians, but typically these people are killed in ethnic wars, and typically they involve other religions such as Islam, a religion that is at least as intolerant of others as Christianity. But in the United States, people rarely die for being Christian.

I'm not trying to imply the opposite is true, however. Atheists in America aren't being killed very often. Christians aren't killing non-Christians. Again, you do hear about it from time to time. There have been cases where a psychotic mother drowns her children because she thought they were possessed by the devil. Or you hear about a man who kills his roommate because he decides he works for Satan. Typically, these are cases of mental illness, though; the murderer is often psychotic and delusional.

In the United States, such violence in either direction is rare. None of us worry about being killed for our beliefs or lack of beliefs (although in other countries the fear is real).

But where we do see violence is when various extremist groups decide that entire groups of people are evil and part of the devil and need to be stopped. During the 1980s and 1990s, for example, clinics that perform abortions were being bombed quite regularly and people were getting severely injured or even killed. People who worked there were fearing for their lives. And doctors who perform abortion have been shot and killed at point-blank range.

I'm not about to generalize and say that all Christians would commit such violent acts. When I lived as a Christian, I would never have done such a thing, and I, along with my Christian friends, condemned those who committed such violent acts. Further, when I was a Christian, I never feared for my personal safety. Christians are everywhere in this country. Why worry?

But now that I am no longer part of that faith, and have spent time with others who are not Christians, I am beginning to hear stories of why non-believers do have reason to worry—not necessarily for fear of being murdered, but for other, less violent but frightening incidents. A young lady I know who is about 19 years old and a college student studying Biology was chased while in her car by some deranged guy in a pickup truck. My friend has a Darwin fish on her car. The man who chased her down was a middle-aged guy holding a little figurine of Jesus out his window, screaming at her that she's evil and working for Satan and that she was going to burn in Hell for "worshipping Darwin." He chased her for miles. She was terrified. She is somebody I know personally.

Many people I know online have received threats from Christians over email. One man who has been particularly vocal in his lack of Christian beliefs has received death threats over email from Christians. A very nice woman I know who is not a Christian received a threat of violence from a good friend of hers who is. The woman I know let go of her Christian beliefs, and her friend who she had known for years made violent statements towards her.

I can tell you firsthand that those of us who proclaim our lack of Christian belief are forced to be careful and watch ourselves. Christians, on the other hand, have virtually nothing to worry about. Again I ask: How many Christians worry about being assaulted for wearing a cross on a necklace that's visible to all those around them?

But what about nonviolence, what about politics and repression? Are Christians being repressed? You hear people complaining about prayer being removed from schools. You hear complaints of the word "Christmas" being removed from our language.

I put the words *Christian persecution* into Google and quickly found numerous websites devoted to the topic. These websites were filled with news articles. But of the four websites I visited, not one article involved Christians being persecuted in modern America. The majority of the articles were about problems in other countries, including Cuba, China, and various Middle Eastern countries, and the few remaining articles were historical articles that took place in ancient times, such as in Rome. I could not find a single article that covered a modern, US incident.

When I modified the search as bit as *Christian persecution "United States"*, I started getting a few websites. This time, I got websites claiming there is Christian persecution in the United States. But the claims I found on these pages are anecdotal and subjective, and largely sensationalist alarmism.

For example, one page starts out by saying that over 150,000 people were killed last year for being Christian (the article doesn't have a date, but mentions the "Clinton White House" suggesting it was written during the 1990s). It then concedes that these 150,000 deaths were outside the United States.

But then the article immediately transitions by saying that statistics are changing and that persecution is increasing in the United States. It follows with stories. This is propaganda at its finest, however, because the stories have nothing to do with thousands of Christians dying for their faith, as the first sentence of the article would suggest. Rather, the stories are silly little stories such as how the Freedom from Religion Foundation is supposedly passing out pamphlets called "We Can Be Good Without God" to children in public schools.*

The article then provides a couple of anecdotal stories about how a woman was told by police she couldn't pass out gospel brochures (called "tracts") from her home on Halloween, and how a United Methodist minister in a remote part of Tennessee was murdered. The article even includes the Columbine shootings, probably because one of the shooters apparently asked one of the victims if she was a Christian before killing her. And the article claims that the entertainment industry portrays Christians as "sewer rats, vultures, and simple-minded social ingrates."† He even laments that some Christian groups have been labeled hate groups. (But it's correct: some *are* hate groups. The well-known church in Kansas that pickets the funerals of homosexuals is a hate group, and their favorite phrase, "God hates fags" pretty much proves

---

* Technically, this did happen, but not as the article would imply. For the full story, visit http://ffrf.org/fttoday/1994/oct/freethoughtchildren.php.

† http://www.worthynews.com/christian-persecution.html "Persecution of Christians Growing in the United States" by Thomas Horn.

that point.)

But does the author present a neutral perspective and mention the many people who have been injured or who died at the hands of Christians bombing abortion clinics? No. Does the article mention a group named Army of God whose web sites (which I won't give the address for out of disgust) celebrate people such as convicted abortion clinic bomber Eric Rudolph and convicted and executed murderer Paul Jennings Hill?* No.

Now I'm not condoning the man I mentioned earlier who murdered the Tennessee minister while condemning the abortion clinic bombers. His act was just as wrong and criminal. But it's clear that this article is anything but balanced reporting and serves no purpose but to rile people up and convince them that they are being persecuted for being Christians, when they really aren't.

Passing out pamphlets and discouraging Christianity is not persecution. Any instance of murder is wrong, but an isolated incident doesn't imply widespread persecution. Persecution against Christians does not happen in the United States. Why? Because it's illegal. People are *not* sent to jail for being Christians; to do so is against our constitution. The persecution is not real.

Of course, one might claim a bit of irony of the truest literary sense in this very book. Isn't this book one big piece of Christian persecution, and am I not claiming persecution doesn't exist while persecuting Christians myself?

No. I am not trying to get the United States to pass laws to prevent people from being Christian. That wouldn't even be possible. In this country, we have freedom of religion, which includes freedom *from* religion. I cannot be forced to go to church or to believe a certain way, and I cannot stop anyone else from believing a certain way. I would certainly hope that others would learn from my mistakes and give up their beliefs after considering the arguments I have made in this book. But there will be no laws stopping them from believing as they wish, and I'm not trying to create any such laws.

But what about the supposed war against Christmas? We hear stories about how a certain retail store has decided not to have their employees say Merry Christmas, and to instead opt for Happy Holidays. But the fact is, the company is a free enterprise, and is free to do that. But there are no *laws* stopping individual people from saying Merry Christmas to their friends.

* Eric Rudolph is serving five consecutive life sentences for several charges including homicide. He pled guilty to avoid the death penalty. Paul Jennings Hill was convicted of murder and given the death penalty. He died by lethal injection in 2003.

Many people are recognizing that there are other faiths and groups who celebrate holidays in December, and they don't want them to feel left out. So they might say "Happy Holidays," for example. But there's no assault on Christmas, as Fox News' Bill O'Reilly would have us believe.

And there's not an assault on Christianity in the public schools. Public schools are mandated by the government, and therefore, by law, cannot promote religion. That means teachers can't lead prayers, and the schools can't require students to pray. But it doesn't mean prayer isn't allowed in schools. Students can still pray before lunch or before a ballgame if they want, provided they aren't required to do so. And nobody is going to go to jail for praying in schools, contrary to what is said in emails that are forwarded and propagated about the Internet.

Yet, all the facts aside, why do people still think Christians in America are being persecuted? I visited a few forums online and it didn't take me long to find Christians insisting that persecution against Christians in America is widespread. Is it because books by Sam Harris and Richard Dawkins are reaching the bestseller list?

Or is it because city councils across the country are ending nativity scenes? Individual citizens are still perfectly free to put up nativity scenes in their front yards, yet people view the city council decisions as an attack on Christianity, when in fact, it's simply a matter of the illegality of a city proclaiming an official religious belief.

Or is it because of other events, such as one that somebody brought up regarding several churches in the Southern US being burned? They apparently overlooked the fact that these were all African-American churches, and the perpetrators were not behaving out of hatred towards Christianity, but out of nothing but racism against Blacks. Again, it wasn't a persecution against Christians. It was hatred towards a specific race, which is certainly illegal and repugnant, but by no means persecution against Christianity.

Perhaps Christians feel persecuted because of all these things, even though they're the majority and are free to keep going to church as they always have, and realistically have nothing to worry about regarding their own safety and will never go to jail for practicing their beliefs. But I have another idea, a hypothesis if you will, of why they feel persecuted.

First, I'm friends with many Christians. I just don't talk about religion with them, and they leave me alone as well. We hang out and just don't bring up religion. Although I've heard people in forums online claim that being

Christian results in being ostracized, typically that only happens to people who are trying to force their beliefs down the throats of their friends. Who wouldn't want such a person to go away? I don't want one of my friends telling me I'll burn in Hell.

But there's a deeper issue at work here. Let's get back to my former co-worker who I mentioned at the start of this section. When he said he would follow Jesus even if he's persecuted, I sensed not only pride, but almost a bit of hope, as if he was *hoping* he'd be persecuted. Why? Let's look at the Bible:

> *If the world hate you, ye know that it hated me before it hated you. If ye were of the world, the world would love his own: but because ye are not of the world, but I have chosen you out of the world, therefore the world hateth you. (John 15:18-19)*

> *Behold, I send you forth as sheep in the midst of wolves: be ye therefore wise as serpents, and harmless as doves. (Matthew 10:16)*

The Bible warns Christians that they will be persecuted, and to stand up for their beliefs. So clearly this guy I knew was hoping he'd be persecuted, because to do so would be an honor!

And I'm not just dreaming this up. One of the websites I found talking about Christians being persecuted actually said that persecution is a "privilege." (In fact, this website also told a story of a high school boy getting attacked by other kids wielding knives and how it was supposedly for being Christian. But it's clear from the story that this poor child was a victim of gang violence and I find it hard to believe they singled him out because he was a Christian, because the chances of him being the only Christian in the school are next to nothing. My opinion, and it's just that, is that they singled him out simply because they didn't like him. Perhaps he was smart and got good grades; I know what it feels like to be singled out for that. It's hard to say. But the evidence that it was because of Christianity was virtually non-existent. The boy was a Christian and he was attacked, but the latter wasn't *because* of the former.)

Indeed, some people want to be able to say they were persecuted, as if they can take pride in it. Do they really want to be harassed? No, I doubt it. But they seem to want to be able to tell people later that they were harassed, and they want to be able to loudly proclaim that they stood up to the harassment and refused to back down from their belief in Jesus. In other words, they like the idea of bragging that they defended Jesus.

At this point, you probably know me as a bit of a cynic, and my cynical response is that they want to proclaim as much so they can impress God and get accepted into Heaven, but if their God were real, wouldn't he see through such hypocrisy?

But the truth is, the persecution isn't real. Consider the fact that the current president as I write this, George W. Bush, has enacted his "faith-based initiative." Christianity is pushing forward as hard as it can, to the point that many local governments have gone beyond what's legal regarding the separation of Church and State, resulting in lawsuits from people trying to protect the separation of Church and State. This isn't an attack on Christianity; it's a challenge to protect our rights.

And consider this story: The United States Department of Veteran Affairs maintains a list of symbols that are allowed to be printed on government-issued headstones of fallen soldiers. For nine years, various Wiccan groups have fought to allow their symbol, a star in a circle, to be included in the list of approved symbols. It finally took a lawsuit, and in early 2007, the VA finally settled and agreed to allow the symbol to be used.[*]

It would be very easy to Christians to see this as an attack on them. It isn't. By not allowing the symbol, the VA was discriminating against a certain religious group, the Wiccans. But such discrimination is illegal, and the followers of Wicca defended their rights and won. (Incidentally, the lawsuit was handled by a group called Americans United for Separation of Church and State, which is currently run by an ordained *Christian* minister named Barry W. Lynn.)

The Cult of Sin

The concept of "sin" permeates all of Christianity. But what exactly is sin? I've used it throughout this book as simply a synonym for any evil act. But really, that's not quite right. In Christian tradition, sin is any act that goes against God.

Consider, for example, the numerous stories in the Old Testament where

---

* This news item is available in many places online, including as http://www.cbsnews.com/stories/2007/04/23/national/main2718944.shtml

God's people were ordered to commit mass genocide, killing every single person in a community or country, including women and children. (Don't believe that's in the Bible? Read all of Joshua 6.)

Many times God ordered his people to kill other people, which his followers happily complied with, brutally and savagely killing people.

Was that a sin? To many of us, sin is simply any act of evil. Today if a town in the United States were to take up arms and go and completely wipe out another town, brutally killing every living being, we would consider that a serious act of evil. And many Christians, I suspect, would consider it a sin.

But in the Joshua 6 story, known as the story of the Wall of Jericho, the people did just that but by *God's orders*. And in the Christian mindset, if people defy God they are sinning; doing what God orders is good and righteous.

Thus, the conclusion is that a Christian would view the mass, brutal killing performed by God's people in Joshua 6 as good and righteous and anything *but* sinful. If the people had not killed the others, then they would have been sinning by refusing God's will!

That, of course, is absolutely disgusting to many of us. How can such an act be justified? Some people may attempt to justify it by pointing out that the people who were killed were horrible people. (Let's not forget that Adolph Hitler felt the Jews were horrible people. Nearly all of us agree his acts were horrendous and certainly not good and righteous by any measure.)

But in fact, the Bible makes no such claims. It doesn't say anything, really, about the people of Jericho. The reason the people in the Bible supposedly destroyed the city and its inhabitants was simply because *it was in the way*. It was sitting in the land they had deemed their Promised Land, and they didn't want that city there. So they wiped it out.

Of course, this is all legend in the Bible and there's very little archeological proof that it even took place. But that's beside the point: Many Christians believe the story happened, and they believe God wanted the destruction to occur, and thus they presumably accept that God determined incidents of genocide were righteous and good. (What would God have done if the people refused to commit the genocide? The Bible doesn't say, but based on other stories, we can be assured that God would have been none-too-happy about such insubordination.)

Clearly, then, there's a distinction between what constitutes a "sin" and what constitutes something that is morally wrong or reprehensible. I consider the genocide of an entire city reprehensible, while the Bible makes it clear that—at least once, anyway—it was good and *not sinful.*

Much of today's ideas about sin come from the writings of Aurelius Augustinus of Hippo, commonly known simply as St. Augustine. St. Augustine lived from 354 to 430 AD and wrote many books about Christian theology that had a huge impact on Christianity throughout the world.

Today, not all Christian denominations agree with what St. Augustine had to say. But many do. And in his works he laid out a framework for what exactly sin is, and where it comes from.

He came up with the idea of "original sin." Original sin is the sin that originated with Adam when he and Eve disobeyed God's commands and ate the forbidden fruit. In doing so, sin originated (and, according to Augustine, was passed down to every generation through the male sperm; I am not making this up).

Other theologians over the years have had other ideas about what exactly sin is and where it comes from. But even when you siphon through all the stories and theologies put forth by various people, it still isn't clear what exactly constitutes a sin—especially when you consider that different Christian denominations can't even agree on it.

To some, playing cards is a sin, and so is dancing. Although there aren't any verses, for example, that specifically outlaw playing cards, there are various verses that some interpret as applying towards card playing. (Although even that's debatable; there are only a couple instances in the Bible where certain games of chance are said to be wrong.)

Or what about swearing? If I say the word "fuck" am I sinning? Is that something that will send me to Hell unless I get on my knees and beg God to forgive me for uttering such a word? A few years back I attended the funeral of a man who lived to be nearly 90. The pastor who preached at the funeral said that the man who died was a great man because he never uttered a swear word.

Is that what makes somebody great? Does that mean that if somebody does say a swear word that this pastor believes they must beg for forgiveness? If another man lived just as good a life as this man, but had occasionally said "shit" and didn't ask God for forgiveness, would that man burn in Hell?

And how does that compare, for example, to a congressman who passes legislation that causes thousands of poor people lose money, causing them to be unable to eat and, possibly, die? This was a very real issue during the 1990s. The Republicans in Congress, with the help of the talk radio hosts, were pushing the nice sounding phrase "personal responsibility." The idea was to push poor people to become more responsible for their own ability to eat. And occasionally they were backing up the idea with a Bible verse: "God helps those who help themselves."

But you know what? *That isn't even in the Bible.* There is no such Bible verse.

But were these conservative pastors saying that the members of Congress, by pushing such ideas of personal responsibility—people who were possibly causing others to die—sinning? Of course not. Children could die from starvation, but that didn't matter, apparently: What mattered more was that these people didn't cuss and swear.

Seriously: Does that make any sense at all? Of course not. But it does to the people perpetuating this nonsense. Swearing is apparently a worse sin than an innocent legislator trying to "better" the country by lowering taxes and causing people to starve.

Now I should probably be realistic here: What I'm describing here certainly isn't true for all Christians. Not all Christians put swearing as a higher sin than causing people to die. But there are a good share out there who do overlook the indirect deaths caused by legislation (and by the people who voted such legislators into office), while focusing on seemingly trivial matters.

But let's go with this for a moment, because back in the 1990s, I met many people who defended the new laws, people who were fundamentalist Christians. When pushed, these people have managed to come up with some Bible verses to back up laws to end help for poor people:

For even when we were with you, this we commanded you, that if any would not work, neither should he eat. (2 Thessalonians 3:10)

Of course, this doesn't exactly apply to the situation. This verse is talking about people who refuse to work. But there are many people who, for various reasons, are *unable* to work and need help and can't get it. And there are people working hard to make sure that such people don't get the help they need. But regardless, people will pull out Bible verses trying to support their claim.

So again I ask: Which is a bigger sin? Swearing or causing people to starve? But again, when pushed, the people I spoke with also came up with a defense that swearing is a sin. It's right in the Ten Commandments:

Thou shalt not take the name of the LORD thy God in vain; for the LORD will not hold him guiltless that taketh his name in vain. (Exodus 20: 7)

But I suppose one could argue that this still doesn't directly pertain to the situation unless the swearing is one of the forms that has "God" in it. (So "fuck" apparently doesn't count?)

But let's just drop it all for a moment. Swearing rarely causes any pain to anybody. Passing legislation that prevents people from eating, however, *does* hurt people.

Of course, in my cynical eyes, there's a bigger issue here that I've so far ignored in the present chapter, and that goes back to the whole issue that the politicians are simply using religion to get their way; by appealing to the religious mindset of the masses, the people happily elect these politicians, having decided that they are moral, righteous, and "one of them."

That, of course, pretty much invalidates the whole nonsense and shows the real problem here, that religion is nothing more than a political tool.

So back to the question: What is sin? It's hard to say. But its concept certainly plays a huge role in Christianity, and even comes into play when religion is used in politics.

Christianity: The Peaceful Religion?

Is Christianity a peaceful religion? Let's first consider Islam.

Right after 9/11, there was a huge backlash in the US (and across the planet, but mainly here) against Muslims. Islamic people were being discriminated against. Non-Muslim Christians would see a Muslim man wearing a turban and get frightened that he was a terrorist. Even people who didn't wear traditional Islamic clothing but *looked* like they might be Muslim were discriminated against.

However, many people, particularly those who tend to lean leftward on the political spectrum, were quick to point out that this is nothing short of discrimination. And they're right. Singling out people because they look like somebody who bombed the World Trade Center, and not letting them on an airplane, *is* discrimination.

But then such left-leaning people went too far, in my opinion, and tried to say that contrary to the acts of these terrorists, Islam is, in fact, a religion of peace. Even George W. Bush (who isn't left-leaning by any means) started falling into this bandwagon and calling it a peaceful religion. In his State of the Union Address in September of 2001, shortly after the attacks, he said the terrorists represent "a fringe movement that perverts the peaceful teachings of Islam."

It's true that there are plenty of peaceful Muslims. In college, I knew several Muslims from the Middle East, and they were some of the nicest, kindest people I've known. And, indeed, many Muslim clerics did condemn the 9/11 terrorists and their acts.

Yet, there are plenty of Muslims who *do* hate Christians and Jews, and who want to kill any non-Muslims. But what do they base their idea on?

Turns out, it's right in the Quran, their holy book:

So when the sacred months have passed away, then slay the idolaters wherever you find them, and take them captives and besiege them and lie in wait for them in every ambush, then if they repent and keep up prayer and pay the poor-rate, leave their way free to them; surely Allah is Forgiving, Merciful. (Surah 9:5)[*]

Of course, in the same way Christians defend verses that seem troubling, Muslims do the same. The Internet is filled with pages explaining how these verses in the Quran are taken out of context, refer to an ancient time, stating that times have changed, or are simply mistranslated from words less severe. Sound familiar?

I've met many Christians who argue against such notions, pointing out that the words are clearly there in the Quran for all to see. Indeed they are. But what about the Bible? These same people ignore the same violence in their own Bible. Turns out, the Bible *also* tells followers of Jesus to kill the nonbelievers. Here it is, right in the book of Luke:

But those mine enemies, which would not that I should reign over them, bring hither, and slay them before me. (Luke 19:27)

That was, of course, Jesus speaking. Jesus said it himself. He's telling his followers to slay the nonbelievers!

Of course, when I brought this up online, several people told me I was

---

[*] There are many online versions of the Quran, and they differ a bit in their wording, just like the Christian Bible. I found this verse at http://quod.lib.umich.edu/k/koran/.

taking it out of context and that I was (same old story) misinterpreting it. They said that if you look at the verses surrounding this one and read the whole thing you find out that Jesus was telling a parable, and that in the parable, it's some king saying this about killing those who don't want him ruling over them.

But was Jesus trying to imply that the king in this story represents Jesus, and so Christians should kill nonbelievers? One could argue that.

But I've stated early on that I refuse any longer to look for the "deeper interpretation" of the Bible to find something that makes it nicer, more feel-good, because if a god wrote the Bible, its meaning should be clear and self-evident. But what I can say is that this verse has been used by many Christians as a reason to attack people who aren't Christians.

And, indeed, history is filled with cases of Christians going on rampages and killing thousands or even millions of people (particularly across Europe several hundred years ago, but also in the Americas where Christopher Columbus was the primary perpetrator, killing millions of Native Americans in the name of Jesus). And consider this: If Jesus, the supposed son of a supposed all-powerful deity named God, created a church, how could it be so flawed, so evil, so violent?

So is Christianity really peaceful? No more so than Islam.

My Reaction to Jesus Freaks

I consider myself lucky that even at a young age I was a little skeptical of what I would today call Jesus Freaks. By that I mean people who have Jesus stickers all over their cars and shirts and proudly proclaim their love for Jesus.

As a child, I never quite knew how to react to these people. I would be torn. On one hand, the Christian in me would try to react with respect, nodding and smiling as if it's a good thing. But I was repressing my real feelings, feelings that frightened me, feelings that worried me. I would look at such stickers and signs and feel disgust. But then I gradually allowed the disgust to come up to the surface.

At first as I'd allow the disgust to come through, I would justify it from a Christian standpoint, viewing these people as people who were displaying their Christianity just to impress the people around them. Jesus had warned against such acts:

And when you pray, do not be like the hypocrites, for they love to pray standing in the synagogues and on the street corners to be seen by men. (Matthew 6:5, New International Version)

But there was still a deeper feeling I had, that these people were pathetic people who were desperately trying to proselytize to others in hopes of impressing both their supposed God as well as the people around them. And that's the idea I've mentioned several times in this book.

Why do they feel compelled to proclaim their faith so loudly? I can only guess, because I've never been of that mindset. Unfortunately, it was *not* being of that mindset that caused me distress as a Christian. Why? Because of the story in the New Testament where Peter denied being a follower of Jesus (Matthew 26). The story made it pretty clear (to me anyway) that trying to hide your love for Jesus was a sin.

And so this resulted in more self-beating, the same self-beating I spoke of early in this book. Shouldn't I be like these people running around proudly proclaiming their love for Jesus? Wasn't I, by being *embarrassed* by such a charade, sinning against Jesus? The Bible suggested that Peter was wrong to deny being a follower of Jesus.

Shouldn't I, then, do the same thing, and sport these loud and obnoxious signs everywhere proclaiming my Christianity? That was what I wondered; that was what troubled me.

Now if there are Christians reading this, they might see this as being rather trite. Come on, they might say. Just because you were torn on how loudly to proclaim your Christianity, that shouldn't be a reason to ditch the whole faith. After all, Jesus also made it clear that the people who stand on the corner praying are being hypocrites and just putting on a show, and that when we pray, we should go in our room and shut the door. In other words, a Christian could easily explain to me—using the Bible—why I was wrong.

Well, certainly, I hope that this book is showing that this is just one tiny issue out of many issues that all came together to finally bring the whole thing down. The Bible is so large that you can pretty much yank anything you want out of it to defend your ideas and beliefs. But the real point here is that because of Christianity, I was yet again feeling like I was doing something wrong, that I was a bad person. And that was interfering with my ability to live a happy and complete life. And that, ultimately, led me on a long journey to seriously question my beliefs, a journey that started with questioning the moral validity of what I was being taught, and on to exploring the mythical basis of the Bible and how it wasn't actually true, and ultimately ditching my faith.

Yes, But What Do You Have to Offer?

There seems to be some confusion among a lot of Christians regarding the people who don't believe in their religion, people I've been collectively calling *non-Believers* (which includes primarily atheists and agnostics). Several times I've heard Christians point out that they're offering eternal life in Heaven, and then they ask what atheists and agnostics have to offer instead. They seem quite amused by the responses from non-Believers: Nothing. Many non-Believers respond by saying they have nothing to offer! The reason they're saying this is that they're saying the claims of eternal salvation made by the Christians are simply not true, and that atheists and agnostics aren't trying to offer an alternate salvation, an alternate Heaven that's somehow different or better. Besides, how can somebody blindly accept the Christians' offer of eternal salvation without first making some absurd leap of faith and suddenly starting to believe it's true?*

However, I would argue that we non-Believers really do have something more to offer. Letting go of artificial beliefs has brought enormous relief and happiness to many of us.

But the issue is actually a bit more complex than that, because the more time spent talking to these individuals, the more clear it is that they see Christianity and non-Belief as *two competing religions*. And so to them, asking what non-Believers have to "offer" is a legitimate question.

But they don't see it from our perspective. They don't understand that they're the one trying to convince people to follow their religion, and we're trying to get people to open their eyes and not follow it. We're trying to get people to understand the reality of this supposed loving and true religion called Christianity. We're not offering a competing religion at all. We're promoting freedom from religion.

They're the ones proselytizing; we're the ones defending against the proselytizing.

They're the ones claiming stories as real; we're the ones trying to get

---

* I've heard that when missionaries try to convert tribal people to Christianity, the tribal people are often given the impression that God is an actual human performing these amazing works, and that effectively bypasses the need to blindly accept supernatural claims.

people to see the stories for what they are: myths.

They're the ones threatening and scaring people into believing in something that isn't real; we're the ones trying to get people to use logic and reason to resist falling for it.

So it should be no wonder at all, I suppose, that they're defensive. They're trying to put us on the defense, by attempting to "debunk" our "beliefs". But how can you debunk a non-belief? You can't. The burden is on the one presenting the belief to convince people it's real.

Try as we might, however, we just couldn't get them to understand our perspective. They're offering a reward of eternal salvation, and they (rather selfishly and hypocritically) want us to convert (so they can gain kudos with God, no less—not because they really give a damn about me and my soul). But the problem is, I'm not about to accept a gift of eternal salvation if I don't even believe in it!

I've been accused more than once of being "angry at God." But that just shows exactly the problem: They don't understand that I don't *believe* in their God and Jesus. How can I be angry at somebody I don't believe in?

One Christian online even presented a list of why he thinks that *we* non-Believers are the ones getting defensive. But how can we be the ones on the defensive when *we're* not the ones making outrageous, impossible offers to try to convince people to blindly follow us?

So what did the list by this Christian consist of? Only two items, and they dealt with the "end times" as predicted in the book of Revelation and how they're supposedly coming true. Then the claim was that we non-Believers are on the defensive because we see the prophecies in the Book of Revelation as actually happening and that we're frightened by them! (And then other people posted replies about us non-Believers experiencing eternal suffering. And unfortunately, some of these nice, loving Christians seemed pretty excited at the idea of me and my non-believing friends experiencing eternal torture in Hell. Such loving people indeed.)

But really now: Why would we be afraid of these end times prophecies we don't even buy into? Any supposed connection between the prophecies in Revelation and modern times are purely coincidental. An awful lot has happened in the last two thousand years; there's certainly room for some coincidental similarities.

And so, what do we have to offer? Well, I say happiness and relief knowing that this threat of eternal damnation isn't real.

No More Worrying!

There's no reason for us to beat ourselves up as I did when I saw the Jesus Freaks and their loud stickers and signs and shirts. It's not healthy or productive. Many of the Christians I know claim their lives are happier and fuller. But are they really? They spend a lot of time denouncing evils. They spend a lot of time nitpicking. And how much time do they spend *worrying*? I can't know, but I think it should be clear that in my case, I was spending almost every waking moment worrying. And I've met many people who are still Christians who say they worry all the time. Somebody I used to know really well was a devout Christian all her life and even as an older woman she lived in total fear that she might have accidentally committed the supposed unforgivable sin and that she will burn in hell forever (even though she was one of the nicest, most selfless people I've ever met).

Is it worth it? Of course, to a believer of Christianity, whether it's "worth it" isn't even the question, because they believe in what they do and can't just instantly stop believing. They truly believe that Judgment Day will come. And so to them, worrying really is worth it, because they will be judged eventually.

But I no longer believe that that will happen, and so now I can look objectively at it and truly ask, *Is it worth it?* The answer to me is Absolutely, No. It's not worth beating ourselves up, living a life of walking on eggshells, dreading every little thing we might have done wrong, things that are, in general, human nature. Instead, I say we should (and can) accept ourselves as we are, and not live in fear, because the fear *isn't real*. There is no Hell; there is no pending Judgment Day.

But how can we let go? How can we walk away from it? For me, the myths were coming together as just that—myths. And the science was making sense. But there was still that problem that I believed in Jesus. Even though the Bible was becoming untrue to me, Jesus was still real. I'll take that up next.

eight

Letting Go and Walking Away

One of the common arguments by the Christians I've spoken to online is that people like me put all our faith in scientists, and they put all their faith in God. They say that our faith in scientists is so strong that it's also a religion and that we just blindly follow the scientists. They say that we, therefore, have no right to criticize them. The fatal flaw in their argument, however, is they are confusing faith with *trust*.

Here's an example of trust: I need somebody to repair my car. I call my buddy who has had his car repaired and find out what repair shop he trusts. I take my car to that shop because I trust my friend's opinion since in the past he has demonstrated to me he is good at finding a reliable mechanic.

> *A casual stroll through the lunatic asylum shows that faith does not prove anything.*
>
> *- Friedrich Nietzsche (1844-1900)*

Here's another example of trust: While my car is broken down, I have my wife drive me to work. She has demonstrated to me several times that she is a good driver and I trust that she will drive safely.

And one more example: If I need a filling in my tooth, I will call my usual dentist. I trust him because in the past he has demonstrated to me that he is a good dentist.

Trust is something that is built up. My friends and family and doctors have worked hard to build up my trust over years.

Faith is the opposite. Faith is where you blindly put your trust in someone or something without any rational reason for doing so. That might sound a bit harsh, but it is indeed true.

Instead of calling my friend for a recommendation on a car repair shop, I could just let the car sit in the driveway and pray to God that it will repair itself. I could have faith. Or I could put a sign on the car that says, "If you can fix it, have at it" and let just anyone who happens to be passing by have a crack at it, while knowing in my heart that the person who comes by will fix it correctly.

When it comes to science, I do not have blind faith. I trust science. There are millions of scientists out there, and they have all worked together to create a modern society filled with medicines that work, cars that run, computers that function. They have demonstrated to me that the science and engineering community as a whole is remarkably competent. Things go wrong and mistakes happen, but as I've explained earlier in this book, science has a built-in method for reviewing its mistakes and correcting them and thus growing and evolving.

My trust in science is anything but faith. Faith is blind. Science has *shown* me that the Scientific Method is sound and competent.

Consider the electron. I've never seen an electron. But science has worked hard to earn my trust, and so I can safely say that electrons are real. And scientists have demonstrated their knowledge of the electron, for example, when they design computer chips that function correctly, sending electrons flying at near the speed of light through the tiny little circuits in the computer chips.

The electron is real.

But now suppose I read about some guy in another country who charges five thousand dollars for a unique cure for cancer.

If I were sick, would I just immediately hop on an airplane and go hand the guy my five grand? If I did, that would be faith, because I have no reason whatsoever to trust the guy. How do I know his method really works?

The obvious thing to do would be to first do some homework and find out what exactly the guy is doing. Call around and get some opinions. Go online and research the method. Find out everything I can about it. And research the guy doing the supposed curing. Is he legitimate? Does he have any degrees? Does he really know what he's doing?

That's wise in all cases. When we need to find a new family doctor, we ask around and get referrals. And slowly, I might be able to build up some trust in a particular doctor. And only then could I make an informed decision about whether or not it would be worth it.

In other words, it's wise to move from *faith* to *trust*. And if I can't find any reason to trust the guy, then I wouldn't bother.

Science is clearly about trust and not faith. I trust the work of the scientists over the past several hundred years. I've studied a great deal of science and understand a lot of it.

But what about the parts I don't understand? I'm not an expert in genetics or biology. So how can I accept something like evolution?

The answer is that I have developed an enormous amount of trust in the scientific method and the millions of scientists who use it. And so when the scientific community *as a whole* (as opposed to just a handful of fringe scientists with an unusual idea) presents me with something that I do not have time to personally verify, I trust them.

And so when it comes, for example, to evolution, I do not have blind faith in the scientists, allowing myself to just sit back and swallow everything they give me. Rather, science has proven their case to me, and after many years of me being skeptical, they have convinced me that they do indeed know what they're talking about, and that I can trust them.

Of course, I also accept that science is sometimes wrong. But scientists do too. Some physicists are exploring an idea regarding the number of physical dimensions of the universe. This idea has been called "superstrings" and some alternate names. Do I blindly trust that superstrings is real and correct and true? No. It has not yet been demonstrated to be true. And the community of scientists acknowledge that. And as such, they have not yet giving superstrings their seal of approval. They have, however, given evolution the seal of approval. It's been shown to be true.

So while people may have faith in God, the same is not true with my attitude towards science. I have trust in science, for good reason.

Faith in Preachers

Over the years, I've noticed something that's shocking and troubling. By and large, people put the majority of their faith in one person and one person only: Their preacher.

During my 20's, I moved around the country a lot, and each time I moved I had to find a new church. During the search I visited many different churches of different Protestant denominations. And I quickly noticed that the preachers at these churches all had different ideas about what the Bible meant, and they all had different educational backgrounds. Some held doctorate degrees in theology; some had no college education whatsoever. And those that did get theological degrees had degrees from different schools that had taught them drastically different ideas.

Although I encountered a few instances where the members of the church didn't like the preacher (usually the preacher was chosen for them), in general people liked their preachers. And they never questioned a thing the preachers said when it came to understanding what God and Jesus wanted. They might have disagreed with non-biblical things, such as how the money in the church should be spent. But they always listened and completely ate up everything the preacher said about the Bible.

Yet, these preachers were giving different stories!

Here's an example: Christians are greatly divided on the notion of whether homosexuality is a sin. There are the extremists who feel that homosexuality is an "abomination before God" and that homosexuals have earned a direct flight to Hell complete with eternal damnation and punishment. Then there's the other end of the spectrum. There are Christians who have made a pretty good case that Jesus was rather indifferent towards homosexuality and that there's nothing wrong with being a homosexual. I suspect the majority of moderate Christians do not subscribe to either extreme; many are either unsure or indifferent or believe it's wrong but aren't very vocal about it.

But look at what is happening! These are all Christian churches and they have drastically different views on homosexuality, and they all back their views up with Bible verses. I've studied them myself; I've seen the verses that call it an abomination for a man to lie with another man; and I've also attended lectures by theologians who looked to the original Greek and Aramaic writings and insist that Jesus had no problems with it.

And so what are people to do? God forbid they look inside their own hearts and minds and see that if two men live together and are causing no problem at all with anyone, then it should be fine. Instead, the people go right to their preacher. So many don't even try to interpret the Bible themselves; they just go to the preacher. And whatever the preacher says is right to them, and they just eat it up. They have complete, absolute faith in their preacher. If the preacher says it, it must be true.

And if chance had caused them to have moved into a house that's down the street from a different church with a slightly different perspective, then they would have ended up believing something different.

People might ask, though, why this isn't a matter of trust. Well, I explained that an important factor of trust is using rationality. Is it rational to trust the preacher?

Think about that in your own journey. Why trust the preacher compared to, say, the scientists?

Consider this: The work of the scientists is all in plain view. There are libraries filled with millions of articles published by scientists; these articles carefully detail the experiments the scientists have performed and the findings. If you have the tools and understanding, you can duplicate the experiments and see for yourself. But what of the claims of the preachers? How can you see for yourself whether their claims are true, especially when two different preachers claim two different things?

Letting Go of Faith

In my own recovery process, identifying where I placed my own faith was one major step to breaking free of the shackles. And it didn't take me long to realize that I was putting faith in a lot of people who didn't necessarily deserve it. I'm not trying to be harsh here, but the fact is, these people I was placing absolute faith in were no different from me: They were only humans.

And so the first question was: Why did I place faith in them? After much inner exploration, I realized I'd had faith in people that I identified as having *authority* over me: The preachers, certain family members, certain friends, and of course doctors and dentists. For whatever reason, I had decided that they were somehow chosen to watch over me and be allowed to pass judgment on me. It was almost as if I felt they were my boss, not in my job, but in life. They were *life bosses*. And I put absolute faith in them. If they said something, it must be true.

Looking back, I realize that this, like so many other things, went back to my childhood. My parents had taught me that certain people had authority over me, and right into my 20's, I submitted to this imagined authority. Many of these people were nothing more than friends. But I can tell you this: If those friends said something as fact, I would accept it as fact, and I would even defend it without question.

I'm not sure if choosing such life bosses is human nature or not, but I see many people doing it. I can't count how many times I've heard people say with absolute confidence that some economical or political situation was going to occur simply because the guy on the AM radio said it would. That's absolute faith, and has no rationality. These AM talk radio hosts are paid well to do what they're doing, and they know that if they change their viewpoint they'll lose advertisers. And they have people convinced that they know the absolute truth.

But why blindly trust people? Remember, they're only humans, too. Are they really an absolute authority? For me, I had a serious awakening when I was involved in a situation on a job where the company got hit with a major lawsuit and every single person involved started pointing fingers and blaming each other. I was ultimately made to be one of many fall guys and was fired from my job. These people at the job were people that I previously had absolute faith in. I not only trusted them, I put my absolute confidence in them, without previously checking them out, only to find what to me seemed like dishonesty. I can't know exactly what was going on in their minds, but from my perspective their behavior seemed dishonest and even malicious.

This was a major awakening for me; I went from treating many people as life bosses to practicing the mantra, "Trust no one."

That, of course, isn't healthy either, and it took me several years to get past it. The mistake I made, though, was to equate faith with trust. It made sense at the time to trust these people when I first met them, even though they had not demonstrated to me they were capable of doing their work. And so I didn't just have trust in them; I had absolute, total faith in them. And when they made mistakes, I went to what seemed to me the absolute opposite: Trust *nobody*.

But it need not be that way. Faith and trust are two separate beasts. Trust relies on reason and logic, and has rationale behind it. Faith uses none of these. If I had kept to a healthy level of trust rather than go to an extreme level of faith, when things crashed I wouldn't have punished everyone around me, including innocent friends, by becoming totally distrustful of everyone. Instead, I would have reacted in a healthier manner. My trust in those individuals would have gone down, but logic and reason would have held up and I would have realized I still had reason to trust other people who weren't even involved in the whole fiasco.

How many times have people had their faith shaken and dropped into major despair? Many times. And I would argue that instead of grabbing hold of blind faith, if they had only used logic and reason to develop a healthy trust, then when something went wrong their whole world wouldn't be shaken.

Look at it this way: We're all only human. We make mistakes. Nobody is perfect. But on the other hand, we're also not a bunch of evil scumbags who must grovel to a deity. Are you seeing what I'm getting at here: When we're on a high point where we have blind faith in people around us and everything is fine, where do we go next? What does the church teach us? The church teaches us we're all sinners. And think how easily that makes it to drop into an enormous slump. If we believe the whole world is evil, then it's so easy to instantly embrace that unhealthy notion, and go to the other extreme of having absolutely zero trust in anybody around us. That's what I did, and that is absolutely not healthy.

So what is the solution? How do we stop having blind faith and adopt a healthier, more sensible level of trust? Easy: We make the conscious decision to do so. We embrace reason and logic. We ask ourselves: Does it really make sense to believe that this person you know is an absolutely perfect, all-knowing individual? Of course not. But does it make sense to suddenly think that this person is the complete opposite, the epitome of evil? No, that's not healthy either. Instead, we recognize that the each person is only human and makes mistakes. And then we can logically ask ourselves if that person is somebody we can trust. Does the person know his or her stuff? Maybe. Has that person demonstrated that he or she is capable of something? Maybe. If so, then perhaps we can trust them.

This is why people have embraced the word *skeptic*. When I first heard people using that term to describe themselves, I felt the term was incredibly negative and definitely not a virtue. Why would somebody want to go around doubting everything and being suspicious of everything?

To answer that, consider the opposite: Is it healthy to *never* be suspicious and to never doubt anything? That's what blind faith is. I know people who have been hurt many times by putting an inordinate amount of blind faith in people. I know a woman who decided to help a prison inmate get his life together shortly before he was let out of jail. When he was finally out of jail, he told her he had become a Christian and she immediately moved in with him. And then he started beating her and forcing drugs into her mouth. Fortunately, her parents came and got her out of the mess and took her away, and he ended up going back to jail.

Now I'm not saying no inmates can be reformed. But I am saying she could have used a little logic and reason, and been a little more careful and checked the guy out to find out for sure if he really was trustworthy. I've known people who have been to jail and who have turned their lives around and become law-abiding, honest people. But it's about being reasonable, and only putting trust in people after they've demonstrated they deserve it.

And that's what being skeptical is all about. It's not a negative thing at all! It's a virtue. It's a positive trait. We skeptics don't blindly accept everything that is thrown at us. We question things.

Here's an example: How many times have you received an email with some crazy story about something that happened to someone, or about something a politician said or did? What do you do: blindly believe it and forward it again or question it? Unless the email is about a topic I'm familiar with and I know whether it's true or not, I don't blindly accept it. I do some research online, checking out the various urban legends sites, and determine for myself whether it's correct or not. (And those urban legends sites that I use, incidentally, have earned my trust over the past few years. I don't blindly believe them either.) And more often than not, I discover the story in the email I received was, in fact, false.

I question everything.

Even evolution. Although I accept evolution as fact, my acceptance has only happened after the scientists who research it have demonstrated to me they know what they're doing. But even still I make sure I keep a healthy amount of skepticism, because there are some issues evolutionary scientists don't yet agree on. And so I don't blindly accept those smaller, questionable aspects until the scientists have done their job and ironed out those few issues.

Indeed, when I was reading Michael Shermer's excellent book Why Darwin Matters, there were paragraphs and sections where I had serious doubts about what he was saying. I said, "Wait, I'm not going to just blindly buy into that." But over the course of his book, he made some excellent defenses. I used logic and reason; what he said made sense. And this helped reinforce my knowledge and understanding of evolution, as well as my trust in the scientists who have done the hard work of figuring out the details of evolution.

That, then, is how we let go of unhealthy, blind faith and move to a healthy skepticism where true, healthy trust is possible. And when something happens where somebody demonstrates they can't necessarily be trusted, our whole world doesn't come crashing down on us.

The answer, to reiterate, is to embrace logic and reason. Question things. Don't just immediately accept what you're told until you have good reason to accept it.

Letting Go and Walking Away

Throughout this book I've presented many ideas on why I do not accept Christianity for what it is. But is it possible to just brush off the problems as the "wrong" Christianity and still believe in God and Jesus and call myself a Christian?

Of course. And for the longest time that's what I did. Late in my days as a Christian, I definitely recognized that there were people called Christians whose beliefs were drastically different from mine. These people were the Fundamentalists. I didn't understand how their ideas could possibly be right. And I did exactly what they did: I decided that they were being deceived by Satan.

Respect yourself and others will respect you.

- Confucius

I held onto that idea for a few years, accepting my own beliefs as correct and true. But one day something interesting happened.

I was going through a time of depression and the doctor put me on an antidepressant. This drug had a surprising effect on me. It actually changed my personality. It made me happier and less depressed. How was that possible? I am me, I am who I am, and I can't be somebody else. Yet...oddly, that medicine (a legal prescription, no less) did indeed change certain aspects of my behavior.

How could it be that a drug, a chemical, could change the way we think and feel?

And then one day I was in the gym working out. There was a TV in there and a commercial came on advertising a CD box set of religious music being sung by choirs. The commercial showed a huge auditorium. The seats were filled with people in their "Sunday best" clothes. The choirs were on stage singing and the people in the audience were having what was unmistakably a religious experience. The camera zoomed in on a conservative-looking man in a suit and tie sitting with his arms in the air, his eyes clothes, and he was waving back and forth to the music. He looked like he was on the verge of fainting, he was so excited.

244   *Christian no More*

To him, he was clearly feeling the power of the Holy Spirit moving him.

To me, he was experiencing nothing more than brain chemicals.

That's it. Brain chemicals. It had never occurred to me before until I had seen just what chemicals can do to the brain. My chemicals were prescription chemicals to improve my mood. Could it be that the brain can emit similar chemicals that give you a euphoric feeling that can easily be attributed to a religious experience?

Absolutely. The brain creates endorphins that can be released at various times based on different stimuli. And clearly that's what was happening. It was so obvious to me. This man was not having a religious experience; he was having a rush of endorphins and nothing more.

And it's true: If there's only one true God, and different Christians have radically different, totally incompatible and exclusive beliefs, how could they both feel such a strong feeling of God's Spirit moving them? And how could people of non-Christian religions also experience such a thing?

I didn't believe that the music these people were listening to was part of the same religion that I belonged to, because Fundamentalism was, in my opinion, based on an extreme intolerance that was clearly wrong to me. And so it seemed that these people were not being moved by any spirit. The only possibility then was that my other idea, that endorphins were creating this euphoric effect, was correct.

Indeed, they were not being moved. They were just experiencing a rush of chemicals and nothing more. And on those occasions when I felt something spiritual happen, it was the same thing: a rush of chemicals, the same rush people get when they go to a concert, or to a really good ballgame, or when they experience something like skydiving.

We Are Not Worthy? Yes We Are!

Shortly after that, I was struggling to find a good church whose beliefs were compatible with mine. And so I tried watching services on TV. One of the local Catholic churches had a "TV Mass" where they did their service on TV. Although my beliefs were based in the Lutheran church, the Catholic service was the closest to what I was comfortable with.

And that's when it finally broke.

I was watching the service, which included communion (for the people actually there at the taping, of course). Prior to communion the priest prayed for forgiveness of our sins. And in the prayer he said, "We are not worthy."

My eyes shot open. *We are not worthy?* Immediately my mind started spinning, going through my life. I thought of the years of self depravation, the self flagellation, where I convinced myself that I must be an evil person.

And it hit me: I didn't do anything evil! I'm human. I never hit anybody; I didn't do things like rob banks and kill and rape people. I'm just a human being trying to live in this world, doing the best I can.

And I am a good person.

I am a good person. I am a good person.

Finally. After all these years of the Church convincing me that I'm fundamentally evil and therefore need to grovel before God and beg him to accept me for doing things that are nothing more than human, I was finally accepting *myself.*

I am a good person.

I really am. Contrary to what these preachers had told me all these years, contrary to what all these Christians were telling me, I am, in fact, a good person.

I am a good person. Why? Because I'm only human. And humans occasionally make mistakes.

What a liberating feeling! What happiness to suddenly think this!

And so there I was, listening to the preacher on TV, having this rush of ideas spinning through my head.

And here's this guy on TV trying to tell me otherwise! I'm not worthy? Who does he think he is? He doesn't know what I've gone through in my life, what situations have led to the decisions I've made, and how hard I've tried to live a good, pure life.

I am a good person. And the next thought entered my mind:

Fuck you.

That's really what went through my mind. I cussed out the priest on TV, that horrible man who has spent a lifetime convincing people that they are nothing but scum of the Earth who need to grovel to God and beg for forgiveness for just *being human.*

In the middle of the prayer, as soon as I heard those words, "We are not worthy," all these thoughts shot through my head, and my eyes snapped open.

The prayer was done, disconnected, over. Finished.

I stood up and walked away and went in my bedroom and just sat there for a long time, thinking.

I was angry. Very angry. This was the beginning of the end.

But I didn't immediately let go. There was more to come. Because I still believed in God and Jesus; I just didn't believe what all these Christians had been teaching me all my life. They were wrong about telling me I was a bad person; that much I knew. But God and Jesus were still real to me.

What followed took several years, about six or seven. I still held on to the idea of God and Jesus, but that's when I started to question what was in the Bible. All those things that I've covered in this book went through my mind, but only after time, only after studying. I realized certain things in the Bible couldn't possibly have happened. I continued my reading and studying, and more and more I found problems, one after another, stories that completely contradicted what we knew to be historically true, or scientifically true.

I researched and read. I explored other religions. I explored the history of the Bible and the history of the Christian Church and the history of Judaism. I explored the history of the stories in the Bible and how they bore remarkable similarities to other, earlier stories, stories that today's Christians consider myths.

And so I went from simply not liking Christianity to deciding the Bible *can't* be true. After all, as I've said many times in this book, just because you don't like something doesn't make it untrue. But the truth of the Bible was definitely falling away.

Ultimately, what I've covered in this book is what made me realize that the Bible cannot possibly be true.

But does it mean God isn't real? And what about Jesus?

One might argue that I've just ended up with a totally twisted perspective of Christianity, and that God and Jesus are real, and that the parts of the Bible I don't like are just allegorical, and not meant to be taken literally, and that other parts just don't pertain to today. I've covered this earlier in the book, however; these are arguments that would likely come from more liberally-minded Christians, people who I tended to agree with when I was a practicing Christian. (Fundamentalists wouldn't make such arguments; they would have already decided I'm destined for Hell.)

This was where the next struggle came before I finally broke away. What about Jesus?

What About Jesus?

Regardless of all the different types of Christianity, they all have one thing in common that is indisputable: The belief in Jesus.

As long as I still believed in Jesus, I was *not* comfortable answering "No" to the question, "Are you a Christian." For the longest time this question would make me hesitate. "Well," I would say, "I'm not the same type of Christian most people think of." And I would beat around the bush like that.

During that time, I still believed that a man had lived named Jesus who was the human son of the deity named God. And so I felt that *by definition* that allowed me to still maintain the title of Christian.

But in Chapter 6 of this book, I made the case of why the Bible is simply not an accurate account of history and why it's nothing more than a re-hash of the same old myths that long pre-dated the supposed time of Jesus.

During the past couple of years, I've done a great deal of reading, which has included books that fundamentalists would probably be terrified to even touch, books that compare the supposed man called Jesus to earlier myths. These books make it pretty darn clear that Jesus was just a rewrite of earlier myths. The evidence the authors present in these books is solid. (I didn't just blindly believe the books.)

As I mentioned earlier in this book, it was common in ancient times to develop myths that involved male gods impregnating human women to create hybrid man-gods that were almost completely human except for certain superhero abilities.

And what kind of superhero abilities would they have if they were created by today's fiction authors? Think of it: Today our superheroes live on the movie screen and in the comic books. They can do amazing things that we can't do, such as flying. Or they have superhuman strength—all sorts of cool things that humans wish they could do.

Jesus didn't fly or have superhuman strengths. But he did do things that at the time would have been considered superhero—or, at least, supernatural—abilities: He healed people; he sent demons out of people; and, probably the single biggest superhero feat: *He walked on water.*

Walking on water is perhaps one of the ultimate abilities fiction authors of two thousand years ago could think of. People weren't so obsessed with being able to fly yet; that came about 1500 years later. Had this story been written around the time of Leonardo DaVinci, then I would expect a god-man to have the ability to fly. But 2000 years ago, an amazing feat would be to walk on water.

And that's exactly what Jesus did.

But that's *completely out of character* for this supposed Jesus guy and for the supposed Messiah that the Jewish people were expecting. It's a huge contradiction. The gospels totally contradict themselves when they build up a character who is supposedly a god-man who wants to let people decide for themselves on sheer faith that he's real.

Yet, right in the middle of it all, what does this Jesus character do? He puts on a huge theatrical performance and comes walking out from the shore to a boat during a terrible storm and demonstrates his superhero powers. He then convinces Peter to try walking on water too. At first Peter has trouble but finally he manages.

But the irony here is that in the lesson he tries to teach Peter about the importance of *faith!* While Peter sinks and is, presumably, starting to drown, Jesus, instead of helping Peter, chastises him about his faith. Finally, Peter develops enough faith and manages to walk on water as well.

And so we have this god-man character who tries to hide his true nature and convince people to use faith, and then he puts on a huge superpower display that convinces people he's a god-man, but at the same moment is supposedly trying to teach people about faith. That just doesn't all fit together in a sensible manner.

Of course, the early writers of these stories had a problem on their hands. They had created this character and wanted him to teach people to have faith. But if they wrote a collection of stories that rely only on faith, then the main character in these stories would have to be purely human in every way, and not a god-man at all. It's hard to say if they consciously recognized this problem, but to get around the problem they gave the god-man character a few superhero powers, like healing people and being able to walk on water—just enough to try to prove that this guy is the real thing, a god-man, while at the same time teaching the idea of faith to the rest of us, who do not possess superhero powers.

But it doesn't work. The god-man character, Jesus, demonstrates abilities that *only a god could have*, while at the same time teaching us that *we* can have those abilities if we just have *faith*. How is that possible? Am I supposed to believe that if I have enough faith, I too can have abilities that only a god could have, like superhuman strength, flying, and walking on water? In the story, Peter was able to walk on water using faith, and thereby perform an ability that only a god should be able to do.

As for the Jesus character, however, his abilities were not the result of faith, now were they? He was supposedly a hybrid god-man who had supernatural abilities that came from being the Son of God. To walk on water, he simply invoked his inborn supernatural abilities, *not* his faith.

But he taught us that we could do the same thing—not because we too are hybrid man-gods, but because we have faith.

And this confusion continues throughout the New Testament. Consider the story of the resurrection, something I haven't discussed much at all in this book. The resurrection has some serious problems, beyond the fact that that its inclusion in the gospels is clearly the result of pagan influence; the early Christians wanted the Greeks to accept the story so it was familiar with their own myths.

A physical resurrection where Jesus' dead body came back to life was never mentioned by Paul, the author of the earliest books in the New Testament (they were written from around 50AD to around 64AD). The first gospel, the shortest one, Mark, was written after that, around 70AD, and it also never mentions a physical resurrection. Clearly the idea was added much later; the idea was briefly mentioned in Matthew and wasn't completely developed until the gospel of John was written around 100AD.

In John, Jesus is crucified, and later comes alive out of the grave. He then goes and meets with the 12 disciples, although one—Thomas—is not present. And once again, the story goes against this idea of having faith, and Jesus physically appears to the disciples. What happened to having faith? Supposedly these guys had to physically see Jesus. And even Thomas didn't believe it since he wasn't there. A week later, Thomas was present when Jesus appeared for the second time, again as a physical human. And Thomas doesn't believe it's him until he tests Jesus. Here's what the King James Version has to say:

> *The other disciples therefore said unto him, We have seen the LORD. But he said unto them, Except I [Thomas] shall see in his hands the print of the nails, and put my finger into the print of the nails, and thrust my hand into his side, I will not believe. (John 20:25)*

And then Jesus lets Thomas touch him and get his proof. Again, so much for faith.

But what bothered me even as a child about this story was that if Jesus came back to life and was once again intact, why would he still have marks from the crucifixion? Why wouldn't those marks be gone?

Yet it's even more confusing, because although Jesus is supposed to be alive, walking around in physical form, he has the ability to walk through walls (again, a superhero ability). In verse 19 of this same chapter in John, the disciples were in a room with the doors shut and Jesus appeared.

But let's be completely realistic here: If there's a Heaven, we know it's not "up there" somewhere in outer space as the ancients would have believed. Clearly the stories of the Bible were written as if Heaven is "up" and if you climbed high enough you would get there. The people back then believed that Heaven was a physical place that you could physically travel to if you had the right kind of vehicle. And certainly they felt that if Jesus were to come back to life and ascend to Heaven, then naturally he'd be some kind of physical being. As such, they needed to explain that Jesus came back to life in physical form before he could go "up" to Heaven.

If there is some kind of spiritual world called Heaven, it's certainly not up in space, and we certainly can't get there in our current physical form. (And again, this is all a big *if.*) So why would Jesus have to come back to life in physical form? And even when he did in these stories, it didn't make sense because he had a more spiritual, angelic quality to him—yet, while apparently retaining holes in his hands where he had been crucified. (And he even ate a fish!) It just makes no sense.

When you combine all the aspects of the Jesus character, it just doesn't stack up to reality. The story is fundamentally flawed in so many ways. And further, I talked earlier in this book about how the story of the virgin birth and other pagan ideas were similarly assimilated into the character so that the story could be more appealing to people of non-Jewish culture, such as the ancient Greeks.

I already mentioned Mithra earlier in this book. The parallels to the Jesus story are uncanny. In the Mithras religion, people were baptized and took part in a Eucharist (what many people today call communion). Their god-man named Mithras was born by a virgin, died and on the third day rose again.

There are also incredible similarities with other mythological god-men as well, including one named Osiris, who also was born of a virgin and rose from the dead. Entire books have been written on the subject, and I couldn't do it justice here. Check out the bibliography for information on where you can read about these myths.

One interesting factor to consider is that many of the Christian temples and churches in Europe and the Middle East (including the Vatican) have been built on top of older, earlier temples that were for Mithras or Osiris or other gods. What Christians who learn about this want to believe is that the local people converted to the "real" religion of Christianity and replaced their temples of their false gods with temples to Jesus.

A more likely scenario, however, is that the religions in these temples just evolved over time into what eventually became known as Christianity, and that today's Christianity is nothing more than a refined, evolved form of these earlier so-called pagan myths.

But I Feel Jesus With My Heart and Soul

I mentioned earlier about the endorphins helping people have what they perceive to be a spiritual experience. But for many Christians (and I was this same way), it goes even further. For many people, Jesus is absolutely real. Just as I described in the very first chapter of this book, I felt Jesus with all my heart and soul. He was very real to me.

Think of somebody you love who you see every day but isn't nearby. What is he or she doing right *at this very moment*? I can think of my wife. I imagine she's sitting at her computer at work, going through the records. But is she?

In fact, I have no idea. I'm not there with her. I assume she's at work, but she could be in a coworker's office, or she could be on the phone, or she could be in the restroom. She may or may not be talking to somebody right now. Or she might even be outside the office, perhaps to make a quick run in her car somewhere.

In fact, the mental image of her in my mind isn't totally in line with what she's doing and thinking right now. But it's easy for me to imagine what she's doing. It's very easy for me, in my mind, to construct an image of her and to see her and to experience her as I do when she's in the same room as me. But that image in my mind is still just that—an *image*. Sure, my brain can manipulate the image and have her talk to me and what not, and that just makes the image even more real. But that image is still a separate thing from the real person.

Our minds are very good at doing that kind of thing. Think of the children who have imaginary friends. Adults with imaginary friends are usually placed in mental institutions, because as we grow up, we get better at realizing the friends were imaginary, and we can distinguish reality from fantasy. But I would argue that our brains still have the ability to create such imaginary friends.

Consider this: I felt I had a personal relationship with Jesus. Jesus was very real in my mind, and he looked like the familiar Jesus in the books and paintings, the guy with the beard and long hair, like some hippy singer-guitarist from the 70s. This guy in my mind would talk to me, and I'd interact with him. He would guide me and offer me advice. And that advice was very similar to the advice laid out to me in the Bible.

But if that image in my mind was truly Jesus, shouldn't he be identical to the Jesus that other people experience in their mind? One could argue that he could look different based on what we, as individuals, expect him to be. Fine. But what about the advice he gave? Shouldn't that be universal? If two people are together and they're both trying to figure out how to handle a difficult situation together, and they each interact with the Jesus in their minds, shouldn't they receive the exact same directions?

But it just doesn't happen that way. The Jesus we feel in our mind is usually the same as the Jesus that was presented to us by our church (or the church that we went to as children), and the advice he gives us is the same as the advice we would expect him to give us based on what we learned from the Bible.

The fact is, it's very easy to imagine somebody in our minds and to feel with total certainty that this person is real. But that doesn't mean he is.

Now combine that with the mythical aspects of the Bible and of Jesus that I've presented here and throughout the book. The Jesus in the Bible shared similarities with earlier man-gods. The Jesus in the Bible followed a religion that was clearly founded in myth, as I explained in Chapter 6. Are either of these people real: the Jesus in the Bible and the Jesus in many of our minds that we have a personal relationship with? And further, if the Jesus in the Bible couldn't have existed in the form described, then why would a current, living, spiritual guy based on that made-up character actually exist?

I now appeal to your logic and reason. Letting go of something like this is *not easy*. Believe me, I've been there. It's not something that you just decide to stop believing. But if you're thinking about an eternal life that's being presented to you by the church, don't you owe it to yourself to make sure what they're presenting is, in fact, *real?* And if you're going to spend all your physical life thinking about it, don't you deserve to at least consider whether what you're believing is real?

Now hold that thought while I talk about God.

Is There a God?

Is there a God? Short answer: I don't know, and I dare say, neither do you.

In Chapter 6, I made what I consider an excellent case why the God described in the Bible can't be real. We can mark off that one guy called God. The angry, jealous, God of the Old Testament is a myth that evolved from earlier myths that we know aren't real. And the supposedly loving, kind God of the New Testament, while certainly an inviting notion, is just a revision of the God of the Old Testament mixed with ideas of the time. The God of Christianity, and of Judaism, and of Islam, which all comes from the Old Testament, is not real. This much I can say with confidence, and I hope, after reading this book, you'll agree with me on that.

> *The opposite of the religious fanatic is not the fanatical atheist but the gentle cynic who cares not whether there is a god or not.*
>
> - Eric Hoffer (1902 - 1983)

But is there a god out there somewhere? Is there some kind of deity? Who knows. I don't know.

But I can tell you this: If there is a god, there's no *reason* to believe he/she/it is in *any way similar* to us humans. How could it be? We're creatures that have evolved to fit this unique planet called Earth. Physically and emotionally we are products of this planet. We breathe air, and we eat food that was once living matter, and we interact with each other using the means we have, and that has a lot of influence on the way we think and feel.

And intellectually, while I like to think we're highly intelligent beings, the fact is, there are things going on in this universe we can barely understand. Physicists who study quantum mechanics would be the first to tell you so. Quantum mechanics defies common sense and is extremely hard to grasp. There are aspects to this universe that our Earthly, human brains simply can't seem to grasp onto. Maybe in the millennia that follow we'll evolve such that our brains can grasp more. It's hard to say. But what this says to me is that if there is some kind of being out there who created this universe, it bears little or no resemblance to us, and we would probably never be able to understand or comprehend it. (And again, if there is, that being certainly wouldn't behave in the jealous, childlike, overly-human manner of the God of the Old Testament.) And again, this is all a big if: I'm not saying such a being exists at all. I don't know.

And personally, for me, that's something to celebrate: Why go through life being terrified of an afterlife? If there is an afterlife and I live on, I'm confident in saying that I will not be transformed into some other kind of being such as a demon where I become completely evil or an angel where I become perfect, but instead will continue being me. And I don't have to worry about appeasing some narcissistic god as featured in the Bible, one who is more concerned that we believe in him than anything else.

So is there a God?

Maybe. Maybe not. I tend to doubt it, but we can't know for sure. So why get all bent out of shape over it? I say, let go of it and don't worry about it. Just be true to yourself. Do what you know is right; treat others as you would have them treat you. (Such irony, considering Jesus gave that instruction as a commandment.) And have confidence that because you're being true to yourself and treating others as yourself, that you are, in fact, a good person. And if there is an afterlife, you'll continue being a good person, and you therefore don't have to worry about some horrid judgment as described in the Bible.

An Embarrassment in History

Any time a country or culture does something really bad, like keep slaves for a hundred years, later generations look back on the ordeal with embarrassment. I've met a lot of Southern Americans who are embarrassed about the former slave days.

And I've also met a lot of people who have predicted that one day Christianity will be gone and a thing of the past, and that the people of that day will look back on it with embarrassment. People will be appalled that there were once billions of people worshipping these god-men created thousands of years earlier, even after modern times kicked in during the 19th and 20th centuries.

And it's already happening. Contrary to what some people claim, church membership is declining. Look at the number of churches that are resorting to bizarre advertising methods to try to drum up membership. (Remember, they can't pay the light bill if people aren't there to put money in the offering plates.)

I've spoken with a number of preachers over the years who have told me that one of their biggest struggles is to get young people to attend church. They often have ideas about why people aren't coming. Some say it's because young people would rather spend time chatting online than meeting new people at church. And maybe that's indeed a factor.

Perhaps the silliest claim I've heard is that young people don't go to church because they don't like organ music! Look at all the churches that now advertise that they have "contemporary" services featuring electric guitars and drums, and that people are welcome to show up in jeans. It's clear that this "organ music" problem is a serious concern to the preachers, if they're going to go so far as to change the sound of the service in hopes of bringing more people in.

But I would argue that's not the real reason people aren't coming to church. The church leaders are in denial about the real reason: People are getting fed up with religion. People are fed up with the close ties between religion and politics. Young people are, by and large, progressive liberals who despise the older, conservative parties and are sickened by the close connections between the churches and the conservative politicians. These young people are disgusted by the way homosexuals, who are finally gaining widespread acceptance, are still treated as lepers by the churches. These young people are disgusted by the wars the conservative leaders are waging in other countries with the support and help of the conservative churches. The young people are the people of tomorrow, and they're just plain sick and tired of churches and what they're doing.

They're also waking up to the absurdities the churches are teaching. And that's good news. At the end of Chapter 2, I talked about the supposed gift of eternal salvation. So many churches act like they're making this beautiful, amazing offer, and all you have to do is come in and accept it. But they're oblivious to the fact that there's an enormous step that a person must take, a step the churches seem to think will happen automatically, a step to start *believing* in the nonsense. And if people either stopped believing or never believed from the start, why would they come in and accept an invisible, empty promise that has no evidence of being real? This is what the young people are waking up to, contrary to what the churches believe.

Even though I ranted in this book about how the Creationists are holding back science education, perhaps the young people are savvy and are seeing through it and not being swayed by it. Perhaps as they grow up they're going to take a stand and announce that they've had enough with the lies. Perhaps they'll take a stand for science and progress so that someday when they have children and eventually grandchildren, the world will be a better place. The world will finally accept science and allow children to excel in their studies and become good scientists not held back by superstition, and perhaps soon the world will move forward and find cures for cancer and for AIDS and for war and poverty, unencumbered by ancient beliefs that have no basis in reality.

That's the real reason church membership is declining. People are tired of it and just don't buy it any longer, organ music be damned.

Finally Breaking Away

But let's return to Jesus for a moment. Because we still have a bit of a problem here: By definition, if one believes in Jesus, he or she is a Christian.

I've met a good share of people who are not Christians who say they at least accept that there was probably a historical man named Jesus upon which the religion is built. However, there is absolutely no evidence that there really was such a man. These people are deluding themselves, unable to let go of that last little tidbit of their religion.

Outside of the Bible and the Apocrypha texts (remember, most Christians do not accept Apocrypha texts as real), there is almost no mention whatsoever of Jesus. There is plenty of mentions of other people from that time, such as Julius Caesar. And if Jesus was as the Bible presented him, there should certainly be a huge number of historical documents that mention Jesus.

But there aren't. The documentation just isn't there. There are no first-hand accounts of Jesus whatsoever. Any mention of Jesus is based on what was read from the four Gospels. And even that's not first-hand, as the gospels weren't written by people who were supposedly right there seeing it.

And as for second-hand information, it's extremely rare. People like to mention the ancient historian Josephus Flavius, because he supposedly wrote a little mention of Jesus in his book called Antiquities. But most scholars today recognize that the sentence is a fraud and was added later by Christians. The writing that mentions Jesus is completely different from the writing throughout Josephus' works, and it is obviously not his own words.

For me, these two problems—that Jesus was based on earlier myths, and that there is no evidence of Jesus having existed—convinced me that Jesus wasn't real.

Everything I've spelled out in this book makes the case clear to me. The myths… the stories that couldn't have happened… the mental processes… He just didn't exist. He wasn't real.

Jesus didn't exist.

And the Jesus we have in our minds, the spiritual Jesus, isn't real. Jesus isn't real.

Thus, by definition, if one does not believe in Jesus, then one is not a Christian. And as such, I've finally had no choice but to accept this simple fact about myself:

I am no longer a Christian.

Final note:
If You're Breaking
Away and Struggling

I can tell you that breaking away from Christianity was one of the most difficult things I've ever had to do. (If you read the final chapter, you understand why I say I *had* to do it. I know Jesus didn't exist, and therefore, I had no choice but to no longer be a Christian.)

Having your faith die is not unlike having a close friend die, and most of us go through a grieving period. I felt I had a personal relationship with this man who lived in my imagination, this man named Jesus. And I had a lot of good times at church. Even to this day, I miss the evenings at church and I long for those times. I miss the beautiful architecture of the churches and spending time in there.

If you're going through this divorce of faith, you're probably having to deal with a great deal of emotional pain, including grieving, along with, quite likely, the loss of real friendships. People who are still Christians have likely turned their back on you and have decided you're some kind of devil.

It's not easy. I've been there. And I can tell you this: The single most important thing that helped me was to find others like myself who have been there. It's been such a relief to know there are hundreds, thousands, tens of thousands of others just like you and me. Meeting these people has been what I would almost like to call a blessing.

If you're active online, you can find a lot of communities and web sites online that you can join. Myspace has a huge community of nonbelievers, and has been helpful to me. You can find me there at:

http://www.myspace.com/RecoveringChristians

I've made a lot of great friends there and have had a really nice time talking to these people and discovering what all we have in common and seeing how they've been through so many of the same things I have. People have had friends and family leave them, and just some terribly hurtful things happen. But at the same time, we've all met each other and have forged wonderful new friendships. There are some truly great people there.

Also, check out the Freedom From Religion Foundation (FFRF). They're a non-profit organization run by a man who was once a fundamentalist preacher but also left just like you and me. He's written several books and the organization has loads of information. They even have local groups throughout the country. You can find out about them here:

http://www.ffrf.org

Other places you can meet some wonderful people are at various Secular Humanist organizations. (Humanism is a philosophy that celebrates being human and strives to advance the greater good of humanity without the need for supernatural deities.)

A family member of mine has joined such a group and has met a lot of sincerely nice, friendly people who meet up in local chapters for various causes that advance Humanism. Check out the web site of the American Humanist Organization; click the Contact Us link and then the Local Groups link to find a local chapter:

http://www.americanhumanist.org

There really are plenty of great people and organizations out there (I have more listed in the list of Web sites in the Appendix of this book), and the more you meet these people and the more time you spend with them, the easier time you will have breaking free. And it also helps to know that you're not alone in this. Many of these people are former Christians, just like me.

And I can tell you firsthand that I've needed people like this. I still occasionally doubt myself: What if the Christian God is real, and this book I wrote just gave me a fast track ticket to Hell? The fears occasionally come back. But all I have to do is remind myself of what I've written here, and that there is *no possible way* the Christian religion can be real. *It isn't.* The myths are just that, myths. The stories in the Bible didn't really happen, and as such the Jesus character wasn't real, and therefore, the spiritual Jesus that so many people claim to have a personal relationship with isn't real. In other words, I let in ration and reason. And you can do the same. Remind yourself of what you've read in this book. And then, by knowing Christianity isn't true and through meeting other people, you can work through it and deal with the grief and other issues that will likely come from breaking away. You're not alone. I've made it, and so can you.

Don't keep the faith.

Instead, have trust in your own logic and reason.

Do this after YOU have let go!

If you've recently let go of your faith and had a church that you used to attend, you might start getting a barrage of fellow church members calling and visiting, wondering why you haven't been around lately.

Here's what you can do. Pull out (or photocopy!) the following page and send it to your church. This should do the trick! (Or don't fill it out and let them just wonder who left. That will be a pretty good message.)

Dear _____
              (clergy name)

Of _____
             (church name)

I, _____ , am no longer a Christian. Therefore, I will no longer be attending your church and will not need to be visited by your church's members. I have given a great deal of time and thought to this, and have finally realized that what you have been teaching me is simply not true. I am still a good person, and I still care about people. I just do not believe in your ancient myths.

If you're interested, I recommend the book called *Christian No More* (ISBN 978-0-9816313-0-1), a recent best-seller, which will provide more information on how you, too, can finally let go of the lies and finally live a happy life free of terror and dread.

Sincerely,

_____
             (your signature)

Appendix A

I felt I couldn't leave this out. I originally wrote it in the main text, but it just didn't fit. So I decided to include it as an appendix.

What's truly bizarre is that while today the Catholic Church has officially admitted that Galileo was right, there are still people today who believe the Earth is the center of the universe and that the entire known universe rotates around the Earth. This is not as uncommon as you might think. Searching online, you can find many people, who are primarily Christian, who hold to this belief. There are entire websites devoted to the notion that the Earth is stationary and that the Sun goes around the Earth.

But what is going on in their heads? Their reasoning is backwards. They read that the Bible states the world is the center of the universe, and from there they want to confirm what they hope is true. (This is known as *confirmation bias*, where somebody searches for answers to confirm what they already believe, and is anything but open-mindedness, and is certainly not scientific.)

Science, of course, works in the other direction. Science sets up the experiments and gathers the data and facts, and determines the conclusions, even if the scientists don't personally like the conclusions. That's the correct order of science and is part of what's known as the Scientific Method. You draw conclusions based on the given data and facts, not on your preconceived notions and biases. Believing the Earth is stationary simply because the Bible says so, and then searching for data to confirm this preconceived notion is not scientific.

The fact that the Earth moves is easily seen using a Foucault pendulum. This is a long wire, often 50 feet or more long, hanging from the ceiling, with a heavy bob at the bottom. Under the bob is a pile of sand which the bob scrapes, leaving marks as the pendulum rocks back and forth.

To understand what the pendulum will show, consider this: When you're riding in an airplane going, say, 400 miles per hour, people sometimes wonder why, if you let go of a pencil, the pencil won't shoot to the back of the plane at 400 miles per hour.

Here's why not: Suppose you are standing on the ground and you put a rock in one hand. You reach back behind you and give the rock a good hard throw. While your hand is moving forward, you are pulling the rock forward. When you let go, the rock *continues* to go forward, just as you would expect. Pretty simple: You throw the rock, and when your hand releases it, the rock *continues moving.* This is a simple fact of nature: Once an object is in motion, it continues in motion.

This simple fact demonstrates the notion of *inertia.* When something is moving, it keeps moving in a straight line until some force slows it down or changes its motion.

The ball that you throw, of course, doesn't keep on going forever. Instead, it slows down due to the friction it encounters with the air, and it falls downward due to gravity pulling it. Those are two forces the ball encounters: air friction and gravity, and they cause the ball to slow, fall, and stop. In outer space, however, the ball wouldn't slow and stop. Instead, it would keep moving forever. (That seems hard to believe, but it is, in fact, true, and something scientists have shown through simple experiments and demonstrations.)

So think about the airplane. When you take off on an airplane, the plane is pushing you forward with it because you're up against the seat. (You can feel this because you're pushed back in your seat as you take off.) And items on the floor that don't have anything pushing on them don't get pushed as much and they slide towards the back of the plane. But once airborne, you are moving with the plane, just as the rock was moving with your hand before you let go of it. And so you no longer feel like you're being pushed.

While you're on the moving plane and you let go of the pencil, it's just like letting go of the rock. The pencil effectively gets thrown forward at 400 miles per hour. But the plane is also moving forward at 400 miles per hour, so the two travel *together.* There's also a downward pull of gravity, which simultaneously pulls the pencil down towards your lap. The end result is the pencil falls right into your lap, *just as if you're sitting still.* It doesn't shoot to the back of the plane.

But what if the plane suddenly turns to the right? You can feel this when the plane is descending towards an airport. Often the plane has to come around the airport as it lands, and you can feel yourself continuing in different directions. The plane is no longer going in a straight line, but your body still wants to be thrown at 400 miles per hour in a *straight line,* so when the plane turns, you feel it. (That's the same as how you feel yourself pulled one way or another when you make a sharp turn in your car.) The effect is that as the plane turns, you keep going forward, and you feel yourself pressed against the different parts of the plane around you, such as the seat and the seatbelt. But since you're buckled in, your legs are pulled with the plane, while your upper body isn't, and you feel a pull across your body as your legs go one way and your upper body continues going another.

Now let's return to this pendulum thing I mentioned. If the Earth is stationary, the pendulum should just rock back and forth, tracing out a single line in the sand, back and forth, back and forth. But if the Earth is moving beneath the pendulum, we won't see a single straight line. Instead, we should see something considerably more complex. And indeed we do. We see a flower pattern.

If you're an expert in math, you can find the formulas online that predict what pattern you should see if the Earth is indeed moving. Then you can go see a Foucault Pendulum at any nearby university or museum and see for yourself the exact pattern the formulas predicted, thus proving the Earth is in fact turning.

Now some people might argue confirmation bias: We were hoping to see the patterns and so we forced an experiment to show them. But that's not the situation at all. Instead, we considered two possibilities: The pendulum will map out a single line as it goes back and forth, in which case the world is not spinning; or, it will map out a complex flower pattern, in which case the world is turning. Then we construct the experiment (or, in this case, go observe one already constructed), and see for ourselves which is the case. (But because this has already been done, I can already tell you which one you'll see.)

Indeed, the Earth is spinning. There is no denying it, even if the Bible says otherwise, and even if some geocentrists (as they're called) deny the realities.

Bibliography and Further Reading

As I had more and more trouble believing the ancient stories, I read a great deal of books that helped me understand the ancient roots of Christianity. I also found many web sites that provided me with information about ancient texts, but I try not to use web sites as original sources. Instead, I try to find the web site's source, which is hopefully a book, and then I check out the credentials of the author of the book.

But some of the web sites I found were written by people who quoted other web sites without actually going to the sources. When you follow the path of sources—from web site to web site and finally, hopefully, to a book—you don't always end up where you expect to. In the parallels between the Garden of Eden and other myths, I found several web sites that referred to a book that makes the rather outrageous claim that a few thousand years ago alien giants came to the Earth and fought battles and finally created people. Well certainly in letting go of my religion, I find it just as hard to buy into ideas like that, ideas that to me are just nonsense. As such, I refuse to quote these web sites and books, because that is not what I would consider reputable, scholarly research. Further, I think works like this stain the actual, real research going on, because it makes skeptics look like we're buying into some kind of new age, conspiracy cult nonsense.

So here are the books I found that are excellent.

Note: Typing in web addresses from a printed book is never easy. For all these books, I'm making use of the simplest Amazon web addresses; type in **www.amazon.com/dp/** followed by the ten-digit code that represents the book (called the ISBN) as shown after each of these books. Then you'll easily get there.

The Christ Conspiracy: The Greatest Story Ever Sold
By Acharya S
http://www.amazon.com/dp/0932813747

Who Was Jesus? Fingerprints of The Christ
by D.M. Murdock (Acharya S)
http://www.amazon.com/dp/0979963109

Middle Eastern Mythology
By S.H. Hooke
http://www.amazon.com/dp/0486435512

The Jesus Mysteries: Was the "Original Jesus" a Pagan God?
by Timothy Freke and Peter Gandy
http://www.amazon.com/dp/0609807986

Misquoting Jesus: The Story Behind
Who Changed the Bible and Why
By Bart D. Ehrman
http://www.amazon.com/dp/0060859512

Letter to a Christian Nation
By Sam Harris
http://www.amazon.com/dp/0307278778

The God Delusion
By Richard Dawkins
http://www.amazon.com/dp/0618918248

Atheist Universe: The Thinking Person's Answer to Christian Fundamentalism
By David Mills
http://www.amazon.com/dp/1569755671

Fundamentally Misguided
By Grace Lyerly
http://www.amazon.com/dp/1604417528

Why I Became an Atheist:
A Former Preacher Rejects Christianity
By John W. Loftus
http://www.amazon.com/dp/1591025923

Why Darwin Matters: The Case Against Intelligent Design
By Michael Shermer
http://www.amazon.com/dp/0805083065

Heretics: The Bloody History of the Christian Church
By Dr. W. Sumner Davis
http://www.amazon.com/dp/0759675376

50 Reasons People Give for Believing in a God
By Guy P. Harrison
http://www.amazon.com/dp/1591025672

The Portable Atheist: Essential Readings for the Nonbeliever
By Christopher Hitchens
http://www.amazon.com/dp/0306816083

God Is Not Great: How Religion Poisons Everything
By Christopher Hitchens
http://www.amazon.com/dp/0446579807

Godless: How an Evangelical Preacher
Became One of America's Leading Atheists
By Dan Barker
http://www.amazon.com/dp/1569756775

The Quotable Atheist: Ammunition for Non-Believers,
Political Junkies, Gadflies, and Those Generally Hell-Bound
By Jack Huberman
http://www.amazon.com/dp/1560259698

God: The Failed Hypothesis.
How Science Shows That God Does Not Exist
by Victor J. Stenger
http://www.amazon.com/dp/1591026520

Beyond these, there are many fine books, all of which are available in the usual places such as Amazon.com. Open up any of the Amazon pages for these books and you'll see a list of other books that you might consider as well.

Additionally, I highly recommend the classic book Cosmos, by Carl Sagan. Presently, all I can find that's in print is a paperback edition, which, frankly, doesn't do the book justice. Rather, see if you can locate the original hardcopy edition, perhaps in a used bookstore, or borrow it from a library.

Excellent Web Sites

There are loads of web sites out there for people atheists and agnostics and freethinkers. First, check out my own web site at:

www.escapingchristianity.com
where you can find many resources, including updated links. And you can find me on myspace:

http://www.myspace.com/RecoveringChristians
and Facebook:

http://www.facebook.com/profile.php?id=1282100921

Then here are some of excellent sites I found run by other people. First, here's a freethinker site:

http://nobeliefs.com
and I especially like this page on that site, which talks about whether a historical Jesus existed:

http://nobeliefs.com/exist.htm
as well as this fascinating page on the site, which talks about the darker side of the Bible:

http://www.nobeliefs.com/DarkBible/DarkBibleContents.htm
And this separate site also talks about the dark side of the Bible:

http://www.evilbible.com/

On a similar note, here's a site that has a lot of discussion showing Jesus never existed. This site makes some fascinating points:

http://www.jesusneverexisted.com/

Here's a site for people who have left religion:

http://www.de-conversion.org/news.php

Here are a couple of the organizations I've mentioned. First, Freedom from Religion Foundation:

http://www.ffrf.org
and next, the American Humanist Association:

http://www.americanhumanist.org

And a huge list of organizations can be found here:
> http://www.freeinquiry.com/skeptic/organizations/

And another list:
> http://www.discord.org/skeptical/

Here's a fascinating web site that covers the entire Bible and provides skeptical responses to a huge number of verses throughout. This site really gets you thinking about how unrealistic the stories in the Bible are:
> http://skepticsannotatedbible.com/

Here's a site about leaving Christianity with an excellent story; but if you scroll down you'll find a huge list of links and other resources. I definitely recommend checking it out:
> http://www.users.globalnet.co.uk/~slocks/decon.html

This is a well-known web site called The Secular Web, run by a non-profit organization called Internet Infidels. It has loads of information. Here's the main site:
> http://www.infidels.org

And here's one of my favorite pages on it, a list of testimonials from former Christians:
> http://www.infidels.org/library/modern/testimonials/

Here's a great blog by a man named John Loftus and several of his friends. (John has advanced theological training, is a former preacher, and has written some excellent books, one of which I mention above.)
> http://debunkingchristianity.blogspot.com/

This site has a lot of interesting information:
> http://www.skeptictank.org/

and it includes a "walk away package" that you can download here:
> http://www.skeptictank.org/walkaway.htm

(The download itself is in a very small font in the middle of the page.)
Here's a site with many resources for helping people escape Christianity:
> http://www.fundamentalists-anonymous.org

And here's a site for escaping the International Church of Christ in particular:

>   http://rightcyberup.org/

and another site (primarily a forum) for help with leaving Christian Fundamentalism:

>   http://walkaway.aimoo.com/

Here's a site that's cool because in addition to having blogs and other resources, you can create your own profile, much like myspace:

>   http://www.secularearth.com/

WebRings are collections of sites that all link together. Here's a list of WebRings that contain many sites that might be of interest:

>   http://a.webring.com/hub?ring=lbafc
>   http://a.webring.com/hub?ring=leavingfundament
>   http://x.webring.com/hub?ring=recoveringfromre
>   http://k.webring.com/hub?ring=exchristian

Here's what is probably one of the most famous atheist organizations around right now, the Rational Response Squad:

>   http://www.rationalresponders.com/

Next, here's another organization, the Skeptic Friends Network:

>   http://www.skepticfriends.org/

Index

Visit our web site for more great books
coming soon!

www.ReasonablePress.com

Visit the author online!

http://www.myspace.com/
recoveringchristians

3622573

Made in the USA